Cioran

A Dionysiac with the voluptuousness of doubt

Ion Dur

Baia Mare Northern University Centre, Romania

Translation
Ian and Ann Marie Browne

Series in Philosophy

Copyright © 2019 Vernon Press, an imprint of Vernon Art and Science Inc, on behalf of the author.

All rights reserved. No part of this publication may be reproduced, stored in a retrieval system, or transmitted in any form or by any means, electronic, mechanical, photocopying, recording, or otherwise, without the prior permission of Vernon Art and Science Inc.

www.vernonpress.com

In the Americas:
Vernon Press
1000 N West Street,
Suite 1200, Wilmington,
Delaware 19801
United States

In the rest of the world:
Vernon Press
C/Sancti Espiritu 17,
Malaga, 29006
Spain

Series in Philosophy

Library of Congress Control Number: 2018966903

ISBN: 978-1-62273-667-6

Also available:

Hardback: 978-1-62273-460-3

E-book: 978-1-62273-576-1

Cover design by Vernon Press.

Cover image: By Photographer of Keyston agency/Getty Images before Rivarol Premium. Photo taken in the last years of Cioran's life-in-Romania, before his definitive transference in France (1947); first publication 1955-1960s. Public domain. https://commons.wikimedia.org/wiki/File:Cioran_in_Romania.jpg

Product and company names mentioned in this work are the trademarks of their respective owners. While every care has been taken in preparing this work, neither the authors nor Vernon Art and Science Inc. may be held responsible for any loss or damage caused or alleged to be caused directly or indirectly by the information contained in it.

Every effort has been made to trace all copyright holders, but if any have been inadvertently overlooked the publisher will be pleased to include any necessary credits in any subsequent reprint or edition.

*In memory of my wife
Doina Marieta*

Table of contents

Preface — xi

Part I According to the original — 1

Chapter 1 — **Shortcuts** — 3
- 1.1 The Cioran effect
- 1.2 Manuscript *versus* definitive edition
- 1.3 "The gift of sorrow" – a phenomenological sketch
- 1.4 *The Twilight of Thoughts* – the context of reception
- 1.5 Cioran and Anselm
- 1.6 Cioran imprisoned
- 1.7 Cioran – the gnostic?
- 1.8 The stigma of biography
- 1.9 Around philosophy
- 1.10 The trial of philosophy: a form of free fall
- 1.11 Loneliness in/for Cioran

Chapter 2 — **The ambiguity of the epistolary self** — 25
- 2.1 Card/letters, work/writings
- 2.2 A thinker in disguise – sincere letters
- 2.3 Homesick, "metaphysical stateless person"

Chapter 3 — **The erotic adolescence of a septuagenarian** — 33

Chapter 4 — **Impervious to the "French spirit"** — 41

Chapter 5 — **The tragic overture** — 45
- 5.1 The sincerity of religious faith and the crisis of fundamentals

5.2 The beginning of an exercise
of *divine disobedience*

5.3 Spiritual drama and metaphysical sadness:
for moral reform

5.4 The absence of measure as vitality

5.5 The tragic overture

5.6 Local Don Quixotism and metaphysical revolt

Chapter 6 **Bouts of insomnia** 57

6.1 Warning signs for a "metaphysical masochism"

6.2 The edge and the fragment

6.3 Vaingloriously atypical.
Re-acknowledging Nietzsche

6.4 Misery, aesthetics and moral rules

6.5 Intuitionism *versus* intellectualism

6.6 Decadence, the mediocre man
and the "knights of nothingness"

Chapter 7 **The irrational, symbolic culture
and a eulogy of madness** 71

7.1 The eclecticism of culture as agony

7.2 Peeling off the irrational through culture

7.3 Beyond culture. The return of the irrational

7.4 In place of a conclusion:
an anthropology of the tragic

Chapter 8 **Between *falling in time* and
*falling into the temporal*** 83

8.1 A fall in (and from) time

8.2 The fall in the temporal.
Prelude - or what history is (not)

8.3 Utopia and lucidity

Chapter 9 **Against "national drowsiness"
– Cioran *versus* Cioran –** 99

9.1 The solution of "national collectivism"

9.2 Reception and contextual ideological comfort

9.3 A pamphlet on Romanian inertia

Chapter 10 **Waiting for Cioran's *reply***   129

Part II Restitutions   *137*

Nationalism, Socialism, Judaism   139

Abstract   *153*

Bibliography   *157*

About the Author   *161*

Index of Proper Names   *163*

"A civilisation starts in myth and ends in doubt"
"For me, refusal has always been more powerful than enthusiasm. Spirited alike by the temptation of the absolute and the persistent sentiment of vacuity, how could I dare hope?"

(Cioran)

Preface

Cioran's code

Reading – or writing a book about Cioran – you cannot but help wonder if Cioran himself would have approved of such an enterprise. To comment on a thinker proclaiming the futility of all things and the primacy of delusion, is not this "the heights" - to use the word in the title of his first book - of futility?

However, it seems that neither Cioran nor other masters of "despair" are indifferent to the reception and posterity of their work. Schopenhauer and Nietzsche vituperated while holding in their hand the still-invisible "ace" of their future glory. Kierkegaard seemed to preach from the pulpit of future recognition – about which he had not a single moment of doubt. Cioran himself is very attentive to the "echoes" of his writings, he censures certain writings, retracts certain theses, cultivates an enormous correspondence with his admirers, encourages studies and academic writings about his work.

Could these people who give us, through their writings, the feeling that they have looked into the shadows of being, into the abyss of existence, be just as sensitive to fame as all the others, as those they repudiate, whose petty arrogance is, in so many brilliant and scathing lines – denounced, deconstructed, ridiculed? How to explain the split between the burning, scathing content of their words and revelations, and this Godforsaken "authorship"?

Above the vain-gloriousness of a writer – no matter how small he is – there stands nothing else except the pride of the Devil. One cannot exclude the idea that it be the origin of the "writing" itself, of literature, for if God is the Word, the Devil – aping Him – "created", by overturning the original, *the written word*. The ancients were no strangers to this fundamental, radical opposition - which we, as modern people give to so many forms of writing, we as *those who write even when we speak*, definitively forgot: the contradiction between *speaking and writing*. Plato evokes it in a number of dialogues, embodying – as on so many other occasions – the "paradox of the liar", he himself being a sophisticated writer who makes the apology of orality, giving – by his (written) homage to the utterance – more credibility to his writing.

The absolutely inflexible refusal of the great teachers, the great initiates to write anything is revealing. As if they knew all the dangers associated with this "devilish" practice, Buddha, Jesus, Socrates, Confucius never wrote a line. The

Islamic religion also rejects the idea that the Qur'an could have been written - it was *dictated* to the Prophet, then *in-scribed* by others in the pages of a book. In almost all traditions, the original word is the spoken word, while writing is secondary and "dirty". Oral teaching predates and prevails over the written tradition, until late in history the oral doctrine is secret, esoteric, and the written one - exoteric, public, secular. "The real truth" is not to be communicated except by word of mouth, and this *true truth* is reflected in the written doctrine as faithfully as a face is by its shadow.

The scenario of the sacred texts, which communicate a primordial *original truth*, is simple: these are the *trans-scriptions* of a previous speech - be it that of a master, or of the deity itself. The "authority" of such texts springs from outside, is inherent in them only to the extent that it is also transcendent. Such "literature" (sacred and sapiential texts) is credible only insofar as it is a literature without an *author* - in the sense that we moderns have in mind. The value of such writing derives from the fact that someone else *has said* what is written in it.

As we shall see, Cioran belongs to the paradoxical category of *enlightened writers*. From this contradiction in terms results the fundamental ambiguity of Cioran's work, as well as the strong fascination which such writing elicits in the reader. Ion Dur notes that Cioran is quick to avoid any possible influence under which could be ascribed to him, whether he talks about Camus, labelled as provincial and half-learned, or about Nietzsche, repudiated as "an iconoclast with adolescent traits". Neither intuitionism nor Bergson, sources little noticed until now and which Ion Dur has the merit of revealing as the main sources of Cioranian thinking, escape from this frenzied denial of all predecessors. What, however, is the reason for this supposed dismantling of any suspicion about the *originality* of his thinking?

Cioran is *constrained* to such an attitude by his *fundamentally ambiguous* situation: the type of truth he professes to uphold, the content of his writing is one that maintains the order of *revelation, illumination* - hence *utterance*. On the other hand, a writer is placed, by definition, by the "grammar" he uses, in a sequence, a timeline, a history. *The enlightened* one *speaks* from the timeless space of primordialism; he is a contemporary only of God and the Devil. The fact that he is not the author of sacred or sapiential texts that replicate his words reinforce, in the mind of the reader, this impression: "an illusion of perspective" which pushes away, into a primordial distance, "the paramount source" of recorded truths. *The enlightened writer* represents a special typology to which Cioran belongs together with Nietzsche, Kierkegaard, Schopenhauer. *The enlightened writer* practices an oral-mystical style (not accidentally Nietzsche's *book* is called *Thus **spake** Zarathustra*), bibliographical, *originary*, therefore, *the enlightened writer* will contest - either explicitly or most often tacitly, in the absence of any referral, or any reference to the forerunners - the truth of any statement predating its occurrence; *the enlightened writers,* like the founders of religions, desire to cultivate in the spirits of their readers the impression that all that was said before them was error, illusion or, at the most, a semi-truth, a stunted sketch of the *integral truth* which, through them, is now revealed to mankind. The terminology of an *enlightened writer* will be composed, for the most part, of *strong* terms such as "climax", "peak", "abyss", "fire", "ice", "illusion", "foundation", "death", "life", "becoming", "being", "non-being", "destruction", "creation", "good", "bad", "last", "prime", etc.

"Paramount - primordial" literature does not support the presence of an author. Its truth-value derives from an external, transcendent instance. Or, in the case of the "enlightened writer", the author is the one who *enunciates, expound*s the truths in his text. It is not by chance that, both in Cioran's case and in the case of the others, we find a preference for aphorism, for "the word of spirit", for the "pointed joke", analogy, "formula" and paradox - that is, precisely for those figures characteristic of "oral style". The philosophers' closed judgments repel them because their writings are rival not of philosophy treatises, but of the Gospels, the Qur'an, and the Vedas.

The special merit of the present volume is the fact that its author has managed to decipher the fascinating "code" of Cioran's writings. Ion Dur crosses, hermeneutically, several of its layers: "the gift of anguish", the "histrionics" of the author, the epistolary "sincerity" exercised in such a way that the boundary between *writing* and *letter* becomes invisible, his persistent loneliness, even amid conviviality ...

What is the "secret" of Cioran, how can one decipher his stylistic code? Could it be understood, as Ion Dur wonders, in the light of that six-month prison experience about which Pamfil Șeicaru tells us, an experience that forever perfected his pessimism and scepticism? Is Cioran a gnostic? Or is it perhaps a fruit of his biography - as he repeatedly wants to make us believe - more precisely of that "original", disastrous experience of disease and insomnia? Or, on the contrary, is it an outgrowth of that bibliography he explored with such an insatiable thirst? And, the question of questions, is Cioran a philosopher or a renegade philosopher, a poetic soul - wandering inside a cuttingly lucid and sharp mind?

Cioran's revelation does not stop here: the secret of his effervescent writing is "the lack of measure as vitality"; his metaphysical revolt is, "in fact", a rebellion against his provincial condition, a condition that marked and pursued him for his entire life. From the list of decouplings, one should not remove resentment, the revenge that Cioran would like to take both in the face of life (which he cannot enjoy) and in the face of death (which he cannot overcome). Cioran's will is broken into two parts - from within, by his own morbid temper, and from "without", by the fatality of death. Between these two irreparable fatalities germinates the resentment or, more precisely, *the vengeful sense of existence*.

Ion Dur reaches a surprising first conclusion: Cioran is the name of a unique game of masks: *disguise is his true nature*. *Mask* and *ambiguity* fundamentally define Cioran. A mask without any face would then be the authorial correspondent of a doctrine of deceit without essence, of appearance in which the essence is, eventually, factitious and possibly factual. *Un-masking* is a potentially infinite process because Cioran would not have a real face. Thus, the break-up with philosophy would "hide" an inability to elaborate a coherent system, just as the break-up of Romanians with Romania has "utilitarian" motivations: a concern that his "shady" past (his adherence to the legionary movement) would be revealed. But, in turn, the latter conceals more and more masks - meant to protect and reveal at the same time his true identity, which is *ambiguous*, protean, the identity of a master of self-deceit and avoidance.

Finally, Ion Dur also draws the second conclusion: Cioran is an author, he is a *writer* and, like any writer, he is also an *actor*, i.e., an expert of dissimulation. Indeed, thus we find the "key" allowing us to decode and decipher Cioran. His essential ambiguity derives from the double status he claims for himself: that of an *enlightened being* and that of *writer*. The "image" that we've been waiting to meet beyond the masks he puts on can only be absent, non-existent - precisely because he is the *very author of his own texts*, of a "primordial" literature which, as a rule, is based on a source located beyond it.

From behind Cioran's writing *speaks no one*, precisely because Cioran alone is the author of his texts. Cioran can rightly be called a "mystic without a God". The divergence between the reader's expectations regarding primary literature, grounded in a transcendent moment, and the *autonomy* of enlightened writers' texts is anticipated, expected and greeted by them through the annihilation of exteriority: enlightened writers are self-styled prophets announcing the death of God, knights of nothingness, preachers of immanence. And their readers are bound to search their writings for an always promised truth, which they *know* they will never find. And to know, along with those who announce it, "just the joy that precedes it, that joy and madness and fear." (Cioran, *The Temptation to Exist*)

Horia Vicenţiu Pătraşcu

Part I
According to the original

Chapter 1

Shortcuts

1.1 The Cioran effect

I don't know whether the fact that these lines are written more than twenty years into Cioran's posterity has any significance. I wouldn't like to think that we are somehow reloading mechanisms which, yesteryear, in various contexts, suddenly brought to our attention the fact that a *famous personality* had been forgotten and that it was somehow appropriate to pour living water on the head of his statue.

In the past two decades or so, Cioran had no need for such therapy, even though, before 1989, the reception of his work was precarious, for his philosophical-literary glory proved uncomfortable for the (not only) cultural nomenclature of the totalitarian regime.

Beginning in the 90's, however, the Humanitas publishing house (later joined by other editorial houses) made Cioran's work, in its entirety, available to the Romanian cultural market (with ample space provided for any surprise). It was a long-awaited retaliation, after the lengthy ideological censorship imposed by the former dictatorship. Who would have thought we would see one day in our local bookstores, shelves loaded with those same volumes that some people, by I don't know what mechanisms of the occult, owned – even before 1989 - as Xerox copies? It sounds incredible, but this is the way our cultural history looked, life-sized, at the time.

Cioran was extensively read after 1990, out of both pleasure and curiosity, and it was mostly the young generation who, in increasing numbers, read his books, avidly and without a trace of snobbery. They were the characters who represented and maintained – and maybe still do – a Cioran syndrome or effect. In fact, the wide-scale acceptance of Cioran's works was underway, an acceptance which, in most cases, was hardly assisted by exegetical discourse (a necessary grid, we believe, for works such as *The Transfiguration of Romania, Histoire et Utopie*, even *Tears and Saints* when Cioran was turning eighty, that we *organised a symposium* in Sibiu which had as its subject: "*Cioran – between a negative mystique and an anatomy of decomposition*" (April 11-12, 1991), a *binomial* which seemed challenging at the time through the Cioranian formulation of its terms. It was, in fact, the first cultural act of its kind devoted to Cioran, followed by a kind of epidemic of festivals of homage, with the notable exception of the Colloquium held in Sinaia. The sponsor of that meeting was the Inspectorate for Culture in Sibiu County; Continent Press and Publishing Group and the magazine *Euphorion* agreed to participate as partners, at least formally.

Coming, beneficially, from the direction of Cioran's text but also from its con-text or sub-text, the guests at that Colloquium proposed either exciting or easily obedient-Cioranian reading hypotheses: Vasile Avram "From shout to aphorism," Adrian Boeriu "Cioran or an exercise in insubordination", Aurel Codoban "Speech and/or nothingness", Ion Dur "Cioran *versus* Cioran", Doina Graur, "Being and Nothingness", Irina Mavrodin "A reading from the inside", Dan C. Mihăilescu, "Cioran's Demon", Gabriel Popescu "Cioran and the hermeneutics of power", Toma Roman, "Cioran S. A.", Doina Uricariu "Syllogisms of serenity" (without proposing a specific topic beforehand, Bishop Antonie Plămădeală formulated, in a short draft, some ideas about the relationship between Cioran and God/the Deity).

After a Noica colloquium, the first of its kind in post-communist Romania, held in the mountain resort of Păltiniş (in December 1990), the Cioran *symposium* tried to measure the degree of his assimilation and perception in the *medieval age* which began with the political hurricane triggered the previous year. We had planned with the Bishop of Transylvania, Antonie Plămădeală, a similar event for the works of Mircea Eliade, to be held in the Sâmbăta de Sus monastery. But it was not to be, the primitive accumulation of financial capital created insurmountable problems.

A dialogue on the edges of Cioran's work, as it was expressed at the time, had outlined some, perhaps meagre conclusions. But, beyond all expectations, it was clear that the Cioran effect could only be at its inception, the "on-call sceptic" of the universe, being, at the time, only superficially known and therefore garbled in a cultural space which had thrown upon him anathemas of all kinds. And if some sort of resolution is formulated from a critical angle, it could not be any other than the need for *(re)-knowing* Cioran. This implies (re)reading, without myopia or long-sightedness, all the books written in the two idioms that, alike, were entitled to claim the author as their own.

I wanted that national *symposium* (which has since become international and reached its XXI-st edition) to have as a guest Cioran himself, a request that I expressed in a letter in which I also requested a text about "his faraway friend", Constantin Noica. Aurel Cioran, brother of the philosopher, knowing his reactions only too well, assured me in advance that he would not come. And this is what happened, Cioran elegantly refusing despite my pleadings, and sending me the following letter: *"The Romanian language is one of the most poetic languages. Unfortunately, it belongs to an almost prehistoric era of my life. A few days ago, I sent Liiceanu a concise text about Dinu Noica. I don't* think it's necessary to write another one. The important thing is his work, not our comments. As for the character, he is complex, fascinating and confusing: impossible to define by a simple improvisation.

How far Sibiu seems to me now! I don't have the courage to see it again" (Paris, October 19, 1990).

Indeed, maybe here, in the last line of the letter, was hidden, in its obvious fragility, the reason why Cioran had not come to our debate in Sibiu, he who yearned relentlessly after the hills of Șanta and Coasta Boacii, or the stones on the road to Rășinari, to say nothing of another symbol so precious to his existence: The Library of The Romanian Academy.

The meeting between Cioran and what we call, perhaps too easily sometimes, his *fatherland* (Eminescu sends us, for the etymology of the term, to the Latin *pater*) could have been fatal. His sensitivity, almost pathological in some instances, would have been able to bring him face to face with an unwanted collapse. He preferred the protective distance and the silent suffering, instead of a live confrontation with the paradise that was not supposed to degrade its ontological condition if it wanted to remain a paradise (such a topos, however – the paradise – is what it is, precisely because it is lost).

1.2 Manuscript *versus* definitive edition

The need for *critical editions* of Cioran's work is keenly felt. Of his works – and we have in view here not just the ones written in Romanian – the one that is always located in the critics' line of fire is, without doubt, *The Transfiguration of Romania* (1936).

It is, perhaps, the essay which has been most colourfully commented upon, because it is one of his most controversial works. In the anthology of (until 1989) Cioran's work through which he was perceived, edited by Marin Diaconu, we can easily see this. But also, in later times, the text which fuelled the most devastating critical attitudes towards the work of Cioran remains this same book, printed in January 1937 (joined, if the truth be known, to the group of interwar pro-Legionary publications).

As is known, the most sophisticated comments emerged not only in Romania (I have only partially excluded from their sphere Marta Petreu's book, *A debauched past or The Transfiguration of Romania*, Apostrof, Cluj-Napoca, 1999, which requires a separate discussion), but also, particularly in France, where criticism of Cioran's work took the form of a so-called media performance, appetizing and intensely spicy. And the main charge of the prosecution was *Cioran's concealed ideological past* in the fourth decade of the XX-th century. Had there been, until now, a critical edition of *The Transfiguration of*

Romania, it could have added a few flat notes to its tendentiously-biased critical reception.

In a comment that we ourselves made about *The Transfiguration of Romania*, we placed this text within the ambit of pamphlets.[1] The book appeared in two editions: the *princeps edition*, printed by the Vremea Publishing house in 1936, reissued in 1941; and the 1990 Humanitas edition, "the only authorized and final version", as specified on the cover page of the volume.

The option for which we plead, therefore, is simply expressed in these lines: at least in terms of the now final destiny of the text, now final, of the essay *The Transfiguration of Romania*, we need a Cioran resembling the original as much as possible. Even if my proposal ignores the will of the one who wrote the book, a critical history of the works of Cioran will have to restore the author, life size, to himself. And, also in line with the original, in other words, it sends us to *the extent of the exercise of hermeneutic reading* that we employ for Cioran's text, the latter always challenging if not downright outrageous, which can lead to exaggeration or even fabrication on the part of any interpreter.

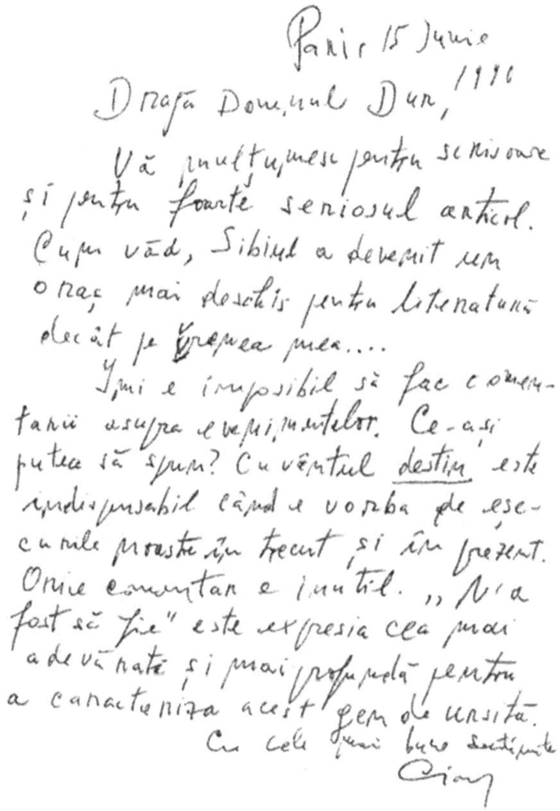

> Paris 15 Junie 1990
>
> Dragă Domnul Dan,
>
> Vă mulțumesc pentru scrisoare și pentru foarte seriosul articol. După cum văd, Sibiul a devenit un oraș mai deschis pentru literatură decât pe vremea mea....
>
> Îmi e imposibil să fac comentarii asupra evenimentelor. Ce-aș putea să spun? Cuvântul destin este indispensabil când e vorba de esecurile noastre din trecut și în prezent. Orice comentar e inutil. „N-a fost să fie" este expresia cea mai adevărată și mai profundă pentru a caracteriza acest gen de nereușită.
>
> Cu cele mai bune sentimente
> Cioran

Figure 1

Letter written by Cioran when the Miners' Revolt in Bucharest (June 1990) was going through its "pampering" final moments

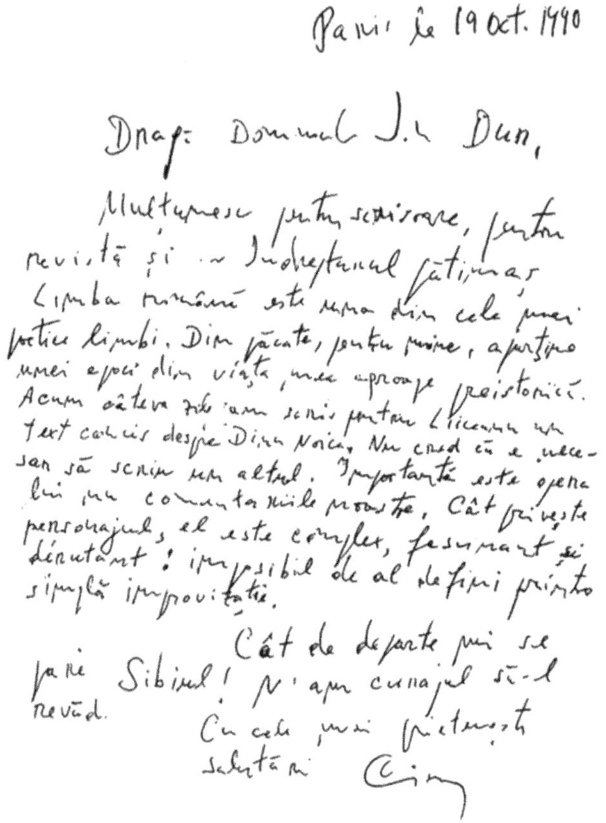

Paris, le 19 oct. 1990

Dragă Domnule J.L. Dun,

Mulțumesc pentru scrisoare, pentru revistă și ... Îndreptarul pătimaș. Limba română este una din cele mai poetice limbi. Din păcate, pentru mine, aparține unei epoci din viața mea aproape preistorică. Acum câteva zile am scris pentru Liiceanu un text concis despre Dinu Noica. Nu cred că e necesar să scriu un altul. Importantă este opera lui nu comentariile noastre. Cât privește personajul, el este complex, fascinant și derutant: imposibil de al defini printr-o simplă improvizație.

Cât de departe mi se pare Sibiul! N-am curajul să-l revăd.

Cu cele mai prietenești salutări

Cioran

Figure 2

Facsimile of the letter sent in response to the invitation to participate in the *Cioran Symposium* in Romania (April 1991).

1.3 "The gift of sorrow" – a phenomenological sketch

The mould of Cioran's thinking has been decoded up till now from various angles: either the philosopher should be a specialist in the problem of death, as he described himself, therefore, a kind of servant at the court of Thanatos, who spoke the dialect of the latter; or he should be the usual sceptic of the universe, as many exegetes have concluded, a spirit prey to utter and radical hopelessness, verging on, if not similar with, the futility of an Ecclesiastes.

Cioran's scepticism remains, however, atypical. We don't have to deal with behaviour loaded with the gestures and reflexes of defence or failure. Cioran is not a loser but has the ontological saturation of an *outraged* and *rebellious man* within the Camusian meaning of the phrase; he is a being always *contrary* or *against the grain* towards everything that has been created from the time of Adam, a radical reformist dissatisfied even with suicide, which will have to be itself reformed. Disease and pain sublimated in suffering which is imbued with metaphysical determination, the boredom and melancholy generated by a too-full existence, lived on the edge of falling out of time – are forms or negative states which engender philosophical reflection.

But together with these main hypostases of Cioran's thinking ego, as a kind of *sapiential state* in which the ones who came before melt and form an active whole, we find that condition which reigns over the mind of the philosopher, a native, state, almost a being-ness, if we can say so: *sadness* or, as it will be redefined in the first book written in Romanian, but in France-*grief*.[2]

A sceptic such as Cioran was never against God, as some of the readers of *Tears and Saints* believed, but incessantly, desperately and exclusively addressed this Great Silent One, the most powerful dialogue partner who fascinated him both by silence and, paradoxically, by absence. In this book, which Cioran preferred among all those he wrote, he spoke of sadness as being located *after* boredom and melancholy, but *before despair*. And looking at its levels, the most unsustainable for inspiration would be the *temperate sadness*, for the frequency of vibrations would later induce states of poetic, musical and, as a last expression, religious sadness. Beethoven seems to have resisted the "temptations of sadness" a bit too much; instead, Chopin or Schumann have often been gripped by a lust for sadness.

Perhaps the first thought exercise Cioran accomplished on the topic of sadness was the one found in *On the Heights of Despair* where, in the paragraph entitled somewhat didactically "On sadness", the philosopher noticed, comparing it with melancholy, that sadness has "a closed seriousness and a painful inwardness".[3] But what he found most revolting was the fact that neither state constituted an igniting inner force, as neither "irritates man to the point of shaking the fundamentals of his being".[4]

Moreover, a significant note for sadness would be its frequent occurrence *after* (meaning: at the end of) "great satisfactions and vital accomplishments" in the category of which Cioran included, in particular, the sexual act, extreme drunkenness or the Dionysian paroxysm. The basis for this explanation can be found in the *losses* – and not the gains – that such feelings or experiences invariably cause. There are excesses that don't leave behind more than a "feeling of the irredeemable and a sentiment of desertion and loss", not to mention, also on the level of sadness, the almost total absence of an aesthetic dimension.[5]

However, *sadness* appeared to Cioran as one of the faces or masks that the agonic nature of life wears, and the cramped mechanism that produces them protrudes into the essence of our being, making us wonder if sadness "is not, somehow, a form of objectifying death in life".[6] In addition, because it facilitates mystery and is in itself an inexhaustible, rich and enigmatic mystery, sadness belongs, Cioran believes, to the category of "mysteries of the infinite, which never cease to show themselves, because they are inexhaustible".[7]

Sadness came thus to represent, for Cioran, a *constitutive obsession* in relation to the human being. The philosopher deconstructed incessantly, almost sickly, the same and yet a different sadness, to which he finally gave a fundamental role in the composition of the human being, and in the manner in which he lives his life. If paradise was corrupted, first, through knowledge, the second time this fragile role belonged to sadness. Only then would the philosopher be reborn under the aspect of the serpent, says Cioran – self-referential, with Biblical and sibylline innuendo – in the *Book of Deceptions*.

And everywhere in this work which displays a voluptuousness of wailing, putting "the courage of deception" to work, Cioran not only speaks about "feeling the music of existence" or of the fact that, through musical ecstasy, we return to the "primary roots of existence",[8] but also notes that our intimate core of sadness, independent of any external shape of such a condition, is "*the sadness of being*, which is the true metaphysical sadness".[9]

Therefore, belonging necessarily to our irrational core – without any chance of being expelled from the economy of our being, for whoever fights against this kind of sadness is fighting against himself – such a sadness, finds Cioran, is "tied to the Being that precedes man".[10]

Such an idea was not new to the philosophical world of Romania if we would just remember Blaga, who sublimated metaphysical sadness and gave it poetic expression and even more. For Cioran neither is this thought an asymptotic flash. He invokes even a project of unexpected meditation taking the form of a *tragic anthropology*[11] (the only one that exists), structured into two main oppositions, so many chapters of such a discourse: the relationship between consciousness and life, on the one hand, and the relationship between illusion and essence, on the other hand.

Our analysis will not linger in this alcove of Cioran's thought, in which work assumptions which diametrically overturn classic normality. Essentialism is irrevocably compromised as long as the essences are declared "a superstition of the philosophical spirit", and their place and rank are taken over by deceptions, for "the fullness of life does not exist except in delusions, because in its substance everything is delusion";[12] and the final sentence states, with its apodictic character: "Delusions are originals; essences are derivatives".[13]

Cioran had a somewhat Eleatic attitude towards knowledge and towards communicating its results as he was building an endeavour in which the paradox was the main figure of a knowing spirit. However, an exception to this *more vivid closeness* of essences remains: "the path of the religious and the obsessed", the one whose guides are suffering and sanctity, those which activate and support the state of *religious sadness*.

Cioran speaks about the *road of sadness*, one that stretches from *the flesh* up to *sky*,[14] a path upon which religious sadness and the sadness of the metaphysical alternate and are organically combined. If *Tears and Saints* is the product, perhaps the exclusive product, of the first, Cioran's other books seem written under the not exclusive spell of metaphysical sadness. With *The Twilight of Thoughts* (1940) this latter form of sadness or sorrow takes the shape or the form of *grief*. For *grief* seems to be a much more personal code for the *tissue* of Cioran's thought, it is a *master-word* (Edgar Morin) which the philosopher, as we will see below, invoked in the title given to the manuscript of his book. Sorrow turned into *grief* is also confirmed by the Biblical quote from Chronicles 2, 18: "*Feed him with the bread and water of sorrow*", a sentence with which Cioran opens *The Twilight of Thoughts*.

Akin to Micaiah, who was resented by the king of Israel, Cioran is thrown into a dungeon, one of tragic thoughts fertilised by the metaphysical sadness of *grief*. And grief, as he says in the phrase which concludes the book, is "a *gift*, like drunkenness, faith, existence and all that is large, painful and irresistible".[15]

1.4 *The Twilight of Thoughts* – the context of reception

Considered to be, until the revolution of 1989, the last book written by Cioran in Romania, *The Twilight of Thoughts* is a book written in Paris, begun in 1938, and printed in Sibiu in January 1940. In a country infected by political leukaemia (just like today) and in a Transylvania disputing its identity (the hijacking of the Northern part of Transylvania), Cioran's volume faced a somewhat precarious reception. But even half a century later in 1991 when the work, thanks to the Publishing House Humanitas, returned to the public, or after its translation into Cioran's temporary-foster language (see *Le crépuscule des pensèe*, Librairie Générale Française, Paris, 1993), *The Twilight of Thoughts* did not have a more insistent and deeper reading.

We believe Dragos Vrînceanu is among the first to issue a verdict on the book, under the significant heading: "Why did Mr. Emil Cioran reach the 'twilight of the mind'?"; he finds in the volume "a disintegration into aphorisms", "dialectical games of the phrase," and the author appears as an "early Seneca of serious reflections".[16] Another exegete, Mircea Mateescu, formulates the issue of Cioran's originality of thought, its metaphysical depth, for which he invokes the similarity between such statements and the writings of a Heidegger, a Kierkegaard, a Scheller or a Jankelevitch. The critic asks himself how thorough was Cioran's reflection, especially when debilitated by some notes from *The Twilight of Thoughts*, a "symptomatic book"[17] for the spiritual evolution of the author.

And, still, inside the same axiological horizon of chosen values of reception, Grigore Popa writes of a "chronicle of ideas" trying to identify a substantial list of the "spiritual family" and claiming Emil Cioran as one of its members. He notes the "vocation of authentic thinker" of an author who was building a "metaphysical diary" after the model of Gabriel Marcel, while the confessions of *The Twilight of Thoughts* were located between "the piety of prayer and fiery tongues of the curse". Cioran is revealed as a passionate reader of the Bible, a great *writer* in whom the expression is "consubstantial with the thought", and *The Twilight of Thoughts* remains a beautiful piece of writing about *the tragic destiny of man*" (the tragic, but also romantic, Cioran was the central point of a note made by the young Victor Isaac), a "metaphysical view of existence",[18] a luminous book that includes a lot of pain and quiet consciousness. In short: a twilight or twilights that heralded *auroras*.

The manuscript of *The Twilight of Thoughts*, which I read in the Aurel Cioran archive in Sibiu, comprises of six notebooks (formatted - 17 cm x 22.5 cm), of which the first is missing. Book II starts with part III of the book: "I have got a heart like wax...", has 70 files written on one side of the page only, with black ink. Without proceeding now to a parallel reading *manuscript/princeps-edition* of the book, we will examine just some significant features. The text of the notebook is relatively clean, with few hesitations, abandoned words or sentences. It's a writing that expresses the stillness of disturbing ideas.

The most important thing, however, is the title or titles on the cover, which I try to decode in their palimpsestic overlapping: initially, *A breviary of grief,* then *Summaries of sorrows* and *Roundup of tribulations*, the final one – *Breviary of griefs* – being reiterated on the covers of the other notebooks. Therefore, *the original manuscript title* of the book *The Twilight of Thoughts* is *Breviary of griefs*.

Shortcuts

Notebook III has 50 pages, written only on one side, in the same black ink, the same clean text, as if it were a transcription. A specific element, however: on the cover, in fine writing, the quote "Feed him with the bread and water of sorrow" (Chronicles 2, 18), the *motto* that actually opens Cioran's book. The identification and invocation by the author of this message from the Bible remain, as yet, an unknown. Could Cioran have deciphered the sense of this Biblical quote after dozens of pages of reflection?! Anything is possible, including the presence of this quote in the presumed Notebook I, which we did not see.

Books IV, V and VI have 50, 73 and, 44 pages, respectively, and are also written on one single side of the page with the same accuracy. The final part of the manuscript is missing about 12 pages, which represents chapter XIV of the book. And another clarification: on the cover of Notebook V, at the bottom, the following words are written and then crossed out: "The gift of grief", a phrase with which Cioran's book actually ends.

Could *Breviary of griefs* be yet another title variant of *The Twilight of Thoughts*?!

1.5 Cioran and Anselm

A meeting with Umberto Eco's writings can never be a waste of time. Even in texts that sometimes seem to disappear in the dust of everyday publications (of course we take into consideration the ones in which he published, and which appeared in Italy), Eco is serious in his thinking, and this when you least expect it. Each of his ideas equates to years of research; his flashes of insight can light up reflexive beginnings. In an anthology of published texts such as *Kant and the platypus* (Constanţa: Pontica Publishing House, 2002), after various discussions, you come across countless references or incredibly valuable allusions. One of them suggests a parallel between Cioran (I was about to write: the Qur'an) and Anselm, in connection with the ontological argument. Here is an area of research unpursued until now in Cioranian exegesis, a path seemingly untrodden so far.

1.6 Cioran imprisoned

I was unaware of this particular issue from the biography of the person who has turned his own "I" into an eternal prison. Pamfil Şeicaru wrote in *Curierul Românesc* in 1961 that, while in Paris, Emil Cioran resigned from the position as cultural attaché at the Romanian embassy, a job to which he was appointed by the Legionary government, and the liberation of France from German occupation would cost him "six months imprisonment".[19]

What happened? To further quote Şeicaru: "In the passionate atmosphere of the first months after the withdrawal of German troops, Emil Cioran was the victim of an error and, as he could not be accused of anything, he was released. It seems natural that those prison months should represent for him a time of monastic meditation, a pessimistic re-inforcing of his Nietzschean individualism".[20]

What "error" could that be? The traces of this episode have to subsist somewhere; in the correspondence of those years, in a page of the diary or, why not, transfigured in a little-known fragment of the *Précis de decomposition* or any of his other writings.

1.7 Cioran – the gnostic?

Everywhere in his work, Cioran seems to relate to the world like a gnostic of the first centuries: the world is for him a kind of grave, a hole into which, by the inconvenience of being born, he was thrown forever.

However, Cioran is not an absolute gnostic, because then he should also consider that salvation can only be accomplished through knowledge. Or, in Cioran, salvation occurs through the therapy of writing, offering him shelter when faced with suicide.

Actually, as we have already said, Cioran is – even if he didn't wish to acknowledge it later in life – a Nietzschean in disguise. In Aesopian terms, he is against Christian morality, and (pre)tends not to have read this anywhere; he wants to escape obnoxiously negative pessimism through negative experiences which he does not hate at all; and turns despair, as his youthful emulator also did (at a time when he was not shy of delightedly acknowledging his affinities), in the most unbeatable hope, located at the end of an almost heroic effort of imagination and willpower. And Cioran also resembles Nietzsche when he converts the aesthetic contemplation of life in lyricism and does it as a *pure-blood fragmentist.*

1.8 The stigma of biography

Any exegesis of Cioran's work can't abdicate from a certain form of biographism, required of any researcher who might be interested in both the personality and the creative output of this author. Ideationally speaking, Cioran's biography underpinned much of his writing.

One can say that Cioran was a *rebellious child*, an attitude which will imprint his aphorisms. He was born in a geopolitical space dominated by the Austro-Hungarian Empire, and his parents were deported by the Hungarians during the First World War, something that should not be ignored when talking about a *complex of the foreigner* in Cioran.

But we should not extrapolate the properties of a part to the whole. Cioran's relationship with Hungarian ethnicity is not so linear and exclusive. He detested, but also almost ecstatically admired the Hungarians: their music, their language and their women. But the alien complex also includes the Russian, and the Jew, and the Romanian, and others, about which Cioran will speak in *The Transfiguration of Romania* and in other books which followed it.

The young Cioran's biography also reveals his special relationship with his father, the Orthodox archpriest Emilian Cioran. Cioran, the philosopher, had certain anti-religious reactions, despite the fact that he was genuinely interested in religious life. It is well known that at the age of 26, when he was a professor of philosophy at the Andrei Saguna Highschool in Brasov, Cioran undergoes a *religious crisis*, avidly reading the mystics and hagiographic works and writing a disturbing book (*Tears and Saints*, 1937, which Cioran regarded as the most beautiful of all his books), after which he will understand that an enormous gap lies between him and religious belief. In his paradoxical style, he will say that he could have been at most an *atheist theologian* and nothing else.

We resume here things which have become *commonplaces* in an Aristotelian way of speaking about the biography of Cioran. At the age of ten, he leaves his native village, Rășinari, with the already famous hill "Coasta Boacii", and moves to Sibiu. He will study at the "Gheorghe Lazar" High School of Sibiu (Hermannstadt) and will start, also biographically speaking, one of the tensest periods of his life. But also, one of the most decisive experiences he is ever going to live. Suffering begins to establish a monopoly in his life. Suffering from insomnia, he knows and lives the biological limits of such a disease. He thinks that he resembles Nietzsche also an insomniac; Nietzsche, who states that *the suffering man is the real man*. He then convinces himself, like the Ecclesiastes, that all is vanity. He is desperate in the highest degree, he has an experience of agony, and he even reaches the brink of suicide, when he eventually becomes "a specialist in the problem of death". He is saved from all this by his writings. *On the Heights of Despair* 1934, is the first evidence of this. From then on, writing a book becomes a *suicide postponed*.

Music will also have all the properties of therapy, rushing in on Cioran's meditation. He admires Beethoven, Mozart and Chopin, but venerates Bach in the highest degree. Without Bach, says Cioran, God would only be a third-rate character.

Biography, in Cioran, becomes work by sublimation, and the work *dictates* its course of action to destiny. A unique and productive symbiosis.

1.9 Around philosophy

For *the generation of the '30s* like that of Mircea Eliade, Cioran appears as a kind of *enfant terrible*. His approach to philosophy was done in an atypical way. The secret lies in the readings made by Cioran the teenager and Cioran the young man. He reads much, and about many things: religious philosophy; Dostoyevsky, who helps him transfer, in the fateful Brasov year of teaching, his *unfulfilled epilepsy* into books; he then reads Rozanov and Shestov, the philosopher of his generation. He also reads Nietzsche, Shakespeare, Schopenhauer, Kierkegaard, as well as many of the so-called minor authors. Some of the reading of a young man of 18-19 is evident in the *bibliographic file* that I compiled together with his brother, Aurel Cioran, and published in 2000 in my book (see *The litmus paper*, pp. 356-364). The authors he frequented remain reference names even today: Fr. Bacon, Julien Benda, N. Berdyaev, H. Bergson, Emile Boutroux. Emile Bréhier, Leon Brunschwicg, E. Cassirer, Shestov, Fichte, N. Hartmann, Kant, H. Keyserling, Alexander Koyré, J. Maritain, Henri Massis, A. Riehl, Max Scheler, O. Spengler, G. Simmel, Max Stirner, Otto Weininger, W. Windelband, H. Wolfflin, W. Worringer, Şt. Zeletin, Ed. Zeller, to identify just the great ones.

He will reach philosophy via a slightly circuitous path, through literature and authors considered unimportant, *secondary* by his generational colleagues.

He writes his first book, which is says Cioran the most philosophical of them all, a book that will be "a sort of farewell, full of anger and bitterness, to philosophy", "an indictment addressing a philosophy devoid of any efficacy in the serious moments of life". We will return to this sophisticated separation between Cioran and philosophy, after considering a few phrases from his first volume.

It was said about the writings of Cioran that they are: "Books to be read, but difficult to write about".[21] *On the Heights of Despair* (1934) is, as we will see in a different context, the journal of an insomniac, a man who lived *the limit* with pain and despair. Cioran is really suffering from insomnia and manages to transfigure this into lyrical-metaphysical texts. The title of the book is characterized by Cioran himself as being *pompous* and *trivial*. It was a phrase which appeared daily in newspapers of the epoch, under the heading "Miscellaneous", where many people wrote that they will kill themselves because they're "On the Heights of Despair".

Obviously, this is one of Cioran's rhetorical tricks, in the same way in which a mock histrionic (comedian, clown) gesture is also hiding in the way Cioran says that he chose his book titles. He had three or four formulated variants, went with them to the cafe or restaurant and asked the waiter which one he liked best (we could deal here with an involuntary gesture of testing the taste of the public, an exploration of the market in order to ensure the success of the book).

Cioran's book was "either the despairing cry of a misfit, or the daredevil gesture of an insurgent of nonconformity; or even the expression of a nihilism with bookish roots", subtly notes the same Gh. Vlăduțescu. And Mircea Eliade would later characterize Cioran's book; "as exciting as a novel, and at the same time melancholy and terrible, depressing and full of excitement".[22] While G. Călinescu notes that Cioran's philosophical essays are written "in Kierkegaard's aphoristic form". Likewise, Cioran's first essays will arouse, as we will see below, the most varied and contradictory reactions.

Cioran becomes, with this debut work, a *moralist*, and he will continue to be one even later, when he becomes a thinker of that *"l'esprit de finesse"* family, with a great freedom in thinking and who also takes huge risks. It has been said that Emil Cioran is a philosopher of the human condition, a creator who stretches the limits of philosophy and turns it into "a space of habitation, perhaps labyrinthine, proteiform, anyway a little disconcerting, being paradoxical, uncomfortable as quicksand, but fascinating as an adventure. And, in a way, as alluring as vice".[23]

1.10 The trial of philosophy: a form of free fall

It's a somewhat Don Quixotesque process, for Don Quixotism also means, after Cioran, "believing that something can still be done, and that we could be comforted by delusions".[24]

But what did *the breakup* with philosophy mean for Cioran? "I studied philosophy" he states "and I did it in all seriousness. Philosophy is extremely dangerous for young people; you become vain, you think you're important, you become terribly fascinating for yourself. Students of philosophy are in fact obnoxious, arrogant, with a challenging, over-inflated self-esteem".[25]

Cioran, however, had the structural nature of a lyric writer and a poet. His debut book representatively and symbolically illustrates the perfect osmosis between philosophy and art. He wanted to be a poet and confessed rhetorically, of course, that he wouldn't have been able to write more than "a rather dubious poetic prose". Cioran says and he feels that the essential experiences of life express our nature deeply and in a complex manner through art and poetry, but not through the use of concepts or conceptual thinking. That would explain why "almost all people write poetry when in love"; they might not express themselves with the help of concepts but using a "fluid and irrational material"[26] (the same things happen with suffering, about whose *monopoly* he will also speak in his first volume).

Cioran will be from the start against *abstract man*, and for *organic man*. He offers, as I suggested before, a eulogy of lyricism, that kind of lyricism unable to exist "without a grain of madness within".[27] To which one can add another eulogy, this one with a rhetorical, peculiar simplicity, and the condition of a genuine-natural state; when asked what job he would have wanted in life, Cioran answered without hesitation that it would have been better for him to be a shepherd's assistant, a locksmith or a forest ranger.

For Cioran, "life becomes the supreme value"; spirit, culture, morals, God himself turn into "substitutes for life".[28] He wants to *detach* himself, elegantly and rapidly, from the world and to *attach himself to the "I"*.

Detachment from the world as an attachment to the I – he will state this in the first pages of his debut book. Cioran makes an apology out of the organic and of the dated, rejecting that outcome which is located at the end of the road of thought. This is why he states that: "A stone, a flower and a worm are worth more than the entirety of human thinking. Ideas never gave birth, and they will never bear anything – not even an atom. Thinking didn't bring anything new into the world, other than itself; which is another world. Ideas should have to be pregnant, fatal and vibrant; to give birth, to threaten and to tremble. For they are not ours, if we don't carry them inside ourselves, as the woman does with the baby". The fundamental objection brought by Cioran against ideas is, therefore, that they are not *ours*: "There are no unique ideas; none of them has borrowed our *face*".[29]

If man manages to be personal in something, that *something* can only be *hatred*. Hate is the thing that divides us, and hate is also the cause of facts. "There is no act without hatred", says Cioran. "Each time hatred shrinks in me, I have the impression that I'm lost to this world, irretrievably lost. Only in hatred do I feel like a creature, only in hating do I belong to God's herd of beasts. And only when hate fills me beyond the edges, do I see the creature in the Creator".[30]

Therefore, thinking serves as an obstacle between us and life, between us and the world. Maybe that's why thinkers stay somehow on the surface of life; they break illusions from truths but remain ultimately *suspended* between them. Philosophers are not able to catch the substance of history, which is made up of *passions*. "History is not the bosom of Abraham", will say Cioran in another meditation.[31]

And here's how, slowly and gradually, Cioran reaches philosophy, doubts its legitimacy and speaks explicitly about "the separation from philosophy" (obviously it's about his breakup with philosophy and a certain sense that he will give the latter). "I never understood why philosophy enjoys a fearful importance, and I never understood the religious reverence people feel for it".[32]

A first finding: "philosophy has no truth", but it is necessary, hence inevitable, for anyone who wants to enter the world of truths, because you get into such a world only if you *"have passed through* philosophy".[33]

To get to philosophy, to go through the lands of this domain, and not to stay here. Philosophy has, therefore, the role of a compulsory interval which should be overcome if you want to get into the kingdom of truths. If you stay inside philosophy and frequent it for itself (the most sterile and useless endeavour in the world), then you have the misfortune to "remain forever in the middle, clogged up in mediocrity as in a destiny".[34] "Philosophers don't live in their ideas, but for them. They lose their lives trying in vain to give life to ideas. They don't know – what the last poet knows – that ideas don't get life. And so many times it seems to me that the last poet knows more than the greatest philosopher".[35] (Incidentally, the examples of poets Cioran calls upon are not at all in the sphere of *last* poets: Rilke and Baudelaire, for instance.)

We should not move too quickly, however, over the accents in this quote: Cioran always relates philosophy to life and to art or poetry respectively, and he accomplishes this by taking living *in the idea* and not *for the idea* as the Archimedean point. Cioran was revolted by the mental neutrality of philosophers, their jadedness. He remembered a disturbing thought of Georg Simmel, whom he admired and whose socio-political philosophy he adhered to, namely: "It is awful to think how little of the sufferings of humanity have passed into its philosophy".

Therefore, when he notes that "you can't do philosophy except in total mental indifference, I mean in inadmissible independence to any state of mind". Cioran himself becomes indifferent to philosophers and philosophy, thinks it is too convenient and easy for one to become a philosopher, and discreetly pities Kant: "Kant was never sad".[36]

Positioning himself in the lineage of Job, declaring himself his *great-grandson*, Cioran notes that he never had need of Kant, Aristotle or Descartes, who only "thought for our safe hours, for our allowed doubts". The meditation of a philosopher is infinitely more mediocre than, for instance, those experiences which cause "the silences in a doctor's waiting room". Philosophers are unable to speak of *the records of life*. Or, if they tried to talk about them, what they said is not even as valuable as "one chord of Schubert's unfinished symphony".[37] Philosophy could thus be defined in just one way: *the anxiety of impersonal people*.

On the other hand, reducing most of what there is to a kind of law of causality and trying to validate *the irreducible and the absurd*, philosophy "satisfies a mediocre taste for the absolute".[38] A creator of poetry, a musician or a mystic can *descend* into philosophy *only in moments of fatigue*. Their philosophizing is a condition with a minor range. Philosophy does not have, like poetry, an *ecstatic vibration* or *the cult of metaphysical nuances*, and what philosophers tell us *is as if it were a long time ago*.[39] Apart from his readings of

Nietzsche, in whom Cioran sees *more than a philosopher*, no other philosopher, once read, makes one feel that he has become *a different man*. The explanation seems to be simple: philosophers are servants of appearances and are far removed from *essential realities*.

And yet, Cioran cannot circumvent the prestige and the attraction exercised by philosophy: "It is strange and inexplicable - why do people turn to philosophy when they feel the need of solace. Why would they think of philosophers, in their most disturbing hour of need?" The philosopher, thinks Cioran, cannot comfort or console, for "any philosophy is an expectation deceived". "*Knowing* and *consoling* can never meet".[40]

Cioran wanted to be a philosopher, but, as he says, he *simply remained an author of aphorisms*, as he also missed the position of a mystic because he believed that he *could not have had enough faith* (an exegete saw in Cioran a kind of *frustrated monk*).

1.11 Loneliness in/for Cioran

Beyond its nature as a code or mark of any creator (in the altar of creation, the author is absolutely alone), loneliness is one of the privileged themes in Cioran's reflections on *life*, a trait that – talking about loneliness – belongs, first of all, to the *person*, but also, partially, to the thinker. Cioran thus browses the *steps of loneliness* with different modulations; from the frenzy on the Coasta Boacii hill, an episode loaded with so much melancholy, the joy of his life starts to fade away. He leaves Rășinari and goes to Sibiu, where he lives the experience of insomnia to its extreme limit, an undesirable and painful isolation, after which he follows the gap of his studies in Bucharest; then, until his death, the *mythological* space of Paris.

To rehearse the landmarks of solitude: The Coasta Boacii hill, the cemetery where he played with the skulls a grave digger gave him (which resembles a game with the ghost or the symbol of death) – insomnia (pushing the limits of the self) – the Luxembourg Garden (significant for his *solitary-ity*), followed by illness and loss of self. Cioran's loneliness is consumed in sinusoidal manner in a paradoxical way, somewhere between simple joy, sadness (and metaphysics), exaltation, excess, maybe some waves of ecstasy, with the latter understood as a pole of solitude for man in the world, a solitude created by the destructuring disease of being.

And here, the biography of Cioran indistinctly mixes with his work, so one could easily say that the steps of loneliness, segmented on the surface of his work, neatly overlap his biographical steps. Alone, lonely and singular, narcissistic beyond measure, he rejected even the idea of marriage as an act of life, which makes us to believe that he was *near* Simone Boué, and not *with her* as his girlfriend, if our observation is not unkind: "There is so much reason and mediocrity in the institution of marriage, that it seems to have been concocted by the hostile forces of insanity".[41]

Cioran's loneliness is consummated in new company: between *meditation* and *silence*: "You can't understand what 'meditation' means if you're not used to listening to the silence. Its voice is a waiver of any call-to-action".[42]

Conceived as an "aphrodisiac of the spirit", akin to conversation for intelligence, loneliness also has socio-historical determinations. A new niche opens here, extremely rich in speculation for almost the entire young generation, by which I mean: the generation of Mircea Eliade. Noica, for instance, speaks very forcefully about loneliness as the background of an intrusiveness of engineering, a factor that will facilitate the emergence of the "one-dimensional man", described by Herbert Marcuse.

Concerned about the irrational, about its upsurge, Cioran contrasts life and loneliness/solitude, the thirst for life being the path that separates man from loneliness.

However, in Cioran, there can be no question of *solipsism* if we try to delineate a philosophical understanding in the concept of solitude or loneliness. We must not try to avoid one thing: the doctrine of solipsism, very often cited under the name of *selfishness* in the guild of XVIII-th century writers,[43] especially Wolf, was claimed, somewhat shyly and with some reservations, by Doctor Claude Brunet in a *Journal de médicine* (1686), where the specific difference between "*le moi personnel empirique*" and "*le moi transcendental*" was vaguely referred to.

In Kant's *Critique of Practical Reason*, section 3, paragraph 3, we find the same concept, signifying here "self-love" (*Selbstsucht*), i.e., selfishness, in the common usage of the term, and the arrogance or infatuation (specific notes, with affinity for those of the *dandy*).

Cioran's loneliness, if we could outbid at least one other category, has only vague accents of asceticism, an intellectual asceticism, because this is where "*vivre dans la solitude*" would lead us: a secluded, lonely, isolated place, in the region of the hermit. Cioran was not an ascetic, but he lived, we believe, in *moral loneliness* He was a lyrical loner, one who scattered his own subjectivity, because being lyrical "means to not be able to stay in yourself".[44] We are all so alone in life, "that you wonder if the loneliness of agony is not a symbol of human existence".[45]

The loneliness of a name: alone anyway, even if there are other people who seem to have the same name; Cioran wanted to have exclusivity even here. He signs his first book in French, *Précis de décomposition*, as E. M. Cioran. Patrice Bolon believed that the attitude of *name solitude* would have been "*une pure affectation"*, an influence coming from a spirit such as E. M. Forster, *"dont il était alors un grand lecteur"*[46] (Aurel Cioran, more credible than Bolon, gives us another option – "M" comes from "Miluţ", the abbreviation of *Emiluţ;* we cannot rule out a Cioranian fad either, thrown towards posterity, to entangle the threads of biographers).

Another step in Cioran's loneliness: keeping the Romanian language beyond the forbidden door and demanding *linguistic asylum* in the vital space of the French language. Two books talk about this episode of Cioran's solitude; *Îndreptar pătimaş* [Handbook of passions] (Bucharest: Humanitas Publishing, 1991) and *Exercices negatifs. En marge du Précis de décomposition,* 'Les inédits de Doucet' (Gallimard, 2005), collection dirigée par Yves Peyré. The latter shows us a Cioran alone in the workshop where he carved the marble block of a book with which was going to enter, triumphant, into the hierarchy of value of French culture (and *the French spirit)*. There are books which hide: one – a rupture; the other, a crisis of beginnings in another idiom.

In addition, the fact that the Romanian language remained in the *linguistic being* of Cioran is shown, among other things, by his correspondence, filled with oases of Romanian words; by readings of the original versions of Eminescu's and Blaga's poems, as well as the Romanian diaspora press; not to mention the debates held – by him, Eliade, Noica, Virgil Ierunca, Monica Lovinescu and other convivialists of the Cioranian attic – on some of the terms in the Romanian vocabulary, for example: the word *"matracucă – old hag".*

Cioran is alone and is with everyone; he is alone among stylists and canonists. He lives what Noica called *solitude in community.* As Cioran's loneliness could be a form of unprecedented narcissism, as well as a radical rejection of any form of otherness – the Ego suppresses itself as personal ego and *imprints* the lonesome plasma of another I (a perverse alterity, will say, perhaps, Cioran?!).

This is how he appears to us, for instance, in a letter to Mircea Zapraţan, in April 1939. Gone were the Sibiu disorders ("ancient despairs in Sibiu"); Cioran was in Antibes, seduced by the charm of the Mediterranean and its clear sky, and the city of his adolescence seemed to be "the most expressive symbol of the immemorial". Reason gave way in front of trivial phenomenality: "From a philosopher of the white nights, you become a whore of the azure. That's my transition".[47] Therefore, he states that the sea, woman, and nihilism would form the triangle of happiness: "When you don't believe in anything, in the shadow of breasts and in marine solace you find the irresponsibility of God before creation. In distances and embraces, I have discovered the sweetness of nothingness. Imagine a sensual Buddhism. (That's the formula of your life.)".[48] There is here the expression of a Cioran alone in front of nothingness, but also of a Cioran who wants to *destroy* almost everything, apart from himself, of course.

Dense pages about loneliness can also be found in *On the Heights of Despair*, *The Book of Deceptions* and in *The Temptation to Exist* (see the chapter "A little theory of destiny"), to which we should add the essay "Loneliness and destiny", but also other texts from the author's interwar publications.[49]

Notes

[1] See "The pamphlet on 'national somnolence", in Ion Dur, "*Hîrtia de turnesol. Cioran inedit. Teme pentru acasă*" [The litmus paper. Cioran previously unpublished. Homework], Sibiu: Saeculum Publishing House, 2000, pp. 221-245. In the present book, *My Cioran*, I extracted and summarised from this volume that which was essential for *a portrait of the philosopher as a young man*. The resumption and the bringing together of texts depend on their ideatic *resistance* in time.

[2] This is *Amurgul gândurilor* [The Twilight of Thoughts] (1940), the fifth book which, as we know, Cioran would have written before leaving for France (*Îndreptar pătimaş* [Cioran, Emil, *Handbook of Passions*] would disturb the pentadic number and provide at the same time a different picture of the relationship between Cioran and the Romanian language).

[3] Emil Cioran, *Opere* [Works], vol. I, edited by Marin Diaconu, Bucharest: Romanian Academy, National Foundation for Science and Art, 2012, p. 54.

[4] *Ibidem*.

[5] *Ibidem*, p. 55.

[6] *Ibidem*, p. 56.

[7] *Ibidem*, p. 55.

[8] *Ibidem*, p. 56.

[9] *Ibidem*.

[10] *Ibidem*, p. 214.

[11] See the entire paragraph "*Gustul amăgirilor*" [The taste of deceptions], *loc cit.*, pp. 195-222.

[12] Cioran, *loc cit.*, p. 195.

[13] *Ibidem*, p. 197.

[14] See Emil Cioran, *Opere* [Works], vol. I, quoted edition, p. 381.

[15] *Ibidem*, p. 994.

[16] See *Curentul literar magazin* [The literary current Magazine], no. 44, 4 Feb. 1940, Emil Cioran, *quoted work.*, p. 1234

[17] See Mircea Mateescu, "*Emil Cioran, «Amurgul gîndurilor»*" [Emil Cioran, "The Twilight of Thoughts"], in "Universul literar" [The literary Universe], no. 7, February 10, 1940; *ibidem*, p. 1236.

[18] See Grigore Popa, "*Amurgul gândurilor*" [The Twilight of Thoughts], in "Sfarmă Piatră" [Stone Breaker], no. 22, May 19, 1940; *ibidem*, pp. 1238-1242.

[19] See "Cazul Noica" [The Noica case], in Pamfil Şeicaru, *Writings*, I, Eugen Frunză Publishing House, 2001, pp. 129-159.

[20] *Ibidem*.

[21] See Gh. Vlăduțescu, *Neconvențional, despre filosofie românească* [Unconventional, about Romanian philosophy], Bucharest: Paideia Publishing House, 2002, pp. 102-105.
[22] See Mircea Eliade, *Încercarea labirintului* [The trial of the labyrinth], Cluj: Dacia Publishing House, 1991, p. 86.
[23] See Gh. Vlăduțescu, *quoted work*.
[24] See *Cartea amăgirilor* [The Book of Deceptions], Bucharest: Humanitas Publishing House, 1996, p. 180.
[25] See *Convorbiri cu Cioran* [Conversations with Cioran], Bucharest: Humanitas Publishing House, 1993, p. 102.
[26] See *Pe culmile disperării* [On the Heights of Despair], Bucharest: Humanitas Publishing House, 1990, p. 8.
[27] *Ibidem*, p. 9.
[28] *Ibidem*, p. 152.
[29] See *Cartea amăgirilor* [The Book of Deceptions], *loc cit.*, p. 167.
[30] *Ibidem*, p. 168.
[31] *Ibidem*, p. 180.
[32] *Ibidem*, p. 168.
[33] *Ibidem*, p. 170, My emphasis.
[34] *Ibidem*, p. 172.
[35] *Ibidem*, p. 170.
[36] *Ibidem*, p. 171.
[37] *Ibidem*, pp. 176, 191.
[38] *Ibidem*, p. 172.
[39] *Ibidem*, p. 173.
[40] *Ibidem*, p. 171.
[41] See *Amurgul gîndurilor* [The Twilight of Thoughts], Sibiu: Dacia Traiană Publishing House, 1940, p. 281.
[42] *Ibidem*, p. 10.
[43] See André Lalande, *Vocabulaire technique et critique de la philosophie*, vol II: N-Z, Paris: Press Universitaires de France, 1993, pp. 1008-1009.
[44] *Pe culmile disperării* [On the Heights of Despair], Bucharest: Humanitas Publishing House, 1990, p. 7.
[45] *Ibidem*, p. 11.
[46] See E. M. Cioran, *Exercices negatifs. En marge du Précis de décomposition*, Paris, Gallimard, 2005, p. 179.
[47] See Cioran, *Opere* [Works], vol. I, edited by Marin Diaconu, Bucharest: Romanian Academy, National Foundation for Science and Art, 2012, p. 1126.
[48] *Ibidem*, pp. 1126-1127.
[49] See *passim* the anthology *Singurătate și destin* [Loneliness and destiny], Bucharest: Humanitas Publishing House, 1991.

Chapter 2

The ambiguity of the epistolary self

2.1 Card/letters, work/writings

The existence of the posthumous work of Cioran has generated a process that until now could be regarded as suspect, and that has triggered not only the redefinition of ideas for which the author has been sometimes unjustly anathematized but also the reconsideration of other aspects of Cioran, the man.

A beginning has to be made, therefore, with Cioran *the man*, who in the twilight days of his life suffered an incredible regression, when only the most primitive layers of the human being control a person's every gesture and behaviour, defeating their rationality (Gabriel Liiceanu spoke about these moments in an eerily beautiful text). There followed, a month after the death of the philosopher, a questioning of his youthful ideological straying, a Romanian past sometimes protected with recklessness and naivety by Cioran himself (an episode which we will examine in the final part of the book).

Unpublished texts, such as *Țara mea* [My Country] (for which I would have preferred the title: *My Homeland*) and the three volumes of the *Notebooks* (now printed in a single volume) have brought testimonies – in a way expected – and instantly processed into corrective views or reading keys for his work. To these were added *pages of correspondence* with all those situated in the space of *home*, parents, brother, friends, acquaintances, those who have opened more and more folds of a complex and contradictory personality

Over all the data, like the ghost of a Dionysian Hamlet (the phrase is inspired by Nietzsche), appears the vivid, always aristocratic silhouette of Cioran *the man*, wandering the depths of the huge laboratory where he created his work, coming towards us on the crests of the many turbulent waves of his time.

Books and letters, here is a binomial which puts into the equation the destiny of a creator. There is, in particular from Kant onwards, a distinction over which no exegete can pass easily: what elements form *the work*, and what are *the writings* of an author made of. Controversies and obstacles difficult to overcome start to appear only when trying a difficult distribution, into one structure or another, of the various elements of creation. For instance, and this is one of the impediments, where would the place of the *correspondence* be (from *corresponderé*, or *responderé*, in the sense of "to be in a relationship of compliance") in such a binary configuration? Otherwise said, what do all the books and the texts that make them up represent, and what do they represent in relation to the epistolary compositions, some more elaborate than others, more circumstantial/circumstantiated, or less subject to a regime of chance, expressing deliberate, natural honesty, and understanding through empathy.

Speaking, self-referentially, about a strange "epistolary mania", Cioran, a "lazy performer" in sending "letters", notes somewhere: "The truth about an author is often found in his correspondence rather than in his work. Most often the work is a mask".[1] Perhaps that's why we find in the letters, as their editor notes, a Cioran "more transparent than the one present in his own works" (we leave aside the disjunction, involuntary or not, between the work and the correspondence).

A cul-de-sac, perhaps only apparent, that we feared and which thus closes the doors right in front of an exegete who is not guilty of any crime. *The work*, therefore, carefully hides the meaning (why and for whom it makes this gesture, we already know now), while *letters* by the same author, sometimes banished from the space of the work, are generous and transparent, eager for easy-going revelations. And of this we undoubtedly convince ourselves, by the intensity and unexpected feeling of pleasure (covered with a hard to hide curiosity) which we experience when we read or – especially – re-read these intimate documents - letters sent or received by someone. The living – or *aliveness* – seems to be present here in the highest degree.

Indeed, in no other part of his writings is the author more authentic than in the lines in the letters, nowhere does he seem sincerer than in these confessions he makes with so much naturalness. The author is – in the private space of the letter– the person who writes in his pyjamas and not in a tuxedo, who writes to someone else (but actually writes to himself), who wants to send his mind elsewhere and – the same as an echo – to have it return to where it has gone (but, if possible, richer and clearer in meaning, free of doubts and more convincing).

2.2 A thinker in disguise – sincere letters

If we reject the work/correspondence disjunction, then the code, and not just the aesthetics of the latter, changes. Since the epistles are themselves an organic part of the work, do they not illustrate a mask – another mask – of the author himself? The letter becomes itself a kind of simulacrum, an honest one if I may say so. The honesty of the epistolary – the honesty of not giving up the mask, while standing with his hand on the props of a disguise – holds, in correspondence, as long as the author, in our case Cioran, confides in those belonging to the intimate circle of his family. From here on the *limits* and the desert of the artist begin. Likewise, Cioran seems to never put the mask aside, day and night; not even when answering letters or talking on the phone; not even when he finishes sketching his next paper, or notes in the *fragmentarium* of those, unknown until now, *Notebooks*.

In a way Cioran illustrates, through his writing, the parable of the famous paradox of the liar: the Cretan Eubulides says that all Cretans are liars (the question being, obviously, what does Eubulides say: a truth or a lie?). The one who hid so much from the others that he risked not finding himself in the end, turned – unwillingly – into a sorcerer's apprentice defeated by his own contrivances.

Through his thinking, Cioran has been permanently located in the riverbed of accented regression, exploring abyssal areas of being, where, as observed, we become, paradoxically, foreign to ourselves. Decoded in other terms, this itinerary meant a huge risk of presenting a less than true identity: by hiding himself in relation to others (here is a natural trick of the writer in front of the Other), he then lived the drama of finding himself with difficulty – or not at all.

The Mask represented, for Cioran, a cheap alchemy through which he tried to portray his disguise as most natural. His rhetoric against the much-maligned subject of philosophy is an eloquent example: "Hatred of philosophy is always suspect: it's as if you couldn't forgive yourself the fact that you were not a philosopher and, *to mask this regret* (my emphasis) harass those who, less scrupulous, or more gifted, have had the chance to build that little implausible universe – a well-articulated philosophical doctrine".[2] It is not difficult to recognize here a peculiar psychological attitude towards philosophers and philosophy: if you can't achieve a "system" of thought, then both the idea of the system and those who embody it have to be blamed, criticized.

And yet Cioran's correspondence – at least in part – seems to have a somewhat privileged status in the context of his work. The letters mark "a major event of loneliness", as it is said in

"Epistolary Mania", and the honesty of the writing displays even more faults. The people at home are nothing other than instances of different degrees of confession, beginning with his parents and his brother Aurel, and continuing with those with whom he fraternized – or not – in the space of ideas, with accidental friends and entourages, with women or with all sorts of "crackpots" who sought, for various reasons, his intellectual company and with whom he entertained a correspondence "*without object*".

While "books are accidents," the epistolary, therefore, constitutes "events", and in such a statute Cioran finds, once more, the "sovereignty" of the letters. But sovereign in relation to what and with whom? If *sent letters* can only partly illustrate a specific independence from their sender, for they finally enter into the skin of a role played by any text that communicates moods, feelings and neutral information to someone (a text that stands out from the author), *received letters*, in exchange (sent, in their turn, by someone) may only be dependent: on the horizon of our expectations, on an intertextuality which the addressee lives in the time elapsed between sending a letter and receiving the answer to it.

It is obvious that Cioran is interested in particular in the texts he receives (of those sent to him, he just keeps "copies of aggressive letters"), but that doesn't mean that they are the most important. Speaking from a value-oriented point of view, the words he sends hide – in a manner of speaking– many of the bookish invariants obsessively reiterated in the letters, with which Cioran the character almost invariably inculcates what he accused Nietzsche of doing in his letters: "*complains*, he is unfortunate, abandoned, sick, depressed" (with due nuances), issues judgments of value, gives medical advice, recommends biographical routes, invokes words of spirit, tells of the little things and minimizes the important ones. In all, Cioran is designing his pragmatic self and projecting his biography upon the others.

2.3 Homesick, "metaphysical stateless person"

It was said of Cioran that he had three *fatherlands*: Romania (for childhood), France (for the language) and Spain (for feelings).[3] We will reiterate here a distinction exposed in a different context: a thinker like Cioran – and the claim could be extrapolated, perhaps, to other authors – *had only one fatherland* (a word that comes from *patres* – i.e., parents) but more *countries* in which he could have established his *residence*. Even if often ambiguous, his countless confessions about his origins have a single and unchanging address: Rășinari, Transylvania, Romania, which he acknowledges with all its specificities: "It's sure that we are marked by the 'cultural space' from which we came. Transylvania retains a strong Hungarian 'Asian' imprint. I'm Transylvanian, therefore...".[4]

Exaggerating a little, it can be said that Emil-Michel Cioran has two origins: one is the *metaphysical stateless person* – in language or, more precisely, in philosophical language; another – the place where he first saw the light. We will examine in more detail these two assumptions.

Even if he will become "more adaptable and more conciliatory" in Paris,[5] Cioran does not stop, even for a moment, being crushed by what the words *home* and *homesickness* mean: parents, brother and sister, close relatives, the Coasta Boacii hill, the stones on the Rășinari road, Șanta, the Library of the Royal Foundation, his improbable and inimitable friend Petre Țuțea, other friends such as Bucur Țincu or Dinu Noica (here we see that "very human, caring, sensitive" Cioran endorsed by Constantin Tacou, whose scholarly work was published by the L'Herne Publishing house).[6]

This is not how he was seen by those who have characterized him, both biasedly and falsely, as a man without a home (*id est*: fatherland), i.e. a "metaphysical stateless person". Actually, where is the homeland of a thinker? Is there, after all, a homeland of thought, one that coincides somehow with the nationality of someone who "lives" inside such a *topos*? Things are a little more complicated because it would be necessary to discuss first the possibility of a national philosophy, a thing we do not propose to do here. Anyway, an appropriate response could be formulated, at least partially and approximately, from the philosophy of Heidegger: the *home* of a metaphysical thinker seems to be, or is, one and the same with his being: *his mother tongue*, more precisely the concrete form of it, namely: language. In other words, *the homeland of the metaphysical individual* called Cioran – the mask of Emil-Michel Cioran – is philosophical language, where he can have Plato, Kant, Hegel, Nietzsche or other thinkers as *fellow citizens*.

When we invoke Cioran's home and homesickness we invariably think about his place of birth, which has no replacement, and the nostalgia, without any substitute, for this space which becomes a mould. If he couldn't bypass – and how could he? – the status of *metic*, in exchange Cioran has never really lived, we believe, the feeling of uprooting; maybe only when he felt refused even by death (an idea of a mainly cosmetic nature, rather a compromise – or a form of complicity – with suicide, because it is a lack of existential morals to bet on a *postponed* suicide, a somewhat suspicious form of self-flagellation). While he was still studying in Germany, Cioran wrote to Ecaterina Săndulescu, a teacher in Ploieşti, that he had tried in vain for about two years to get some "roots in the world while remaining 'a world in the world; *hors la lui metaphisique*" (22 June 1935).[7]

And yet, how should a man who spends the last sixty years of his life away from everything that means the topos of birth be called?! If our wording is not paradoxical or contradictory, we can say that Emil Cioran was not really an uprooted person (or was one who kept his roots in the formaldehyde of his native language, the one which boycotted him in the last days of his life), but he lived the drama of not being able to catch (any) other roots. "I miss seeing you all again and I'm anxious for news",[8] – here's a thought that is repeated obsessively, in different forms, throughout the whole correspondence, a sentiment forever left unfulfilled.

Maybe that is why Cioran lived the drama of uprooting as a continuous postponement of the homecoming, which - in the plan of creation – was converted in fertile charge for the spirit. After 1989, the reasons for his refusal to return to his country, not so many, were minor as it seems, except for the fact that he feared the enormous shock caused by meeting with everything from his past ("The city of Sibiu is so far away! I don't have the courage to see it again" – as he wrote to us, in a fugitive letter, in the fall of 1990).

In spite of homesickness, which might have been less burdensome in the proximity of Romanians in the diaspora, Cioran will have, more than once, a somewhat equivocal attitude. On July 5, 1946, after what were in all probability unpleasant experiences and after lamenting that no friend in the country had contacted him, he wrote to his parents: "I'll keep myself apart from the Romanian colony here, where there are only intrigues and conflicts". And he did not feel otherwise the following year either: "The Romanians I avoid as much as I can: in general, they are schemers and spread false rumours" (September 13, 1947). And in the letter of February 19, 1948, in the full fever of publishing the *Précis de décomposition*, he is completely disappointed by "a few malevolent compatriots" who would have prevented his getting a scholarship from the French state; after which he states: "Paris became a centre of Romanians; I don't look for them and do everything possible to avoid them; they can only bring inconveniences; they go from morning till night from one to another carrying words and creating illusions".

This wilful isolation seems to have other connotations too; among others, that of a discreet detachment (or separation?) from a past that remained ominous: "As for me, I live very discreetly. Here, various persons have tried to use my name in different combinations, more or less political. But I cut it short. I don't accept being a tool for anyone. I got bored of any form of commotion and convinced that all the unpleasantness in life comes from participation in a group". Everywhere in the letters, sent home or to friends, reappears the reason for Cioran's relationship with the Romanian diaspora in Paris and the *ambiguity* which characterized him in a fundamental way.

Nietzsche says somewhere that the mask protects a man only if he's weak; the strong don't need such a travesty, because they are immediately recognized. Where will we recognise, however, Cioran? Probably in both poses. The second is illustrated by his gnomic work, where the artist Cioran hides until he gets to style. But the literary man – and Cioran can't be anything else – is the "fundamental actor",[9] and as for any actor, the mask is indispensable. As regards the first condition, that of a *weak* Cioran, it is the one portrayed by the world of letters, where the author of the texts abruptly expresses the fact that he "suffered from life"[10] and that, even in *writing* letters, he cannot give up the game of disguise.

The *Correspondence* of Cioran can be perceived, among others, as being (also) the expression of an *ambiguous I*, always tempted by the mysterious breastplate of accenting. Being another *"symbol of identification"*, as it was understood in the assembly of masks, the one worn by the Cioranian epistolary self has, however, the predominant function of disclosure, and only occasionally the meaning of protecting true identities, hidden pathways towards an authentic self, or of disguising the true meaning expressed by gestures and words.

I wear a mask, therefore I am: here is Cioran's postulate, not just as metaphysical thinker or writer, but also of one who had the "epistolary mania", the mask being a kind of doppelganger – proteiform in its states – haunting the work / writings and, as we assume, the correspondence too.

Notes

[1] Cioran, *Scrisori către cei de-acasă* [Letters to the folks back home], Bucharest: Humanitas Publishing House, 1995, p. 9.
[2] Idem, *Exerciții de admirație* [Exercises of admiration], Bucharest: Humanitas Publishing House, 1993, pp. 80-81.
[3] Verena von der Heyden-Rynsch, "Entre Therese d'Avila et Don Quichotte", in *Magazine littéraire*, no. 327, Dec. 1994
[4] Cioran, *Caiete* [Notebooks], III, Bucharest: Humanitas Publishing House, 1999, p. 59.
[5] Cioran, *Scrisori către cei de-acasă* [Letters to the folks back home], quoted edition, p. 18.
[6] See Marta Petreu, "Constantin Tacou", in *Apostrophe*, no. 2 (129) 2001, p. 5.
[7] see *România literară* [Literary Romania], no. 43, 1-7 November 2000, p. 10.
[8] Cioran, *Scrisori către cei de-acasă* [Letters to the folks back home], quoted edition, p. 15. The following quotations, without reference, come from this source.
[9] See Fr. Nietzsche, *Știința voioasă* [The Gay Science], in *Works*, 2, Bucharest: Humanitas Publishing House, 1994, p. 245.
[10] *Ibidem*, p. 308.

Chapter 3

The erotic adolescence of a septuagenarian

Cioran's correspondence, therefore, is an organic part of his work and his writings, as his letters are, for the most part, literature. Umberto Eco notes somewhere that almost anything an author writes – of course, if he is genuine, authentic – is literature, except for shopping lists for the market or shops. But even these lists of products or things that will be purchased have what the critic Eugene Negrici would describe as *involuntary expressiveness*.

In a rich and varied correspondence, Cioran's *epistolary* mania was incarnated in tens of hundreds of letters, available to us now for the most part due to the efforts of the editor Marin Diaconu.[1] Therefore, even in volumes III and IV, we do not yet have all the correspondence sent and received by Cioran.

A special segment is what we could call *love correspondence*, sparse epistles or, sometimes, a small sentimental continuum, like that between the thinker and a teacher of philosophy in Köln, Friedgard Thoma.[2]

As Nora Iuga, the translator of the book from German, says, Cioran appears to us, in this last erotic outburst, just as a Hyperion almost-ready to abandon his immortality for a few moments of terrestrial good luck. The man inside him gives up, humanly, all too humanly, in the face of the philosopher. It's like in that anecdote which depicts Aristotle being ridden like a horse with a Creole on his back; when seen by Alexander of Macedon in the garden with olive trees and plane trees, he tells the latter: I wanted to show you at first hand and warn you what *aberration* might befall you one day.

The dialogue between the two took place between 1981 and 1989 and was published in German (2000) when Cioran was no longer alive. The Romanian language version (2005), lacks, however, eight letters – it does not say why and who *censored* them – which is not the case in the German or Italian editions (we don't know in what other languages the volume might have been translated).

Cioran gets to know Fr. Thoma at the beginning of the ninth decade of the last century. At seventy years of age. The exchange of letters and the physical meeting of the two, the physical touches, such as they were, the fleeting looks, the similar cultural inclinations and apparently self-understood empathies disturb the philosopher in a big way, awakening the *organic man* asleep inside him. I was under the impression that this time, too, he would proceed as in other segments of correspondence with *those at home*, with friends or other acquaintances, with personalities who marked his destiny. I meant – referring to the adventures he experienced with his works, making allusions to their metaphysical code. I was wrong. Outside of some precarious references to the nature of his work – a *mixture* of philosophy and poetry, in which the latter prevails, a mixture which comprises *scraps of theology contaminated with the language of the mystics*, nothing metaphysical slips into the letters. Most of the correspondence with Friedgard Thoma, in particular, that of 1981, revolves around the *body* of the woman who awakened in Cioran emotional reactions of an adolescent, even schoolboy type.

We can tell, without any trace of aesthetic protectionism, that Cioran is, as he actually signs some letters, "the Loser", but even here the aroma of a wicked metaphor is never far from an inhabitant of Rășinari. (I can think now of the correspondence, also new, between Martin Heidegger and Hannah Arendt.) The difference in age is not something that matters much in this relationship, but the German woman's *attitude* towards her *friendship* with a philosopher who is, in equal measure if not even more, a poet. She relates to Cioran through the music they both admire, through his aphoristic essay works, through other cultural references. The erotic magnetic field of the teacher enters in resonance, almost exclusively, with these vectors. There is thus, for her, a Platonic and, I would say, "indestructible conspiracy", a "deep friendship" of a spiritual-cultural nature. If Noica impressed us by having read Kant's *Critique of Pure Reason* five times, Friedgard Thoma is moved by the intellectual efforts Cioran made to rewrite, also five times, the *Précis de décomposition* (1949), the book with which he made his debut in French culture and which established his place as a thorough-bred stylist.

Not the same cultural armature motivates or (over)excites Cioran. His erotic imagination works, most of the time, more intensely than upon musical options shared with his girlfriend, music being, however, an essence superior to life and death alike. It is in this manner that we assume and feel Cioran, as a *body* heated up, ignited during and after the first meeting between the two which took place in Paris, when Simone Boué, the philosopher's counsellor and life companion was away from home. Even if she is spiritually seduced, Fr. Thoma is reserved, prudent, does not follow her affective impulses or the allusions (allusion as a metaphor?!) coming from the flamboyant Cioran. The quiet resistance of the German girl begets a glaring fierceness on the part of Cioran. Sudden, intense, unsettling.

In 1981 Cioran lived in truly *sincere*, frantic states (with the sincerity of a highly refined stylist). A riot of hyper-senses seems to have taken him over. He begins to suffer from "sensual addiction", a state which appears so clear after he confesses abruptly, not at all metaphorically, on the phone, that he wants to bury his head forever under her skirt.

In oral or written language, we rarely have anything to do with any productive ambiguity of the epistolary self. With few exceptions, purged allusions or metaphors usually disappear. It is more of a disarming, naked sincerity of writing, similar – I choose here an extreme case, which may be relevant because of its extremity – to texts or statements on the walls of public lavatories.

One who looked ten times in books and maybe once in life, one who felt between his fingers the warm or frozen sensation of a pen wakes up, all of a sudden, face-to-face with a *devastating sensory and sensual actual.* Concrete, therefore with destructive impulses and a final generator of barely masked disappointments.

The two lovers, Emil and Friedgard, talked on the phone a lot, a good way of amplifying eroticism, and wrote a lot in the years 1981 and 1982, but deep silences and pauses also occurred between them, for as long as a year; they met time after time in Cologne, in Paris or who knows in what forgotten resort. Cioran wants to extract from her various confessions, intimate things, "more personal" as he says; he is as anxious as the servant waiting for the return of the master from moment to moment, a reason for which he suggests the use of a *poste-restante* address, a mechanism of keeping secrets away from the eyes of his *flat-mate* Simone Boué.

He himself writes like a hellhound, uncensored by any epistolary style, he is organic and too erotic in his language. A few weeks after they first met, he writes that he's suffering so much because of her, a suffering which frightens him a little; he says, with adolescent purity and gentle despair, that he wants to escape with her to a deserted island and cry all day. In another epistle, he wishes to die with her and, all childish because of so much loneliness, to be buried in the same coffin. He imbues her, offhand, with edulcorate epithets, telling her she's a "perverted nun", she is the goddess of one who believes in nothing (not even in Aphrodite?!) and that she represents for him "the greatest happiness and unhappiness ever experienced".

Cioran *dixit*, Cioran according to the original. He strolls, hand in hand with his girlfriend, through the Luxembourg Gardens, a sort of philosopher's living room or a substitute of those places where the ancients took their peripatetic walks, takes her to receptions to which he is invited; she is present when he meets his publishers; they visit Montparnasse cemetery where Cioran wants to show her his future burial place, a moment filled with that special kind of humour Cioran has: better go to visit your tomb when alive, rather than…

Undoubtedly, we have to deal here with a Cioran whose senses are fully inflamed, an extremely fragile lover, with an – I do not know whether genuine or *played* – extreme vulnerability, a Cioran hungry for the carnal, imbued with a Homeric sensual lust, a man who does not want to hear about the asceticism that makes the hermit look at a woman's thigh and think only of the meat in it and nothing more.

Could we have here the figure of an intellectual angst, bored by that shared solitude, a philosopher wary of any *ontic* experience, filled with existential frustration?! The fact is that Friedgard (Thoma) and Emil (Cioran) do not appear to us as intimate beings, as genuine lovers. The masks were not thrown away at all. It's rather a kind of playfulness mixed with unfulfilled juvenile desires, a duel between two people – one of which is deeply aware of the too-fulness of life, while the other bites discreetly and elegantly on it. In addition, Cioran's a tiger who has reached the golden age, and Thoma – a calm and elegant tigress, with a boyfriend beside her, another reason for high-school jealousy from Cioran.

It's weird and paradoxical, but the lovers always talk in *the second person plural* and this is not from simple coquetry or civility, but because that's probably how they feel. But against and over these somehow dividing segments, Cioran is openly and intensely possessed by the idea of possible carnal relations. The young teacher of philosophy, Friedgard, is for him no more and no less than "a sister for whom I feel an incestuous inclination" says the somewhat perverse Cioran. Or, he continues with the meaning of a known complex, had he been her father, he would never have allowed her to belong to someone else. "As a brother", perorates the possessive Cioran, "I must submit to the inevitable and suffer compromises and hide a few tears" (without having to think now about *saints*).

Not physically seduced by Cioran, only meta-physically, Friedgard's reply is extremely harsh and cold, noticing that while he is interested in the *immediacy of an epidermal, physical relationship* she wants "the erotic duplicity of a 'spiritual' relationship. She often specifies, on a subtle-categorical tone, that the ties between her and the Rășinarian-Parisian philosopher could not be those of the flesh. "Love does not ever compromise" says the translator on the fourth cover of the volume "love destroys; our memory always preserves the one who loves more – *the loser* – because he has been through hell" (one unpaved, or paved only with stones, as was the road from Rășinari after which Cioran longed unto his death).

I don't know if Emil Cioran, the septuagenarian, truly loved Friedgard Thoma, but it is certain that this relationship brought to his life, as he himself says *music and poetry*. "Better hell with you, than the blessings of solitude. You are my unavoidable curse."

Much too precarious, in the derogatory and not biblical sense, any *communication and communion* between the two convinces us that both are *partak-*

ing of the wafer of the same measureless love. After the fateful year of 1981, phone calls and letters are becoming increasingly rare, a certain *protocol* sneaks into their dialogue, seemingly more distant and colder as time goes by, the questions are getting thicker and the answers are still few. From "my frolicsome girl", an exciting and frisky appellative, one gets to "dear lady". The erotic tension tends to reach zero. Should it be all about the twilight of an alleged and impossible love?! Or maybe we have the tragic twilight of an unfulfilled love, one in which *the loser* was lost even to himself and wandered into an irreversible valley of complaint?! Possibly, something from all of them, but your heart is purely and simply breaking when you witness, at the end of this long twilight emptied of any trace of eroticism, the image of Friedgard Thoma sitting, impassive and compassionate, beside Cioran's wheelchair in the Broca asylum-hospital where Bergson the philosopher tried to live, only he knew how with the unforgiving illness that had befallen him.

The present becomes the past in the very instant it occurs; we know this. And everything is present, as everything becomes the past. In the septuagenarian adolescent, madly in love, only a few memories still survived the fangs of time. A year before starting the eternity of another life, before leaving for *the day with no twilight*, Cioran doesn't recognize his girlfriend of yore, Friedgard, the one who charmed his being and troubled him for the rest of his mundane life. Cioran's face, notes the professor of philosophy, "lies languid and seemingly asleep in the little 'Broca' park, next to the ruins of a monastery, where he is taken when the weather is good, in a wheelchair. A ruined being next to the ruins of a place of worship, what a heart-breaking juxtaposition. A philosopher arrived at the end of his life - prolific and exceptional in terms of the cultural - a thoughtful private thinker who, as he confessed, would have killed himself long ago if not for the idea of suicide. This is the supreme *argument* offered to those who could blame Cioran that he talked of suicide, even pushed some into its chasm, but never made the definitive gesture himself.

A "hunter of skirts" for his whole life, as he defines himself, lover of talk about brothels and cheap thrills, but also about the practices of brothels, living with Simone Boué a kind of *solitude in duo*, absolutely in love with both life and death, perhaps seeing in the latter either a void or a new beginning, after the expression of Levinas, but a better beginning than the original one, however, Cioran remains an irreversibly and indisputably original writer.

Indebted to the carnal and sensual, to the bodily vice gripped by the shame of the *human all too human*, the correspondence between Cioran and Friedgard Thoma seems to be saved, from a literary point of view, by its stylistically inimitable oases, even if we have to deal, again, with stylistic precariousness and metaphorical poverty. The truth here is abrupt, and it triumphs, an organic truth which doesn't aspire to become a metaphorical one.

Not for anything in the world. A love of Cioran's is a sad book. And tragic because of its painful messages. It's really all about *another Cioran, in and between its lines*. A portrait which stretches its fabric between, on the one hand, the exuberance with which the suddenly-in-love septuagenarian, blushing when facing the fervour of his senses, jumps and yells at the joy of the desired pleasures of the flesh; and, on the other hand, the tragedy exuded by the position of an insensitive octogenarian, inert to any internal or external stimulus, confined for the rest of his life to a hospital wheelchair.

At almost the same period (1985-1989), Cioran begins a correspondence with Alina Diaconu, a Romanian living in Argentina.[3] This time the letters have a different form, with a different stylistic brand. The letters breathe epistolary civility, balance, cultural meaning. He gives an interview for his Argentinian readers, and when finding out that she got a scholarship, he is sincerely overjoyed and advises her to circumvent the "scholarly environment – in America and elsewhere. As a writer, it's more profitable to sit down and talk with a driver than with a teacher" (13 July 1985).

In another letter, of November 29, 1985, he confides with affection: "In fact, you're right to consider me a sentimentalist. So I am, of course, since I love everything that is grandiose, I love Patagonia, I love Hungarian music and the *fado*" (*fádo* is a genre of popular Portuguese songs). And he returns to the thought of his correspondent's scholarship: "I remember that you had a scholarship, I don't know in what university. Whatever it may be, don't take it seriously, because there is no greater danger for a writer than attending this kind of institution".

That he was not so virile at that age, while still a bachelor as I said above, is apparent from a different confession, made on another occasion: "Lately I've had some trouble with my health. Now I'm better, but the result of the trials I went through will probably disappoint you: I've decided not to talk about myself anymore, to give up interviews, in short, to learn humility. This does not mean, however, that I will not be overjoyed to see you again, only that it will be without 'dialogue', without arguments, without a purpose...

Write a book about Patagonia. It's a topic that haunts me and which I find more interesting than the Balkans and their representatives" (March 16, 1986). In the same *lightning letter*, he thanks Alina Diaconu for sending him a poem by Borges dedicated to Susana Soca, the Uruguayan poet (1906-1959), stressing that "she would have deserved more, perhaps, but even this is not too bad". Cioran understood a little Spanish, Eugen Ionescu – none at all, which is why he recommends to his companion to write - if she wants to do it – a novel, but in a different language, because it would be a shame to devote such a creation to "two old, ignorant and, on top of everything else, exhausted little men".

The disinterest displayed towards *the public reception* of his books was a common practice of Cioran's. Referring, probably, to *Aveux et Anathèmes* (1987), he writes to his correspondent: "My last book is a *best-seller* thanks to television (obviously, I haven't participated in the programs). I believe this 'success' to be a real defeat, the most painful of my life. Old age is a series of surprises, I mean, of all kinds of humiliations" (March 31, 1987).

In letters written two years later, he's talking to Alina Diaconu about the surprising printing, in Romania, of a volume with translations from his books in French (see the translation made by Modest Morariu: E. M. Cioran, *Eseuri* [Essays], Bucharest: Cartea Românească Publishing House, 1988), and he also remembers "an excellent booklet by Mariana Şora" about his work (January 20, 1989). The year was 1989, which would see the Romanian revolution, and Cioran senses the shock waves announcing a political earthquake of epic proportions. He is up to date with everything that happens in his "native inferno" and, congratulating her for living at the other end of the world, he believes that "to the drama of existence is added the drama to belonging to the most unfortunate of peoples. And there's nothing more humiliating than to hear some – (and this happens frequently, Romania being, for quite a while now... fashionable!) – speaking to you with pity and with an easy contempt about an ethnic group that endures everything without protesting" (April 2, 1989).

But immediately after *the exploded Romanian polenta* (December 1989), Cioran gains some enthusiasm in his appreciation for the Romanians. It was not the Hungarians who made the revolution in Romania: "The revolution was in the air. It would have happened anyway, even if later. For the Romanians, however, it was humiliating to see that the Hungarians were the only ones to revolt. And this humility triggered the insurrection, which rehabilitated them in their own eyes, and, alike, in the eyes of the world". As for the *residues of communism* in Romania, he has serious reservations: "There is no doubt that the years of slavery endured by Romanians have left strong traces – both for the better and for the worse. I want to say that from now on their frivolity will have a different dimension".

Starting in 1990, Cioran's French works were to penetrate massively into the cultural world of Romania, through translations initiated by the Humanitas Publishing House. The loop of history was closing and the creation of the Romanian philosopher, who lived his inner and outer exile in Paris, could now be known in the altitude and amplitude of its value.

Notes

[1] See Cioran, *Opere Works*, vol. III and IV (published works, interviews, correspondence), Bucharest: Romanian Academy, National Foundation for Science and Art, Romanian National Literature Museum, 2017.

[2] Friedgard Thoma, *Pentru nimic în lume. O iubire a lui Cioran* [Not for anything in the world. A love of Cioran's], Est Publishing House, 2005; we will quote from this source without giving a full reference.

[3] See previously unknown texts published by the *Saeculum Magazine*, Sibiu (Hermannstadt), 2-2017, pp. 47-60.

Chapter 4

Impervious to the "French spirit"

I discovered Emil Cioran in a comment that publicist Pamfil Șeicaru made about him, in 1961, in *Curierul Românesc* [The Romanian Courier] (new series, Paris, no. 193 and 194). Having been sent by General Ion Antonescu, in August 1944, to support Romania in the West by means of a bilingual publication (in French and English) which was never printed, Cioran finally took up residence in Palma de Mallorca, in Spain (in 1945).

There, he starts to write, as feverishly as when he was a journalist in Bucharest. Pamfil Șeicaru will publish a series of portraits, mainly of Romanian political people, but it will also be interested in the "Exile Files" as one of the sections of the above-mentioned publication was named. Here he is interested, in 1961, by the "Noica case", a text in which, to fix the beginning of such investigations (meaning it almost has to be read with its police associations), Pamfil Șeicaru reproduces – but also comments – on Cioran's *Lettre à un ami lointain* (published, as it is known, in N.R.F. on August 1, 1957) and the epistle – from which the end is missing – to Noica: *Response to "Letter to a faraway friend"*.[1]

This epistolary duel, as well as the comments, not a few, which it has occasioned are already well-known. Cioran's text, entitled "Sur deux types de société", was to become, in 1960, the first section of the *Histoire et Utopie* (on the copy that he offered me at the beginning of the 90s, Cioran made, in green felt pen, a footnote on the first page of the letter in question: *"This 'letter' was fatal for Dinu"* – the Security Services in communist Romania were vigilant), and the Romanian translation of this book comprises, in the Addenda, Noica's text: "*Răspuns al unui prieten îndepărtat* [The answer of a faraway friend] (see Cioran, *Istorie și utopie* [Histoire et Utopie], Bucharest: Humanitas Publishing House, 1992). But Șeicaru's reaction, of its time, deserves, in itself, not only to be known, but commented upon and annotated. His perspective is emphatically memorialistic, he writes rather about Cioran the man and does it in the manner of a spicy narrative, with the description of some relatively cheap biographical episodes without any relevance for the work, although, as self-proclaimed exegete, Șeicaru sometimes pronounces a severe verdict on the latter.

It is true that, had I not read Șeicaru, I wouldn't have ever known (if his information is correct) that Emil Cioran was *the guest* of a prison for about six months. For economy of discourse, I will repeat here the information: after having resigned from the post of cultural attaché at our embassy in Paris, a job to which he seems to have been appointed by the Legionnaire government, in the intense *atmosphere* created by the withdrawal of German troops, Cioran "was the victim of an error; and as nothing was proven against him, he was released. It is natural that those months would have been for him months of meditative hermitage, accenting his Nietzschean pessimistic individualism".[2]

But Șeicaru is, most often, a thesist. Meaning - he does not formulate hypotheses which he then puts to the test, but puts forward a thesis with axiomatic value. He does not deconstruct, which would have been natural for a researcher, a linguistic performance in Cioran's French environment, and does not even want to hear of his wilfully filed *divorce* from the Romanian language, but decides that *Précis de décomposition* expresses the extent to which Cioran "operates with the French language" and that "he was permeated by the subtlety of literary language, but not by the spirit of the French, that nuanced scepticism, that virtuosity of misconstruing ideas by multiplying with voluptuousness the aphorisms of uncertainty". After that he asks himself, rhetorically: "is it possible for someone to acquire a spirit that does not enter into his spiritual dimensions?"

What should we understand from this? If I formulate according to my apperceptive horizon, I understand that Emil Cioran was adopted by the language of Racine, but he is *allogenic* to the spirit of the French. He remains thus a divided creator: he speaks and writes in French as one of the greatest stylists of 20th century France, but still thinks as a Romanian from Rășinari, Sibiu. Fortunately, Șeicaru reveals, without any intention and without saying so, a truth: the brand of thinking cannot be forged (at the most it only creates the illusion of a change) even by the most sophisticated stylistics or scripts.

At other times, memory seems to play tricks on Șeicaru Cioran's debut, *On the Heights of Despair*, appeared in 1936 (and not in 1934), when the memorialist believes this "bizarre book of imprecations against a social order towards which it was in a total antagonism" appeared. He names three thinkers who might have influenced Cioran, namely: Kierkegaard, Max Stirner and Nietzsche, who, "through I don't know what strange assimilation", would have led him to write "a kind of *Thus Spake Zarathustra* for the Legionary movement; a total negation of the past and a delirious nationalism". Șeicaru believed that Cioran's *theory* about a kind of Saint Bartholomew's Night for everyone over 40, travelled through 1937, "as a sinister 'Mane, Tekel, Fares'". Of course, the work Șeicaru was talking about was The Transfiguration of Romania and not *On the Heights of Despair.*

In his letter to Noica, Emil Cioran must have appeared to the newspaperman transplanted to Spain as a fabricator of our history.

And when he succeeds, however, in making a small contextual comment, Șeicaru is inevitably otiose. He finds "stylistic ribbons" in the writing of Cioran, that transform the author into a character resembling the policeman Ghiță Pristanda (!?), the same Cioran who leaves the impression of an "intellectual upstart" who despises the Romanian people.

But so many labels applied to Cioran, and not only to him, are to be found in the too-long the text of Pamfil Șeicaru. Reading it, I did not have the impression that it is, as he says, an indictment led by the desire to snatch the "Noica case file from the silence organized by Emil Cioran, Mircea Eliade, Brutus Coste, and Neagu Djuvara".[3] I did, however, have the incessant feeling that Emil Cioran is undeservedly disinherited and banished from the courts of the French spirit, as did those who turned him (few in numbers, and not in the West, as it is exaggeratedly being said) into an ideological punching bag. What remains then for Cioran? A posterity and something more, in which Cioran seems to be half-French, half from Rășinari, meaning: Romanian.

Notes

[1] See Pamfil Șeicaru, *Scrieri din exil, I, Figuri din lumea literară* [Writings from exile, I, Figures of the literary world], Bucharest: Saeculum I.O. Publishing House, 2002, pp. 483-526.
[2] *Ibidem.*
[3] *Ibidem.*

Chapter 5

The tragic overture

5.1 The sincerity of religious faith and the crisis of fundamentals

In 1931, young Cioran believed that the religious movement of the past two decades was animated by great and largely vain illusions, for beyond the fact that it was more than artificial, it had done nothing except to destroy "any confidence in the *sincerity* of religious experience".[1]

The word we emphasise here attempts to suggest exactly where this temporary failure arose. It was just the feeling of a collapse, because religious belief would involve in the 1930s, at least in the spiritual climate of Romania, large masses of people, feeding, especially through the *pro* stream created by the *Gândirea* [Thought] journal, the substance of Romanian nationalism (to be Romanian would mean, for the theorists of this attitude, to be Orthodox; moreover, even the contrary concept was true).

As early as 1931, Cioran himself would fit the words he said about Erwin Reisner: "Courage in ideas leads to limitations; only he who has inner possibilities can resist." Here was an author who, in a discreet way, seemed to interest him. In 1927, one of his books, entitled *Selbstopfer Der Erkenntins* focused Cioran's attention on a significant issue: that there is only one single problem, namely the problem of death, and that it is the only singular object of thinking (Cioran will become – did he know it then ?! – a specialist in the problem of death). From that time on, Cioran seems to have understood that history is, as the same Reisner said, the eighth day, *the day without evening*, that followed the fall into sin.

Judged in relation to the productive background of modern culture (a rationalist and individualistic culture), the religious movement betrayed, as Cioran believed, its meaning. It tried to compensate for some kind of inner exhaustion of culture, its inability to produce new values, to make the act of creation *spontaneous and free*. And this, at a time when the cultural process was simply obsessed with a sort of historical perspectivism, and threatened, in its organic purity, by eclecticism.

Influenced perhaps by Spengler's vision, the essayist explained this cultural impasse in relatively simple terms: "Religious orientation in a less-than-religious culture proves the decadence of this culture, its approaching death, a process of breaking internal balance, or [...] breaking with the assumptions of that culture".[2] A collapse brought about either by the degradation of cultural metabolism, or a caducity of the foundations, of the elements that establish that culture. The observation sheet that the 20-year-old youth filled in an imaginary hospital of culture was far from optimistic. The modern, optimistically tenured and active man did not perceive the culture-religion *caesura* for the naturally simple reason that his religious sensitivity was not that of a contemplative spirit, or "because of a lack of orientation towards the essential, a total lack of sense of eternity".[3]

Adapted, transfigured, not emerging from an irrational life structure, without having its own specific difference and without being an *organic form of living*, religion – and the religious movement with it – was targeting, as Cioran thought, the *sterile expression of a will to believe*, in which the intellectuals hid their desire for the *Absolute*. The consequence of this reaction was a disintegration in the sphere of culture, especially in axiology, for the will to believe was, in fact, a division of values by their creators, a "division of elements that should be primarily unified. Value creators have here the perspective of values, not their living embodiment".[4]

5.2 The beginning of an exercise of *divine disobedience*

Cioran's approach to the sphere of religion and religious belief was not the first of its kind. There are early texts, perhaps the first written attempts of adolescence, where ideatic troubles take the naive but often profound form of a Cartesian need for clarity and distinction in fundamental questions of life (a clarity which the author will later detest). And life meant, even then, "inner life" or "inner style".[5]

Cioran was a student in the first year of college. His philosophical readings, perhaps unsystematic in their shape, annoyed him and stirred him to reflection. The 18-year-old youth slowly gathered a robust inner protest against the masters of thought. Cioran the uninitiated rejected almost any guidance with a discreet impertinence. The only *magister* that this rebellious teenager, resenting everything and everyone, accepts – a master to whom he is obedient – is *rebellion*, the permanent struggle against the current.

Cioran will now start an exercise of divine disobedience in front of any supreme court, an adventure whose avatars – equally experienced and theorized, especially theorized – will not alleviate the tone of his meditation, for at the end of this *thinking a-rebours*, we find Cioran almost *inquisitorially* interrogating *the Evil Demiurge*.

The notes[6], unknown until the present from the end of 1928 and the beginning of 1929, with all their simplicity and didacticism, largely formulated the author's favourite subjects, the tough nucleus of obsessions to be reiterated in the journalism and books of the fourth decade of the past century. These unusual texts express a *scriptor* who enters the scene as a disheartened, frowning actor, who demands that the fanfare and trumpets are immediately stopped, announcing with organic anticipation the topics of his present and future dissertations.

Being conjured by an expansive and excessive ego, with an internal but aggressive fury which filters from the inner darkness of intimate thrills to the page written as a wild whirlwind, Cioran, the young man, is like a volcano whose eruption is always imminent. He is sincerely disturbed by the tragic character of life, trying to explain the immanent contradictions of Christianity, but without reaching the coherence and insolence of the essay published[7] in 1935; he wants to capture Europe's spiritual unity amid pluralist doctrines that have induced the germs of anarchy.

These early texts, not prepared for printing and seemingly written in the first person, do not have an elaborate form at all but seem rather naive meditations on a given theme. Hence the tension and the stumbling blocks of speech, hence the non-productive ambiguity of some formulations, the superficiality of some ideas, the weak, even lazy reasoning, in which the conclusions are partially obstructed by too facile laws of inference, all of them justifying, in essence, the laboratory character of such attempts.

5.3 Spiritual drama and metaphysical sadness: for moral reform

This is the way in which we also perceive those texts Cioran wrote in the winter of 1929, some of them probably presented at faculty seminars, others intended for conferences. He is concerned, for example, with Christianity, more precisely Christian metaphysical determinism, which he tries to judge by referring to the pagan one. Seeing, too, the cause of the *Fall* (the first Fall, Mircea Eliade would say, because there was a second Fall of man) in man's detachment from the original unity, from the symphony of that happiness, Cioran says that the energy that would have pushed him to such an act would have been the *nostalgia of knowledge*. It was the living and accentuated gesture of a pessimistic man (from *whence* came, however, the consciousness of this state !?), a kind of ghost, equally repugnant and discouraged, placed at the end of all our illusions and who "revelled in, and fed upon, knowledge", which would transform human existence into the mixture of the tragic and desperate futility to which it was condemned.

Such a destiny inevitably sentenced Man to the ethical-existential status of a *despondent being*. Cioran notes that Christianity has argumentative mechanisms to protect its structural and ideological unity. Even if he was condemned, Man cannot have the character of a tragedy, for he has an ideal: he will be redeemed. There will be a fusion of Man with the Divine, which will mean a destiny in which there is no place for tragedy and pessimism. Christianity thus had its fulfilment, Cioran believes, in ethics, in its metaphysical orientation towards the Divine, and ultimately through a philosophy of history in whose warp there is a lot of metaphysics. This process of divinization of humanity, analysed by a thinker like Berdyaev is basically one in which the loop of a Christian history closed, and there is a return of the human to his original hypostasis: the Divine.[8]

It is obvious that Cioran the student was incited by an analysis of the religious phenomenon, which the scientific orientation of that time approached with a dry and arid dogmatism. Essentially interested in Man's temptation by the Absolute, the religious phenomenon attracted him because it perfectly illustrated the spiritual drama of consciousness, whether individual or collective, a drama to which his *metaphysical sadness* was osmotically linked. Cioran thought neither about a destiny marred by his girlfriend's desertion, nor about *misery or failure*, but about the spiritual-metaphysical drama generated by the search for God and the failure to find Him, a situation reserved for the *chosen one*, the one who "has the right to live in the metaphysical, transfiguring the real and adapting it to his spiritual structure".[9]

Therefore, seclusion in a barren dogmatism was not to be regarded as the only value of the religious phenomenon, but also its specific spiritual dramatism, the torture, the inner struggle it brings with itself (for Protestantism, for example, the religious experience, which cannot be ignored even by the scientist, who seems satisfied only with the raw data of the concrete). Cioran emphasizes not only the experience of living the religious phenomenon but also its recognition, its valorisation as a reality: "Religious experience is tried by some; the rest have found another solution to the problems that trouble them".

And he immediately analyses, in a text (dated: Tuesday, February 26, 1929) the new vision of life brought by Protestantism, in radical opposition to Catholicism. Judging the latter by the manner in which it places the relationship between Man and God, the young Cioran observes a fundamental fact: the value of man is lost in the metaphysics of Catholicism, for here we find the nostalgia of raising man towards divinity, and equally "breaking his exaltation by the rigidity of Divine eternity".[10] Instead, Protestantism gives man a meaning and value that far exceeds divine grandeur. The centre of this religion with its *air of heresy*, as Maritain would say, is inhabited by Man, not by Divinity. And who made this return if not Luther, who converted his own states and inner troubles into theological truths (a form of "metaphysical egotism," concludes the French philosopher).

Cioran believed that Maritain exaggerated when he elaborated a doctrine, akin to that of Protestantism, on the exclusive basis of the subjectivity of an anarchist who resisted Catholic authority. German mysticism (Eckhart, Luso, Tauler) and the psychology of the German people (with features specific to Nordic man, inclined towards individualism) were found in Luther's attitude and were bolstered by his doctrine, one that preferred the Devil to the Saviour.

But Protestantism conceals, after Cioran, an organic contradiction. Man, in Luther's vision, appears to us as a divisible being, for he has, on the one hand, an ascendant in front of the divine (the exaggeration of human value would come from that humanism so loved by Luther), but man is also a *corrupt, devastated being*. An antinomy from which Luther's doctrine tried to escape by stating that, even if man is corrupt, he has the certainty of salvation. However, Protestantism as a doctrine, Cioran sentimentally concludes, is prone to pessimism: "The individual feels the demon of loneliness and isolation in the cosmos floating above his head. I do not know if you've ever known, between a compressed cry of desperation and a sigh of resignation, that feeling. The lines of reality blur; the contours are lost in the vague imprecision of a chaos that you never want to update; over and above this nothingness, you would want to see the leaden wing of the angel of death floating; and in this desperation there is something of the collapse of an angel ...".[11]

Protestant individualism thus brought about, by transforming authority into an illusion and by separating being from communication, what would later be called the "solitary romanticism of total isolation". The danger that threatens the values of the church should also be added, because, after the advent of Protestantism, every Christian is a priest and he can enter into communion with God without any intermediary.

This latter dimension conceals, according to Cioran, the secret of Protestantism's lack of resistance over time. Protestantism did not last because "the ideological abstractions of the doctrine lacked the concrete pillar of an institution" namely: the Church did not have a mystical significance anymore, but remained viable only through its social side. German Idealism was thus a degeneration in which the Protestant spirit entered, and Nietzsche was amongst the first to provide a solution to all the anxiety that stirred the *disequilibrium of Protestantism*.

Heroism, as conceived by the author of the *Will to Power*, appeared to Cioran as a trap in which the individualist spirit collapsed. Nietzschean Nihilism had the "pessimism of force" as its ultimate toll, for heroism meant "accepting the struggle on the surface of the world of appearances," "raising wings on heights of tragic loneliness", "the romantic madness of undisciplined frenzy", "the expression of an absurd and paradoxical Don Quixotism.[12]

Cioran's disappointing conclusion was that not even Nietzsche's philosophy[13] was able to bring the "balm of self-reconciliation" to modern consciousness, just as Spengler was no more than a pessimist who did not offer any direction for spiritual reform at all. The latter solution – under which the young student was probably preparing his conference "On Protestantism" – lay in a *moral reform*, in the cultivation of an equally ethical and intellectual ideal. Only thus, Cioran believed, could Spengler's sinister prophecy be overcome, and a Europe divided by the vertigo of so many doctrines become able to re-establish its spiritual unity. What has happened to Europe in these years, since 1929, and what point of spiritual unity has it reached – are obvious issues.

5.4 The absence of measure as vitality

What is evident in these first attempts is what we call the absence of measure as vitality. A self-diagnosis Cioran had in a certain way already stated when he said - in both sincere and protocolary words which he had been asked to write as a preface to an anthology of journalistic texts - in that nonchalant, Don Quixotesque spirit of a conquistador searching for an Atlantis of the Absolute: "My secret was simple: I did not have a sense of measure. Essentially this is the key to any vitality" (Paris, July 16, 1990). *The hand that writes*, to invoke a known syntagma, is seemingly controlled by a director who seems to have no patience. The temperature chart of young Cioran's creative struggle expresses an obvious spiritual suffering, which impresses upon his writings an obvious sincerity. (Mircea Eliade had, at that time, similarly prompted a discussion on *authenticity* in creation).

Physically speaking, Cioran's writing (from this age) shows us – through the graphemes of letters and words – a nervous and agitated hand that greedily fills the entire space of the page. The rectangle of paper that carries his thoughts without any trick appears, almost inevitably, as a space in which he no longer has anything to add, because there is nowhere left. At the top or bottom of the page, left or right, you could not add a single letter or word because everything is occupied by hurriedly scribbled signs.

The page, or Cioran's notes, and we talk here about those from the age of 17 to 18, turn into a kind of container in which the words are poured out to excess. There is manifestly a feverish search for a vital space for writing, a frenzied studying transformed into a plan beyond the physical, that is, into the metaphysical, into fertile obsessions for its own philosophical meditation.

5.5 The tragic overture

Existence appeared to Cioran just as he would later admit in his thinking about Nae Ionescu: a *fall*, something that no one could convince him was not a decline, a self-indulgence, a satanic voluptuousness.[14] He explored a range of sincerity in utterances, even when it was "the foundation of a rich lyricism," as he would say on December 11, 1928.[15] And the existence in which he would practice his meditation was marked by *the daily tragic*. In other words, he intended to write about the "Tragic conception of existence", as it emerges from a fugitive note – which we transcribe here in full:

1) There must be, in the individual, values that raise him above the mass; these values are embryonic in the crowd which only pre-feels them. For it, they are floating in the air - it feels them flicker without knowing their essence.

2) The crowd feels life as something serious - it does not notice its eminently tragic character. - This is the role of the individual.

3) Life conceived as a striving towards happiness is a nonsense - since once acquired, happiness will look like a mirage for which concrete values must be substituted.

4) Concrete values can only be the spiritual - and therefore concrete - units that are fixed in unity.

5) The unity – including the abstract diversity of individual consciousness – must converge towards a tragic - that is, profoundly serious – concept of life"

The individual positioned above the mass (or crowd) through concrete values (which end up being surrogates for happiness) – this is the hypothesis, yet ambiguously, impressively formulated, of the essentially tragic feature of life.

Such a thought spurred the mind of young Cioran on the soil offered by what he himself called the *daily tragedy of personal existence*, as a sign of the inability to reach the essence of everyday projects, promises, overflows and impulses; as an illustration, in other words, of the vain effort to catch the "final meaning of so many scourges and spiritual lusts".[16] "There are days" – Cioran thought in December 1928 – "when the most beautifully dreamed ideals felt like a pile of seeds blown by the madness of the wind". The drama of Cioran's ego had begun its first act triggered by the *daily tragic*, one that left "the traces of a lion escaped from its chains", a drama maintained by triviality, which, being the same but repeated under other masks, conceals "the same essence of platitude accepted with bowed head and tearfully closed eyes." This self of which we are speaking and which is revealed to us by Cioran's first written texts is undoubtedly of a sufficiently Dostoyevskian nature, at least by the fact that it aspires to overcome the state of a life in which there are no peaks, heroism or Don Quixotesque voices through nothing more than the conventions of *spiritual suffering*. "For only suffering is creative – that is purifying; it adds charm and novelty to life, gives it wings and the height to grasp new horizons. It is its own affirmation because only through it do you feel closer to life in general, to that life that thrills throughout humanity. It is not the physical suffering that tortures human flesh and mistresses in the houses of lust, but the spiritual suffering, the anxiety that drips in the soul the demonic and somatic charm of a nostalgia for great transfigurations, great transformations".[17]

This was Cioran's confession at age 17, one that included both romanticism and truth. At 17, when, as he says in another note,[18] "the tragedy begins", that is, "selections are made, the elements are separated", when some "begin to regenerate" in a confrontation with the *engrenage* of those "eternally unsatisfied passions", unsubstantiated by uncertainties, gnashing and convulsions, broken impulses and delays. In short, the tragic state of mind that characterizes the age of seventeen would have been the struggle between "metaphysical sensitivity, guided by religious recrudescence, and uncertainties ankylosed in materialism and nihilism".[19]

However, the earlier stages of this optional state; the first, recorded at the age of 15, when any adolescent is more or less nihilistic (otherwise he lives this stage of life only chronologically), the second one at the age of 16, when the adolescent is fatally and inexorably materialistic, identifying for the first time "a dogmatic point of view": "The real is only that which falls under our sensory perception. The absurd and poetic ideal opposes the smile of a mentor enamoured of the concrete and the direct. If he did not read Conta, he surely knew, at least by word of mouth, about Büchner ... He read a page from M [ax] Nordau or from Zola and now believes he possesses the totality of human wisdom. His sufficiency gains its last expression of stupidity and imbecility".[20]

5.6 Local Don Quixotism and metaphysical revolt

The purpose – or valorisation – of the spiritual experience in the regeneration of adolescence, the transgression of the contingent, of uncertainties, so that it can bring to the soul *the balm of purification* – this is what preoccupied Emil Cioran, the nostalgic student of philosophy disabused by the agitated rhythm of the capital, and attracted by the clean air of the provinces without the fumes of cars and lorries, even though the provinces were also despised: "In my provincial misery, with silent streets and smiling local braggarts, quarrelling with simple and normal reality ...".[21] But it was an opportunity for him to trace, not only the *psychology of the provincial*, but also the unique, albeit faint, profile of his character - sometimes reflecting the figure of the author himself.

The capital-provincial polarization is devastating to the nature and projects of one who lives in the latter. Cioran sees in any provincial a sort of Don Quixote, but "a degenerate one: without the sadness of the Sad Knight, without the human universality and the generosity of a hero transformed into a symbol", "that generosity which is giving itself up for an ideal formed by the intersection of all the rays of human nostalgia". Putting aside the versatile provincial ("one moment lacking proper decorum, the next - ready to kiss your hands") or those who are simply disturbed, he puts under the magnification of the microscope the person drawn towards the *mirage of singularization*. Probably consumed by the relationship between the individual and the absolute, without agreeing to the monotony of the mundane, of the phenomenon, which he rejects, and in the rhythm which he does not want, nor can he consume his existence (such an acceptance of the phenomenon as the only reality would be a sort of recognition of an "organic personal limitation"), illustrating that "local Don Quixotism, a nostalgia for the absolute accomplished in limited frames" and incapable of perceiving the tragedy of human existence, the provincial suffers, in essence, from a disease of egocentrism: a *hypervalorification of the ego*. Henceforth all his frustrations come from breaking any connection with life, self-claustration, the illusion of a defiant superiority to which no mortal can aspire, and the Utopian projection of a world above reality.

Cioran warns us about the illusion of this illusion: "Do not believe that this personal world would be the construct of an inner exuberance, of a greater-humanity that cannot be compressed". Such a world, created by the provincial, is both the effect of an impossibility to close tightly in upon himself and the fruit of a tendency to transcend the real. But this solipsism turns the provincial only into a dreamer who contemplates his *miserable, irreducible* self, accepting one of the two possible solutions: the "individualistic claustration of the Ego".

But the same provincial, tempted by the mirage of singularization, can still choose the other method or remedy, radically opposed to the first: it is the variant of "confusing by identification in total consciousness, the most potential expression of the destruction of the Self". Cioran identifies himself, silently at first but then quite overtly, with the latter provincial specimen, who "cannot accept the troubled life lived in a phenomenon, a life that is not absolute, but accomplished in the tragic" and that is why, as he says at the end of this "provincial letter", he chooses "the destruction of the real" instead of its *transcendence*.

Young Cioran entered, after that, on an offensive against existentialism. In the search for perhaps the best of all possible worlds, he certainly was fixed not upon the implosion of the self, which he wanted well-protected, but the abolition of the real, even its annihilation. What he wanted to put in its place – is a question that remains unanswered for the moment, even for the simple fact that it was only a momentous decision in Cioran's life. His choice, however, pushed him towards a strange mixture of *or* with *and*, for *I prefer* assumed that, in the context of the conjunction, he would exercise the pleasure of the freedom of disjunction: "I prefer destroying the real to its transcendence."

This was the beginning of a decision to resist, as he would later say, all that has been created since Adam. Maybe we cannot be wrong if we place here and now, in lines written at this age (texts that do not have to be excessively overvalued), the first manifestations of a *metaphysical revolt* lived by Cioran. In his provincial position, wishing to overcome that local Don Quixotism (this fascination of Cervantes' hero will never cease, Cioran seeing his own destiny as a dispute between the figure of the Sad Knight and Faust), the young man, aged 17 or 18, feared not so much the adventure of transcending the real as the consequence of such an act, namely: "collapse, resembling that of the albatrosses crashing from the height of their own loneliness".[22]

Cioran will, in fact, remain a provincial all his life; and his work, despite all the changes it went through, arose from the radical revolt of this inauspicious solitude – or isolation – of the provincial. The nostalgia with which he parted from his native village in order to go to the school in Sibiu, the longing for the Boaca hillside and for every stone on the road to Rășinari are also signs of an incurably provincial frame of mind.

Notes

[1] Emil Cioran, „*Voința de a crede*" [Will to Believe], in *Mișcarea* [Movement], year XXIV, no. 76, February 25 1931; see *Singurătate și destin* [Solitude and destiny], Bucharest: Humanitas Publishing House, edited by Marin Diaconu, 1990, pp. 9-11.

[2] *Ibidem*.

[3] *Ibidem*.

[4] *Ibidem*.

[5] Also, in the publication *Mișcarea* [The Movement], he will make a frustrating analysis of what "a form of inner life" means (see No. 184, 8 July 1931, see *Singurătate și destin* [Solitude and Destiny], quoted edition, pp. 21-23), in which the intellectual is the key character and that is why he undertakes such a superficial phenomenology (see. „*Intelectualul român* [The Romanian intellectual] and „*Psihologia șomerului intelectual* [The psychology of the unemployed intellectual], No. 80, March 1, 1931; No. 134, May 8, 1931; *see Singurătate și destin* Solitude and Destiny], quoted edition, pp. 12-20).

[6] The observation was made in 1995 and 2000 (see note 1) and remains current even though some of the texts are now being edited (see the two volumes of Cioran's *Works* [Opere], Bucharest: Romanian Academy, National Foundation for Science and Art, 2012).

[7] See Emil Cioran, "*Creștinismul și scandalul pe care l-a adus în lume*" [Christianity and the scandal it brought to the world], *Vremea* [The Time], year VII, no. [418], Christmas [December 25] 1935; *see Solitude and destiny*, quoted edition, pp. 294-299.

[8] See the previously unknown text entitled *"Despre creștinism"* [About Christianity], in *Saeculum Magazine*, new series, Sibiu, no.1-4/1996.
[9] As per Emil Cioran, *"Despre Protestantism"* [About Protestantism], previously unknown text, *loc cit.*
[10] *Ibidem.*
[11] *Ibidem.*
[12] The sometimes-apparent *inflation* of quotes may have its explanation, perhaps even its *justification*, in the fact that the identified texts have long been unknown and unedited, until the appearance of some of them in the two volumes of *Works*, published by the National Foundation for Science and Art (2012), under the aegis of the Romanian Academy.
[13] A very good introduction to the work of the German philosopher is: Mircea Braga, *Ecce Nietzsche. Exercițiu de lectură hermeneutică* [Ecce Nietzsche. Hermeneutical reading exercise], Bucharest: The Romanian Academy Publishing House, 2015.
[14] See Emil Cioran, *"Nae Ionescu și drama lucidității"* [Nae Ionescu and the drama of lucidity], *Vremea* [The Time], June 6, 1937.
[15] See the previously unpublished text *"Tragicul cotidian"* [The daily Tragic], *Saeculum Magazine*, Sibiu, new series, Year I (III), no. 1, 2000, p. 89-90. These notes, as well as others we are going to refer to, are, as indicated, from the Sibiu archive of Aurel Cioran, the brother of the philosopher.
[16] *Ibidem.*
[17] *Ibidem.*
[18] Emil Cioran, *"Adolescența"* [Adolescence], previously unpublished text, *Saeculum Magazine*, new series, Sibiu, no. 1, 2000, pp. 90-91.
[19] *Ibidem.*
[20] *Ibidem.*
[21] See previously unpublished manuscript, Emil Cioran, "Provincial Letter", *Saeculum Magazine*, new series, Sibiu, no. 1, 2000, pp. 91-92.
[22] *Ibidem.*

Chapter 6

Bouts of insomnia

6.1 Warning signs for a "metaphysical masochism"

Thickening at least the outline of a portrait, we can see that, even at the age of 17-18, Emil Cioran had been drawn into the swirls of a *metaphysical riot*. He pulled over his face the mask of a *dandy* à la Camus and was vituperating - not against the fall in time, which will come later, but against the fall into the ridiculous, which any provincial lived in full. In reality, fighting with himself, but also with the Other in order to escape the arcana of this implacable anathema Fate discarded upon him. That he could never escape from the mental space of a provincial, is proven by his evolution: he remained, for his whole life, a marginal: from his birth in Sibiu's *Mărginime – limes*, through his reading projects which countless times included minor, marginal authors and marginalized, trivial works; to the philosophy in which he tried his forces, lying on the edge of systematic metaphysical reflection. (Later, in a letter to his brother, Aurel, dated November 25, 1979, when *Ècartelèment* appeared, he will state, troubled: "*Je ne m'en suis jamais plaint; au contraire, j'ai accepté très bien me condition de marginal*". And a little further, with self-irony: "*Si je n'étais pas si vieux, je retournerais à la philosophie. Elle a du moins l'excuse ne pas être accessible aux journalistes et aux bonnes femmes*".[1]

At 20, Cioran seems thus to illustrate the aspect of a spirit akin to the abstract art of Oscar Kokoschka, an artist about whom he wrote, in the autumn of 1931, a *small chronicle*. In resonance with the anxiety and churning of the age, young Cioran, like Kokoschka's man, is not coming from somewhere in the world, "but fell, disoriented, in an existence foreign to his own nature",[2] he has the premonition of a nonreligious apocalypse generated by despair and - like the signs in the painting *Der irrende Ritter*, in which Cioran mirrored the recognition of his own obsessions – the impact of what chaos could be for man: "a voluptuousness in despondency, a crazy excitement in the process of its own collapse, an ecstasy of nothingness".[3]

In short, Cioran's intellectual biography can be placed now, in this existential segment at the beginning of the fourth decade of the last century, under the seal of a hardly camouflaged *metaphysical masochism*, whose signs were already apparent, we believe, at least physically, in the experience of insomnia lived by the adolescent Cioran. It was a moment of *terrible crisis*, but that *systematic insomnia*, as the philosopher recalled in the fall of 1990, constituted a kind of "appetizer of the inferno...".[4] Cioran mortified his spirit in order to protect the body: he wrote *On the Heights of Despair* with the therapeutic aim of curing himself from suicide.

It was a form, albeit benign, of metaphysical revolt, similar to the one Albert Camus invokes when he speaks of "the Sons of Cain": "To rebel against nature is to rebel against yourself. It means to hit your head against the wall. The only coherent revolt is thus suicide".[5] Everything Cioran composes now comes from the accidents of a *too-full organic*: "There are thoughts that you have each day. And there are ideas that come in fits".[6]

6.2 The edge and the fragment

Cioran placed himself, with a clear intention, on the edges of a systematic philosophy. The quality of *mărginean* [marginal] of a community morphed into his early option for a certain way of philosophizing. Since 1932, when he was in the last year of college, he found that only a few *anachronists* still believed in the idea of a philosophical system, in "its ability to encompass the real, to exhaust its complexity and multiplicity".[7] An attitude refused by those integrated in reality, who gave new meaning to *the idea of life*, this rigid mechanism of philosophy was inadequate not so much for the theory of knowledge, where it could find, perhaps, a somewhat formal justification, but rather for the sphere of ethics which, located in the plane of an abstract, pure normativity, had ended up in an irreducible antinomy with life.

The influence of Bergson, Nicolai Hartmann and Nae Ionescu was all too evident. Cioran exalted *subjective experience, the intuitive understanding*, the irrational, *living experience* that facilitates actual knowledge and provides a frame in which the whole contents of life, meaning its manifestations, are not to be conceived in isolation, in an abstract series, but "lived in the continuity of their quality". The precariousness of the old way of philosophizing was accused in relation to the spirit of the system; irrational metaphysics hasn't given up totally on the system in the sense that it does not cease to be a construction which has altered its physiognomy and structure in relation to the exigencies of history. Philosophy meant, for the young Cioran, a test, and that's why it took *the form of the essay*, a much more fertile topos and network for the *interrogations of metaphysics*, where the metabolism of a giant scaffolding is substituted with fragmentary sketches that "expose ideas".[8]

This attitude was peculiar to Cioran's mentor: Nae Ionescu. In a text published in *Societatea de mâine - Tomorrow's Society* (see. no. 16, 1926), the "Teacher" had spoken of those "philosophers pure and simple, who philosophize because they can't do otherwise; they are the servants of philosophy; their perspective, philosophizing". Well, through his transparent rhetoric, young Cioran tells us that he also became, with the passing of time, not an exile from, but a *slave* to philosophy.

Rejecting now the spirit of the system, Cioran denounces its rigidity and ossification, but does not give up its *solutions to problems* or its *attitudes*, especially when it comes to philosophical anthropology, where "life breaks those forms that tend to shut it off". History, consisting of "life taken out of the plan of irrationality",[9] made us all unbelievers in this transcendent structure – meaning: static, unchanging and unhistorical – called *system*.

6.3 Vaingloriously atypical. Re-acknowledging Nietzsche

Cioran's revolt had specific characteristics. Being at the same time the bow and arrow, question and impossible answer, his reaction was we believe, the result of the collision between two orders which, involuntarily and without noticing their respective weights too much, oppressed him and assaulted his self-awareness: the order of the mundane, whose limits and mad chaos he tragically discovered, and a supposed but uncertain metaphysical order, both universes sitting under an absurd and sterile logic.

Cioran's resistance seems to deviate from the canon of Camus. This attitude was not basically different from that of a man who, consumed by the great conflagration of the First World War, had the feeling that he lived in a desacralised world, one in which God was dead. Except that young Cioran did not feel solidarity with all those potentially living the rebellion of man located before or after the sacred. He was alone and lonely or at least believed himself to be so, isolated in an existence that did not intersect with anyone and with anything. Or, after Camus, "any rebellion which allows itself to deny or destroy this solidarity immediately loses the name of rebellion and coincides in reality with a deadly consent".[10]

The individual in revolt, therefore, is linked to the collective being: "The evil felt by one man becomes a plague for the collective". Which snatches the individual from the clutches of solitude: "I rebel, so we exist",[11] but does not banish him from the communitarian space of solidarity. One such individual can, however, for the young Cioran, be confused with total consciousness through a destruction of the self.

The case of Cioran is only apparent at the limit of the anamnesis of Camus's rebellious man. Because otherwise, his attitude would inculcate all the determinations that are essential for the latter. The Cioranian self refuses to accept his condition, defies and denies, wants to talk to God under equal terms and there is no way he can ignore the Other – or Others – that he feels are always present in what Noica would term *his communitary loneliness*.

The authentic aspect of Cioran's self, however, is not at all that of a *revolutionary*, as it is not that of a *dandy* either, despite the fact that its image is often maintained through an "aesthetics of singularity and of negation",[12] which sometimes is not just superfluously rhetorical, because when "dandies don't commit suicide and don't go crazy, they have a great career and enter posterity".[13] We detect here vague *(s)elective affinities* between the Cioranian self and Nietzsche-type nihilism.

The rapprochement between Cioran and the author of *Zarathustra* seemed to G. Liiceanu to be the fruit of "a passion of first youth, subsequently abandoned". Cioran's own opinion is cited as support, in a conversation with Fr. Bondy in February 1980, where he says that he had "ceased for a long time any trade" with Nietzsche because he found him to be *too naive*. "I blame his passion and even his moments of ardour. He tore down the idols, only to replace them with others. A false iconoclast with the traits of a teenager, with a bashful way of being, with an innocence that was inherent in his loneliness. He only observed people from afar. If he would have studied them up close, never would he have been able to invent and propagate the concept of the Superman, a funny, ridiculous, if not grotesque vision that could only take birth in a spirit that didn't have time to grow old, to know the long-filtered nausea.

Much closer to me is Marcus Aurelius. I don't hesitate, not for a moment, between the lyricism of frenzy, and the prose of acceptance; I find more comfort and even more hope in a tired emperor than in a philosopher who throws thunder and lightning bolts".[14] In 1986, in a dialogue with Fritz J. Raddatz, quasi-rhetorically rejecting the association Susan Sontag made between his image of history and that of Nietzsche, Cioran would assert: "There is, if I may say so, a resemblance of *temperament* between Nietzsche and me: we're both *sleepless spirits*. This creates a *complicity*".[15] The temper that Cioran talks about is no more than *style*, that is *De l'interieur*.

Synthetically speaking, for the work of Cioran, the relationship with Nietzsche's philosophy is fundamental. Things are more different than Cioran thinks when he speaks to us still with a mask on his cultural figure. The one who wrote about *Tears and Saints* was and remained, from his first to his last book, a Nietzschean, even if this kinship of vision was denied by a sophisticated technique of dissimulation.

Accents of this influence, however, were visible all over Cioran's creation. Nietzsche and Cioran, Cioran and Nietzsche – these are the two stages of conjunction of two great spirits; the first, illustrated by the work of Cioran up to *Syllogisms of Bitterness* or maybe even up to *The Temptation to Exist*; the other form of the conjunction (Cioran and Nietzsche) covering the rest of creation ("and" is here a coordinating conjunction, which induces, however, a vague vectorial-axiological hierarchy between the terms).

This "Bogomilic Nietzschean" (Şerban Cioculescu) first developed, as an apprentice, a love speech in relation to Nietzsche (this is Cioran's iconodule hypostasis), only to convert this attitude into its opposite, later: into iconoclasm towards the one who had been the "great liberator", the thinker who sabotaged the style of academic philosophy and attacked the ideas of the system.

A less-than-perfect disciple, Cioran also lowers – in *On the Heights of Despair* – philosophy into physiology, speaks almost exclusively about *organic man*, without transfiguring organic disfunctions into concepts yet, but offering just the *descriptions* of such notions.

A specialist of disguise, Cioran becomes what he already was, which was a dandy in revolt against Nietzsche. He fakes his own *elective affinities*, turns around in front of the magister, rebels and prepares his spiritual parricide with the same quiet wickedness and meticulousness with which he arranged his suicide for his whole life. Nietzsche begins to seem (after he organically assimilated him) "naive", "worthy of compassion", "a reporter of eternity", "a phony mystic". And the idea of the superman becomes an elucubration, an "absolutely giddy invention" that, in *The Transfiguration of Romania*, will become "accurate as experimental data", as he says in *Syllogisms of Bitterness*.

Through the frenzy of negation, by the fragmented way in which he was thinking about the world, becoming - like Nietzsche – a fragmentist, but also by the tendency to relativize everything, to re-evaluate any value – Cioran proves contamination and convergence with the thinking of Nietzsche. *Gott ist tot* – God has died or is dead – has, in Cioran's thinking, the same role as an axiological reform; but, incidentally, Nietzsche's phrase is, most often, quoted as especially biased, eluding any further partaking of Nietzschean ideas: *because we killed him* (*Gott ist tot! Gott bleibt tot! Und wir haben ihn getötet*)

Cioran feeds on the illusion that one can live without believing in anything. It's not a systematic nihilism, for the suppression of faith is not replaced by any method (I don't even think that Emil Cioran has come, finally, to any methodical denial, as I don't think he would have practiced methodical doubt).

For the young Cioran, the revolt of metaphysics will not, however, start by *Gott ist tot*, but by a general relativism and a bland attempt at self-damnation, together with an incisive examination of Christianity. (Even a few years before his death, he confessed to a doctoral student drafting a thesis on the subject of Cioran: "Everything related to Christianity seems to me to be so much nonsense...".[16]

Rigorously speaking, Cioran is not numbered among those who believe in nothing, but rather among those who don't believe in what is. He will much more resemble Nietzsche in the second part of the fourth decade of the last century, but also in last years of his life (even if he was rhetorically trying to deny consonance), when any rebellion ended in an exaltation of evil.

6.4 Misery, aesthetics and moral rules

Morals, not only Christian morals, were always the target of young Cioran's reluctance. Undermined by philosophy, the belief in morality and its rules were, in the early '30s, also eroded because of poverty, which simply blocked the human spirit, without seeing, in this result, either a fad or an unwonted aestheticism. "In the face of poverty, aestheticism becomes an inadmissible form of life. (...) Poverty makes it impossible to perceive the spectacular concept of life, because poverty, pain or disease exclude the possibilities of objectivity, exceed the intentions of any dualization, cancel the perspective effort that maintains a continuous separation".[17]

So, the anthropological imperative, and not priorities of an economic nature, silence our spirit in the presence of poverty and threaten culture with collapse. A serious consequence of this condition reflected, thought Cioran, on young people: "An early aging, a spirit of boredom in front of the old forms of life, insecurity and the premonition of tragic tremors, a melancholy gravity, all these replaced that naive spontaneity, that momentum toward irrationality, which characterize true youth".[18]

The same anthropological reasons are invoked when Cioran, based on a psychological view on life, observes the existence of two morals, generated by the abstract isolation of morals from anthropology and the specific needs of man. He proposed revisiting and reinterpreting, through the vitalist grid, the living morals of an individual, having as a basis the immanent configuration of the given space in which it exists. "We have to start from man in order to understand the ascension and the value of morals, not from morals towards man".[19]

In this latter way, he preceded both classical morals and that which, says Cioran, *circulates daily*, their lack of elasticity and of understanding of reality coming from their garbled way of understanding man: as being "fixed and rigid in form, for whom life has lost the consistency of the spiritual".[20] Such morals did not follow a folding on the existence of time, but, on the contrary, its rules expressed resistance in the face of reality, and wanted to adjust the attitude of a somewhat static, limited and closed form of life. Such morals, concluded Cioran, were permanently "a weapon of the "self-sufficient", those people who "look at life retrospectively, for whom life no longer means living, but memory".[21]

On a background of timely debates covering the foundations of ethics, the purpose of the Cioranian reflections on morals will be clearly formulated, namely, "to know if those who want to rise have any morals, and if it does not create a dualism". Citing the instability and the obtuseness of the criteria of morality, the incompatibility and contradiction that abstract human morals establish between the plane of *must* and that of *is*, because it is unbound by time, "by the concrete and irrational living-ness of time" (it does not have, in other words, orientation or *dynamic direction*), the young Cioran searched for arguments allowing him to justify the morals of those who progressively give up morals and, in equal measure, advocate the violation of moral rules which do not fulfil an effective social function.

In fact, he thought that giving up a form of morality, for instance, that inculcated through education is the result of social experiences that reassess the very principles of morals. Between morals and life lies a *tragic paradox*:[22] morals "can only exist where life ceases, and is refused where life asserts itself".[23]

6.5 Intuitionism *versus* intellectualism

The philosophical atmosphere of the fourth decade of the last century was, as we all know, emphatically marked by concerted attacks against rationalism, starting with the Cartesianism. Confidence in rationality had diminished enormously after the absurd triumphed with the First World War. As young Cioran noticed, "the concept of the rational was excessively narrowed",[24] to the sphere where the question of religion was almost unthinkable. It appeared all the more clearly that the real against which the man of the interwar period measured himself did not fit at all into the Procrustean form under which reason appeared after the catastrophe produced by the first global war.

The face of the latter became more and more hideous and anathematized by all those who did not understand – but could one understand the reason which explained how man became overnight a wolf towards his fellow man?! – how was that possible. People had turned their eyes to the sky, where they believed they could learn not only the answer to what had happened but also find hope on the road leading to the glade of the good. Religious knowledge was, in this sense, both the road and the guide, and any detailed debate about its mechanism was covered by that guidance published in philosophical thinking under the name of *intuitionism*. (In the manuscripts kept in the archive of Aurel Cioran, there's a more detailed study about *Contemporary intuitionism*, the graduation thesis of the student Cioran.)

Therefore, in terms of the existence and possibilities of religious knowledge, intellectualism was radically threatened by the defenders of intuitionism, including Cioran, still a student in philosophy. A fertile perspective for an appropriate conception of the truly religious because, when going beyond the specificity of religious sentiment by blind faith in the universal virtue of the genetic derivation (the single source of the religious sentiment of fear, etc.), understanding religious knowledge as being of an intuitive type was much closer to the truth, for it decoded the specific difference and unique, unrepeatable items of religious sentiment.

Rational knowledge remained in the sphere of theoretical dogmatism, where religion has a systematic and unitarily developed character. In religion, observes Cioran, because we are dealing with a system, "the constructive spirit of rational knowledge prevailed".[25] Intuition remained fundamental and essential in the plan of the religious experience.

But what were the specific determinations of religious intuition? The subject of such insight (characterized by the intentionality of orientation towards something, a feature much analysed by phenomenology) targets the absolute that transcends sensible reality and establishes a relationship of empathy with the subject of religious experience. The mechanism generating such sympathetic links is "the implicit belief in structural identity between the knower and the known object, beyond the multiplicity of forms of reality".[26] Therefore, it does not concern a substantial identity between man and deity, but one of structure, in which not only man is a being oriented towards God (who he knows, since he is made "in His image and likeness"), but the divinity also proves to be an active sense of turning towards man. Going beyond the way of relating to the real through concepts, as intellectualism does, intuition, as a direct path of knowledge, means certainty, a folding upon the living, dynamic and irrational element. This happened with the great mystics, for whom the absolute was untouched by the wings of historicity.

Religious knowledge is sometimes also supported by symbol, which, unlike myth, is the static "determined expression of something un-determinable"; the symbol is also a sure sign of the road that stretches from intuition to expression.

6.6 Decadence, the mediocre man and the "knights of nothingness"

The problem of religious intuition, addressed in a naive and school-like manner in a text from the *Theological Magazine*, constituted, in its substance, a necessary corollary of the way in which Cioran, fascinated by the presence of a spirit such as Nae Ionescu, understood the weight and the sense of the irrational in the fabric of practical life. Cioran believed that the many forms of life proved a mutual affinity and were participating in an essence of ideal nature. "Plunging deeper into 'life', in the process of intuitive knowledge, is actually an immanent relationship which individual experience develops towards the ideal plan – existing only for consciousness – of life. Only the multitude of forms of life are real".²⁷

A peculiar metabolism makes some forms of life appear, others disappear, in a ceaseless process of devouring itself. Forms are historical, while life is not. (At times, it seems as if we hear a journalistic Eminescu talking: "New forms, but a forever old spirit".) Such an uninterrupted productivity of life, says Cioran, is "an inextricable demonism of creation and destruction", which shows the expression of a kind of imperialism of life, an expansion which never tires. Without any sense, not even a transcendent one, being a deployment inside immanent space, the life of *forms* can only be maintained by self-destruction, not doing anything else except cancelling "any faith in the creator of life",²⁸ as creation is understood in history. A hypothesis that is not far from that acceptance of evil; rather: it will foster, we believe, a more and more frantic adhesion to it, as illustrated by Cioran's publications, after 1933.

Such a demonism of life itself, of life as life, involves at the same time *expansions* of the variously concrete forms of life, "without any intentionality, towards their transcendence." This demonism hides the irrationality of life, pushing "forms, in an imperialist manner, in various directions without any sense which transcends them".²⁹ Thus, the forms of life do not have sense, but direction. Hence the relativity of the contents and, in equal measure, forms of life.

This is the way things are in the sphere of culture and its historical forms, where relativity means the individualization of historical moments, "the separation of values from the anthropological foundation bearing them, from excessive exteriorization, from the subjective energy which produced them".³⁰ Later, culture, through its acts of creation, leads to a weakening of the irrational in life. "The spontaneity of irrational life is opposed by culture's block", the same culture even having the tendency to become autonomous in relation to life.

The separation between culture and life is a pretext – an excuse that Cioran will invoke countless times in his reflections. It is one of the fixed ideas of his generation, particularly during the second half of the fourth decade. An influence stemming, in a roundabout way, from the Spenglerian theory of the asphyxiation of culture by civilization; but Cioran will be passionately interested, this time, in the hypothesis: *any bad thing can lead to something good.* Indifferent to transcendent purposes and values because it's irrational, *life*, which consumed its energy and got sick, may favour the emergence of cultural elements. "We owe our understanding of the world more to suffering than to enthusiasm", says the Dostoyevskian Cioran.³¹ When it manages to convert disease and pain into cultural creation, life is sublimated into consciousness. The road from the irrational to the latter does not pass through concepts, but through "the shaking of fundamental and essential energies of our life".

The spirit of man passed through an identically autonomous process of birth and empowerment, isolation from the past and life disruptions leading it towards experiencing the tragic. Conscience has thus become, by breaking the balance given by the irrational, something that generates pain. Man permanently slides back and forth between the two forms of existence, permanently reflecting either on life – becoming sceptical; or on death – reaching resignation.

Detachment from the irrationality of life has a limit and can generate the most unusual consequences. It's debatable, after Cioran, whether the future will still see the emergence of great cultures, but man, with his accentuated removal from the irrational, can exhaust himself and disappear. Wanting to soar, to reach the ideal, man gets to design his own collapse. He no longer wants to exist inside the frames of life but tries, adventurously, to reach towards the ideal. He wants to achieve the ultimate transcendence of the irrational at any price, even, sometimes, that of decadence. And this descent, suggests Cioran, might be, for man, "a return to that irrationality of life from which he broke off".[32] Which outlines a tragic destiny for man, who only renounces life in order to repentantly return to it. An existential horizon which can only be eminently pessimistic, and that is actually the price which man pays for culture, because to the nervous imbalance from which it sprung,[33] he now adds another, of an ontological nature.

The immanent nature of the irrational in life generated difficulties for those trying to reach the roots of the real. This irrational world, both beastly and demonic, reveals itself, says Cioran, extremely difficulty, especially to those who have situated themselves in a rational understanding of life. He drew attention, in a text in *Calendarul* [Calendar], to an extremely important phenomenon, which illustrated a manifestation of the irrational life, namely: "the destruction of the best and better equipped",[34] an aspect that should be the subject of any tragic and pessimistic anthropology.

What elicited rebellion in the young Cioran was the aggressive *mediocrity* of those who "live the possibilities", those who can't pass beyond life, who didn't discover anything that makes any sense in life, "incapable of happiness, destroyed and irretrievably lost", people imprisoned in an "optimistic platitude". However, mediocre man is one who enjoys life, the only one who has this privilege, while all the others are part of the so-called order of the *knights of nothingness*. The latter, especially if they want to be fulfilled, must go beyond the frames of life, must *crash* on the heights, "where salvation is impossible, either by life or by death."

The working hypothesis from which young Cioran started was destructive: the essence of social life is injustice, a vision not in accord with the rationalist theories of optimistic idealism, unable to reach the understanding of destiny as "immanent reality and inner fatality", helpless in answering the question of why remarkable people fall, while the mediocre remain (Cioran's exclusivism is obvious). The justification, but not the solution, will be one for which the specialist of desperation permanently opted: it's not the exaltation of a man that is impressive, but rather his collapse, his destruction, the comprehension of such a state demanding an anthropology, tragic and pessimistic in equal measure, one which, revealing the irrational mechanism of life, fights against counterfeiting the latter.

In agreement with the conclusion of a German biologist, Cioran characterizes man as a *dilettante of life*, which signifies that he is a being - and here he especially considers endowed individuals – thrown, as a prey, to destruction and death. Most people do not fear death because they live in the world "as if death did not exist".[35] "Anguish in the face of death is only felt by those for whom death is a problem. Philosophers are either false when they say they are not afraid of death, or too proud to confess. In reality, they are shaking more than you can imagine".[36]

And all of these, says Cioran, happen on Earth, a place which the sun, in its grace, hasn't yet refused to light.

Notes

[1] "I have never complained about this (he talks about the failure of books written until then – we note, I.D.), on the contrary, I have accepted my marginal condition very well." "Were I not so old, I would return to philosophy. At least it has the excuse of not being easily accessible to journalists and housewives"." – see Cioran, *Scrisori către cei de-acasă* [Letters to the folks back home], quoted edition, p. 175.

[2] Emil Cioran, "*Oscar Kokoschka*", *Gândirea* [Thought], no. 7-9, September – November 1931; the text is included in the anthology *Singurătate și destin* [Loneliness and destiny], quoted edition.

[3] *Ibidem.*

[4] *See* Fernando Savater, *Eseu despre Cioran* [Essay on Cioran], Bucharest: Humanitas Publishing House, 1998, p.168.

[5] Albert Camus, *Omul revoltat* [The Rebel], Bucharest: RAO Publishing House, 1994, p. 233.

[6] Cioran, *Entretiens*, Paris: Gallimard Publishing House, 1995, p. 185.

[7] Emil Cioran, "*Sistem și viață*" [System and life], *Floarea de foc* [The fiery flower], no. 5, 6, February. 1932; the text is included in the anthology *Revelațiile durerii* [Revelations of Pain, Cluj: Echinox Publishing House, edition supervised by Mariana Vartic and Aurel Sasu, 1990, pp. 47-49.

⁸ Over fifty and something years in the future, Cioran would redefine this moment of his intellectual biography: "I started writing in my youth, after finishing my studies of philosophy, at the age of 21. At that time, I was starting to no longer believe in philosophy, which until then had been everything to me. Ah, philosophy, German philosophy in particular, the major systems of philosophy... The rest I was indifferent to, including poetry. But during that period, I realized that philosophy has nothing to say to people who are struggling in difficulties – inner ones, obviously. I understood that it teaches you to formulate problems and questions, but then it leaves you prey to your fate, because its answers are always questionable" – see *Secolul 20* [The 20th Century], no. 4-5-6/88, pp. 36-37.

⁹ Emil Cioran, "*Sistem și viață*" [System and life], quoted work.
¹⁰ Albert Camus, *quoted work.*, p. 226.
¹¹ *Ibidem*, p. 227.
¹² The quoted expression belongs to Camus. One can speak of a *dandyism* of *the 30's generation*, and Emil Cioran is a very convincing example of this.
¹³ A. Camus, *quoted work.*, p. 255.
¹⁴ *See* G. Liiceanu, "*Cioran – sequences of the itinerary*", *Secolul 20* [The 20th Century], no. .4-5-6/88, p. 38.
¹⁵ see Cioran, *Entretiens*, Paris: Gallimard Publishing House, 1995, p. 167, we note, I.D.
¹⁶ Fernando Savater, *quoted work.*, p. 171.
¹⁷ Emil Cioran, "*Reflexiuni asupra* mizeriei" [Reflections on misery], *Floarea de foc* [The fiery flower], no. 4, 30 ian.1937, *see Singurătate și destin* [Solitude and destiny], quoted edition, p. 51.
¹⁸ *Ibidem*, p. 53.
¹⁹ Emil Cioran, "*Cele două morale*" [The two moralities], *Floarea de foc* [The fiery flower], no. 8, 27 Feb. 1932, see *Revelațiile durerii* [The revelations of pain], quoted edition, pp. 50-52.
²⁰ *Ibidem.*
²¹ *Ibidem.*
²² *Ibidem.*
²³ *Ibidem.*
²⁴ Emil E. Cioran, "*Structura cunoașterii religioase*" [The structure of religious knowledge], *Revista teologică* [The theological magazine], no. 2-3, Feb-March 1932; see *Singurătate și* [Solitude and destiny], quoted edition, pp. 58-63.
²⁵ *Ibidem.*
²⁶ *Ibidem.*
²⁷ Emil Cioran, "*Iraționalul în viață*" [The irrational in life], *Gândirea* [Thought], no. 4, April 1932; see *Singurătate și destin* [Solitude and destiny], quoted edition, pp. 80-89.
²⁸ *Ibidem.*
²⁹ *Ibidem.*
³⁰ *Ibidem.*
³¹ *Ibidem.*
³² *Ibidem.*

[33] See observations on the archaeology of culture that Cioran makes in "*Scrisoare din singurătate*" [Letter from solitude], *Calendarul* [Calendar], no. 140, August 27, 1932; see *Solitude and destiny*, quoted edition, pp. 106-109.

[34] Emil Cioran, "*Un aspect al iraționalității vieții*" [An aspect of the irrationality of life], *Calendarul* [The Calendar], no. 195, Oct. 21 1932; see *quoted work.*, pp. 118-121.

[35] Emil Cioran, "*Despre stările depresive*" [About depressive states], *Calendarul* [The Calendar], no. 210, November 5, 1932; see *ibid.*, pp. 122-125.

[36] *Ibidem.*

Chapter 7

The irrational, symbolic culture and a eulogy of madness

In almost everything Cioran wrote – either in Romanian, or in the foster idiom of French – there subsists a feeling of revenge against life with its kaleidoscope of inconveniences, but also against death, that he thought he could endlessly fool through *postponed suicides*, as he would define the purpose of writing.

A complex-ridden provincial with discrete joys, equally narcissistic and resentful, with a sensitivity exacerbated by the edges of a partly simulated pathology, an intellectual whose genetic code was imbued by nature with the substance of violence and sadness[1] – this seems to be the inner profile of Cioran the publisher and essayist, especially in his juvenile writings.

7.1 The eclecticism of culture as agony

An almost obsessive pretext of Cioran's journalism can be found in the spiritual *figure of the Romanian intellectual*. The structure of ideas in the frameworks in which he judges is given by the network of lived culture (not just read about), where cultured and intelligent youngsters grind up their energy under the gaze of the ghosts of success, marked by a psychology specific to the unemployed intellectual.

Culture represented, for the young Cioran, a temporal structure (time belonging here to the plan of immanence), with individual historical moments which, by their symbolic nature partake of a *native and specific foundation*. (When he speaks of symbolic culture Emil Cioran does not have an original understanding of the symbol as it happens when considering the constitutive symbol of religion – see "*Simbol și mit* [Symbol and myth], *Calendarul* [Calendar], no. 256, Dec. 25, 1932 – but targets its formal, *abstract-decadent character*, conferred by modern culture.) Comparing it to what happened in the modern period, Cioran revealed, in contemporary culture, a trend of great syntheses, as well as the claim of universality illustrated by eclecticism, in an axiological world devoid of unity, in which values are external to and transcendent of man, and where "all productive energy was exhausted," and "possibilities have been drained".[2]

Cioran's considerations were in tune with Nietzschean and Spenglerian axioms about culture. In eclecticism he sees a sign of the agony of culture, while the higher spirits, who managed to protect themselves from the influences of such an environment, could transform contemplation, weariness and sceptical reflection in defining features for their spiritual existence. The decadence of culture, i.e., its ageing, is a consequence – unless it generated the phenomenon itself – in particular, of historicism and psychoanalysis (especially of the kind promoted and cultivated by the public), which led to the schematization and ossification of life.

The time frame in which Cioran described the evolution of culture in such terms coincided with his graduation thesis on *Contemporary intuitionism*, where the analysis focused on a criticism of Bergsonian philosophy. Framing the intuitionistic movement in contemporary culture, he was talking even then about the decadence of philosophy, and not in a moral sense, but "in so far as it is unable to produce new values".[3] The attitude was clearly one of consonance with Spengler, to which was added a kind of riot with radical zest, inculcated primarily by Nietzsche and other nihilists of the previous century.

Salvation from that imbalance of struggling culture was to be found, according to Cioran, in intuitionism, which could cause a break with modern culture and its spirit, concentrated in the synthetic expression of rationalism. He explained without prejudices and without excitement that the violence with which philosophy reacted against rationalism had an objective justification: "A form of spirit does not become depleted, does not consume its possibilities because another tends to take its place, but because any form of spirit is in itself insufficient, it is limited, closed".[4]

An argument obviously originating from Bergson, also able to invoke an anthropological reason, justified by the fact that "man, wearing certain forms, reaches a point when they no longer satisfy, when they are built in a ratio of exteriority from him; when, from an organic and living coating, they become matrices of the inorganic and death, which oppose his spontaneity." And he concluded: "The process of objectification of natural forms which takes them out of irrational and subjective living, therefore depends on the nature of these forms, as well as the nature of the man who lives them".[5]

A sad complexed provincial, still a student, Cioran was attracted more by anthropological psychology than by a philosophical anthropology, seeing man, his contemporary, as a tragic person, suffering from *the boredom of the culture*, tending to approach "the original, the purely given, unadulterated by categories" (the shadow of Bergsonian ideas followed him everywhere). The energy that steered him was coming from the volitional effort of *believing*, which made him live, in a way, the illusion of *authenticity*, the expression of an *inner torment* originating mainly in the inability of man to adapt to religious values.

To a Nietzschean relativisation of cultural values, the young Cioran added the phenomenon of devitalisation, generated by the so-called democratisation of culture, when values broadcast on a large radius are *homogenised* and lose their specific differences and their character of *organic structures*.[6] His workhorses – and not some Trojan horses – were, for Cioran as well as for Nae Ionescu, rationalism and rationalization, ways blocking the access of the individual to the actual, to the unique and irrational character of the real. And the analysis that he tried to accomplish, on the state of contemporary culture, aimed to undo other small folds in a possible conception of the tragic existence.

7.2 Peeling off the irrational through culture

The relativism of the first decades of the XX-th century inevitably generated tendencies trying to rebuild in a specific way the balance between man and existence. The (also) irrational essence of the latter – of *nature*, as it is expressed somewhere by Cioran – was a pretext for the metaphysical discourse of some thinkers, not many, who accepted the irrational and wanted to explain the different and unusual depths and diversity of life (the example of Lucian Blaga, who, from a desire to overcome the only-rational understanding the world, sought and cultivated a sense of *dogma* is perhaps the most representative). In such a reaction, one could read a kind of Platonism, but only circumstantial, as sometimes Cioran leads us to believe, through which the transcendence of ideas can be substantiated.

But young Cioran does not join such Platonic trends in order to understand and deconstruct the actual structure of life, *the pit inside* of it. He will put in parentheses all those interpretations of life seen through the viewfinder of the transcendent (such as finalism, for instance, which wants to organize the world a priori), together with any illusions a historicist attitude might have when facing life, guidelines which required an optimistic outlook but, in exchange, could not reach the secret of that antinomic human structure disputed between the "irrational impulses and tendencies towards transcendence and rationality of the spirit".[7]

Interested by the sense of the irrational in life, Cioran issues a defining Bergsonian question: "Do the forms of life represent a *sense* or a *direction*?" The *irrational* proved to be incompatible with the first highlighted notion because, being a venue in the plane of immanence, a life "has no meaning outside of it", this being the cause for which, in the process of *demonic budding*, the creator item does not find its place, but only the destructive one; life is maintained only by destroying it. What takes place, instead, is a diversification of the actual forms of life, which outlines directions, as an illustration of a kind of imperialism under which the irrationality of life manifests itself and, with it, its relativity (an obediently-Bergsonian demonstration).

Designed in such a way, the irrationality of life is, you might think, unmastered and invincible. And yet, man tries to transcend it. Through culture, the irrational can be decreased (the position here somewhat resembles the one expressed by Blaga, with the difference being that, for him, the irrational takes on the appearance of the unconscious), the acts of cultural creation being those which commit inevitably the consciousness of man and substitute, and at the same time, the living content of life for the process of thinking about it (and its consistent understanding). A mechanism that was opposed to the culture of life, or transformed the latter into a *negative* premise, necessary for the development of the other: "Only when it (life, we note I. D.) consumes its own energy when it gets sick, may there appear some elements of culture".[8]

Cioran reiterated here one of his favourite theses (borrowed, of course, from the great nihilists he almost organically assimilated): suffering – and, in a lesser measure, joy – is the source of human creation (pain or disease constitute normal conditions that make it possible and enrich it). As he also stated, in another thesis: consciousness, a fatality, meant an exit from the steady-state time of the irrational in which man was originally assimilated, and the beginning of a tragic journey of *isolation* from life, *dividing* the latter in relation to the spirit and its products (it was an imbalance that Cioran often heard about in Nae Ionescu's courses, but also part of his own intuitionist-Bergsonian obsession).

Detachment from the irrational could also be accomplished by meditating upon death, organically linked to life, a reflection which can bring resignation, but which, in certain situations, materializes in cultural acts (Cioran believed that death is just apparently something transcendent, because, in fact, it is immanent in life as such). The same detachment from the irrational would be produced by those horizons which man needs to touch. Ideals thus become a form of exit from the normal frames of one's own life, the *greatest adventure* undertaken by man.

Of fundamental interest to Cioran in the conjunction of culture and life were facts, but not as "they would result from a negative attitude towards the phenomenon of culture, or from a romantic conception of life"; rather those facts that give substance to actual life and death. In short: "The tragic destiny of the human detached from life and turning towards it, not the rigid categories of a doctrine".[9]

7.3 Beyond culture. The return of the irrational

By *great adventure* one could understand, among others, an itinerary that some people can follow without fearing the fatalities of life, or its *metaphysical seed*;[10] as it never happens, says Cioran, with the so-called *culturals* - who anathemize the philosophy of life and see primary biological determinants only as dead ends. The man that young Cioran believed capable of such courage was not suffering from *metaphysical bashfulness*. For such a person, culture can never be a set of symbols (which limits the ontological access of the human to being), meaning a universe of "cold, sterile and non-vitalizing forms". On the contrary. The philosophy of life involved overcoming this comfortable and protective cultural setting and confronting the "big issues" and "the ultimate consequences", those which can even lead "beyond culture".

It Is obvious that such a vision of culture is not so easily accepted – either then, or now. The boredom of culture converted, for Cioran, the dissatisfaction of a specific way of understanding values and of making culture. He advocated the return of the cultured, authentic human inside the fertile space of the irrational, where we all once were and from where a certain culture and rationalism banished us.

The relationship of man with life needed to be de-falsified and an intuitive understanding of the irrational was the optimal path for this (Cioran didn't leave, not even for a moment, the frames of Bergson's philosophy, as synthesized in his graduation thesis). Here, our biology is becoming *transfigured*, absurdity and excess are allowed, as from all of this *primordial confusion* and *initial chaos* arise the musical feeling of life, the state of lust, the drama and the real sadness.

The threshold of the philosophy of life is thus reached, a state where you can have "in every moment the consciousness of the beginning and the consciousness of the end", when you can be *barbaric and apocalyptic* and when optimism, due to a tragic sensitivity, forever converts into pessimism. This condition has a name: *metaphysical madness* (a form of decadence of man turned towards the irrationality of life from which he broke away).

The way in which young Cioran was talking about the philosophy of life inevitably relates to his student readings and, of course, the influence that Nae Ionescu had on him. At the age of 17-18 he had read Georg Simmel (*Grundfragen der Soziologie*) and commented on it; in college he resumed and deepened H. Bergson, and also E. Cassirer and Nietzsche (*Der Wille zur Macht* suited Cioran like a glove).

Thoughts about overcoming culture bring to mind, however, a romantic philosopher such as Ludwig Klages and his body-soul-spirit triad (doctrinally speaking, L. Klages has had a substantial influence on the metaphysical vision of Nae Ionescu). An irreconcilable enemy of life, the spirit would have a tendency, as observed by Blaga, "to separate the body from the soul, meaning to dis-animate the body and de-materialize the soul; and in this way, to ultimately destroy life itself".[11] Being, therefore, a kind of intruder, the spirit will try to annihilate life. Therefore, the German philosopher reverses the action of the bitter vector and turns life into the centre of existence and value.

The only thing you have to cherish with frenzy, after L. Klages, is *the vital principle*.

The last consequences of Cioranian man could occur in this world of Klages, where the inhabitant is none other than the Pelasgic man, manifesting himself through instinct, through intuition (he has a kind of vision of ideas), through emotivity and a domination of the image. It is on such a matrix of genetic-behavioural invariables that Cioran places his subsequent elaborations, essentially variations on the same theme, just changing the points of support or the weight of elements in the geometry of the structure. In trifling doses, for instance, this matrix causes a *comfortable balance* to be installed in a small culture and people. But it is an abnormal balance, a *shameful normality*, because it comes from "lack of courage to live, to assert oneself, in the absence of that energy which lets you soar irrationally and without motivation, leading you either to the ultimate transfiguration, or to the final collapse".[12]

This happened, thought Cioran, in interwar Romania, a country of *mitigated people*. "To be Romanian means to be a human being with a lot of water in the blood".[13] And if we wanted *the solution* for our improvement, we only needed to overcome the state of dilution, to increase the dose, to increase the concentration or the proportion of components in the above-mentioned matrix module; meaning we could be saved "by excess, by madness and by absurdity".

Cioran was, through this conception, in pursuit of that *spiritual energy*, if we may use one of Bergson's syntagma, required by a community desirous for sweeping, radical gestures. "In this country," he said about Romania "there are too many normal people. That's why you can't find a musical genius, a dictator or a serial killer".[14] And because he couldn't find that *vital fluid* which would lift Romanians into the sphere of the irrational, that pathos with which they would fight first against themselves, in order to escape that convenient *balance*, Cioran was fatally disappointed: "That's why I had moments when I was ashamed of being Romanian. But if I regret something, it's these moments. Were I Romanian only through my defects, I'd still love this country, against whom I am embittered from unavowed love".[15]

Cioran thus offers, in logical concordance with the premises of his theory, "a praise of passionate people", those self-appointed *enthusiasts of negativity* (a kind of "deviants of passion"), the ones who turn restlessness, agitation and possession into *modus vivendi*. "Passionate man knows only the spermatic truths, only the truths of fertility, which stimulate, which have a vital source".[16]

The exacerbation of the sensible (of the individualized), of perception to the detriment of reporting to the real through intelligence – this concept was, of course, stemming from the intuitionism of Bergson. In a conference about the perception of change held in the University of Oxford (May 26, 1911), the French philosopher, mindful "not so much of change itself as of the general characteristics of a philosophy interested in the *intuition of change*" (we note., I.D.), said that "the perfect being is the one who intuitively knows all things, without need for reasoning, abstraction and generalization".[17] And due to the failure of the faculty of human perception, philosophy appeared – and, through it, the approach through reasoning. Only perception remained paramount. "No matter how abstract a conception might be, it always has its starting point in perception.

Intelligence combines and separates; arranges, disrupts, coordinates; it does not create".[18]

Hence, probably, Cioran's distrust in *Romanian intelligence* (which he qualified as "a plague of our culture"), and in those who illustrated the *Romanian vacuum*. His objection was fundamental: they organically lacked despair, great insights, searing passions, madness and momentum; in other words, everything that the last consequences achieved by an individual due to the intensity of psychological states and the multiplicity of states of consciousness could mean, as Bergson showed in his analysis.[19]

Cioran, the one who was against intelligent people,[20] listened, as it seems, to the call of the French thinker: "Suppose that, instead of rising above the perception of things, we want to get submerged in it, to deepen and enhance it. Let's assume that we involve our will too, and that by amplifying it we would also amplify our vision of things".[21] Would an apology for barbarism, for ecstasy, for nothingness, or, otherwise said, metaphysical madness, be more than a step away?!

The relationship between culture and life that Cioran was talking about in the final part of his graduation thesis represented a permanent pretext for his rebellion. A binomial which, understood through the grid of Bergsonian vitalism, was pushing him to advocate, as I said, the (re)turn of the man of culture into the irrational; hence, that sense of the superfluous in the face of a scholastic kind of philosophy and culture which, feeding only on books (which contain borrowed and not experienced ideas), betray an inorganic nature.[22] An attitude stemming from the meaning given to intuition as such, where we can observe life in all its fullness, its native character and its purity, which "represent primarily a function of experience. As such, it is irreducible and irrational", allowing its targeted object "to be extracted, in the act of living, from any relationship with others"[23] and individualized.

At the same time, intuition supports the development of metaphysical constructions, because "metaphysics – about which we have to say that it maintains itself with the condition of no longer being meta-physical, I mean no longer maintains its substantialist speculations, has absolute need of an intuitive substantiation interface, keeping it in close contact with the roots of nature".[24]

It is exactly where Cioran wants to lead us, back to the roots of nature, where we can observe life in all its fullness, its native character and its pure *given*, the metaphysics to which he adheres, rooted in this place and making best use of experience (it's not, however, the integral experience of Bergson, who - Cioran thinks – exaggerated a little) which man assimilates inside himself. And because the emphasis is on the values of subjectivity, the culture-life rapport becomes much more intimate. Intuitionism wanted to destroy an artificial polarity and to overcome the antagonism introduced by the Christian tradition of modern culture, which saw in culture "a kind of resistance to life".[25] The metaphysical point of intuition was, in this manner, fulfilled.

Is clear, therefore, that many of the texts published by Cioran in the first part of the fourth decade of the XX-th century, including his first book, revolve in various ways around the irrational, an obsession for the first half of the XX-th century. Let's not forget, for instance, the fact that Blaga printed in 1934 part III of his *Trilogy of knowledge*, namely: "*Transcendent censorship*", where he fixed the role and place of reason and the irrational in knowledge.[26] It is also here that he will give an exposition of that analysis of the relationship between spirit and life, as it appeared in Ludwig Klages (in *Der Geist als Wildersacher der Seele*, 1929) and Max Scheler (with *Die Stellung des Menschen im Kosmos*, 1930), thinkers who also attracted Cioran.

Even when he reads Hegel, Cioran is still thinking about the irrational and intuition. The author of the *Phenomenology of the spirit* offered an example close to the limit, if not right at the limit. A rationalist, but not in the contemporary sense of Cioran, who irrationalized the concept, or – differently said – revealed the "irrational through the concept",[27] Hegel had perhaps the most philosophically developed sense for the variety and depth of historical life (Cioran quotes words the German philosopher said somewhere: "History is not the realm of happiness. Its only happy times are in its empty pages").

7.4 In place of a conclusion: an anthropology of the tragic

The depth and complexity of the irrational could not be, after Cioran, perfectly explained and depicted by humanist anthropology, for which man means a balanced and harmonic human being, located outside of any conflicts or antinomies. How could such a vision understand the decay of the human, what would it say about the destiny of man? Only a pessimistic anthropology of the tragic would decipher these meanings because it has as its object the issue of the destruction of man and destiny seen as "immanent reality and inner fatality". Man, in such a vision, is a being "thrown to destruction and death", one that, by his contradictory nature, includes in his grandeur and humanity the secret of decadence, of the regression of the human. There is, in this existential equation, something of the conception of a German biologist with whom Cioran agreed, a theory that defined man as a *dilettante* of life.

It can be said that one of the hypotheses of human decay, perhaps the most significant, is *depressive man*, a man whose being is possessed by antinomy and despair, for whom "tragedy is ongoing in the organic background of his subjective existence".[28] Cioran was asking himself about this man's vision of the world, a category which included Kierkegaard, Tolstoy or Michelangelo. But – and this must be clearly understood – he does not refer to any of the possible maladies of the spirit, but to those who can update the provisions of a primary disposition.

Young Cioran's concept was clear: what to some seems pathological – see the *major organic depressives* mentioned above – is nothing else than the way in which they can get to the irrational, the essential structures of nature. Disposition, whose eulogy he offers in this way, is the mechanism that transforms human subjectivity in "a theatre of continuous tragedy", and the depressive type in an individual who can understand better than all the others the phenomenon of death ("the common world is not afraid of death, because it lives as if death didn't exist.").

Man forgot, however, how to have an existence in the irrational, and the most obvious and convincing sign of his powerlessness to live like this is, after Cioran, *the emergence of consciousness*, proof of a vital disability of humans. "In man, life has reached a bankruptcy. The forces of Eros, which stems from the very essence of life, have lost intensity; the assimilation of organic-in-the-making was replaced by the irremediable breach of subjectivity from objectivity; immediate reaction to qualitative diversity has been replaced by an abstract perspective which homogenises and cancels specific and individual items".[29] The crisis represented by the rationalism and rationality of life, as Cioran believed, is obvious in these reproaches. Human decadence found an essential outlet in consciousness, and all its avatars were translated, by identity loss, in wanderings of the human being (Cioran spoke of the centrifugal trends of consciousness). The source of the tragic in the world will be thus detected in the phenomenon called consciousness, for which "the road of ascension is the path of decadence".

Any determinations presented so far are just part of the actual composition of the physiognomy of *Cioranian man* who is none other than *desperate man*, one who will speak particularly in the first book of the author. And culture, accepted culture, is not always ready to serve democracy ("democracy and culture constitute two opposing terms"), but that which is made for the few, *for* and *by* the *elite*. A culture where the *French feeling of existence is not welcome* since the existence of clarity has become futile and ridiculous. French literature and philosophy, a style of life specific to this space that Romanians have borrowed without censure, severs any roads to mystery, to the "infinity inside".

"Too much clarity!" – shouted Cioran, who condoned prolific confusion and didn't choose the geometric spirit of *finesse*, but something else: "I prefer a thousand times the momentum of a barbarous, explosive and overflowing spirit to the completely unavoidable distinctions of subtle spirits, the ones who love differences in the light".[30] Between the eulogy of insanity and that of subtlety, Cioran now chooses the former. Many years in the future, in France, he will become a *hack of the hue*, after an expression he himself used.

But philosophical anthropology, so enticing for Cioran, had also in its structure a cognitive dimension. If Nae Ionescu had researched the *epistemological function of love*, Emil Cioran would be attracted to *the gnoseological function of ecstasy*, as he confessed in 1936 when he requested a scholarship for the elaboration of a doctoral thesis from the French Institute in Bucharest: "*En France je voudrais m'occuper de plus près avec ces problèmes* – he was talking about the study of differences between rational knowledge and intuitive knowledge, we note, I.D. – *et préparer une thèse sur la condition et les limites de l'intuition. En même temps je tacherai de connexer les idées sur l'intuition avec une certaine catégorie de problème que l'intuitionisme contemporain a mis particulièrement en lumière: la fonction gnoséologique de l'extase*".[31]

Knowledge through ecstasy takes place by means of the symbol, in which an overflowing content of reality is condensed, and which performs direct and substantial communication. Specific to religion and being an actual embodiment of the universe, having in a way the status of Platonic ideas, the symbol belongs, by its very nature, to religious sentiment, attaining a significant link between it and mystical experiences. "The most complicated and most difficult to understand symbols stem from ecstasy, because ecstasy, which is a paroxysm of tension combined with an enlightening drunkenness, deploys a paradoxical diversity of symbols which cannot be understood by a mentality evolved in normal categories".[32]

However, even though the symbol, Cioran followed with the same grimness his usual target: to touch the irrational and to rationalize it. Biographically speaking, Cioran proved that he had an irresistible attraction for the originary or irrational. The place in which he was born was invariably located "in a very primitive environment", "a really barbaric village". From Romania he loved its "intense, extremely primitive side", and had a dubious preference for uncultured illiterates; psychologically, he paradoxically felt very close to the tastes and habits of the Hungarians. "I'm a mix of Hungarian and Romanian",[33] he told Fernando Savater. So, we can finally ask ourselves – which part of Cioran's writings does not participate, discretely and directly, to the composition of a *Book about the irrational?!*

Notes

[1] "If the sources of violence and sadness ever drained from me, I'd give up writing forever". Cioran, *Caiete* I, Bucharest: Humanitas Publishing House, 1999, p. 91. And also, here: "I am, in my heart of hearts, a provincial" (p. 89).

[2] *Ibidem*, p. 68.

[3] Emil Cioran, "*Intuiționismul contemporan*" [Contemporary intuitionism], previously unknown manuscript, page 4 (see Ion Dur, *Hîrtia de turnesol. Cioran inedit. Teme pentru acasă* [The litmus paper. Previously unpublished Cioran. Homework], quoted work., pp. 331-349).

[4] *Ibidem*, p. 5.

[5] *Ibidem*, pp. 5-6.

[6] Emil Cioran, "*Sensul culturii contemporane*" [The meaning of contemporary culture]; see *Singurătate și destin* [Solitude and destiny], quoted edition, pp. 70, 73.

[7] Emil Cioran, "*Perspectiva pesimistă a* istoriei" [The pessimistic perspective of history], *Calendarul* [The Calendar], no. 70, June 18, 1932; see *ibidem*, p. 90.

[8] Emil Cioran, "*Iraționalul în viață*" [The irrational in life], *Gândirea* [Thought], no. 4, April 1932; *see Solitude and destiny*, quoted edition, pp. 84. Cioran associates the irrational with the non-existence of transcendent purposes and values: "Concerning the most intense expression of the irrational in life, it is not paradoxical to say that, for humans, the sexual act is an occasion for metaphysics" (*Ibidem*, p. 85).

[9] *Ibidem*, pp. 88, 89.

[10] See Lucian Blaga, "*Despre gândirea magică*" [About magical thinking], in *Trilogia valorilor, Opere* [Trilogy of values, Works], 10, Bucharest: Minerva Publishing House, 1987, p. 251. The same thing had been advocated by Blaga in 1934, when he printed the "*Transcendent Censorship*".

[11] See Lucian Blaga, "*Despre gândirea magică*" [About magical thinking], in *Trilogia valorilor, Opere* [Trilogy of values, Works], 10, Bucharest: Minerva Publishing House, 1987, p. 251. The same thing had been advocated by Blaga in 1934, when he printed the "*Transcendent Censorship*".

[12] Emil Cioran, "*Țara oamenilor atenuați*" [The Land of mitigated people], *Vremea* [The Time], no. 306, September 24 1933; *See Solitude and destiny*, quoted edition, pp. 229-230

[13] *Ibidem*.

[14] *Ibidem*, p. 231.

[15] *Ibidem.*

[16] Emil Cioran, *"Elogiul oamenilor pasionați"* [In praise of passionate people], *Rampa* [Ramp], no. 4712, September 28, 1933; *ibidem*, p. 235.

[17] Henri Bergson, *Gândirea și mișcarea* [Thinking and movement], Iași, Polirom Publishing House, 1995, pp. 142, 143.

[18] *Ibidem*, p. 144.

[19] See Henri Bergson, *Eseu asupra datelor imediate ale conștiinței* [Essay on the immediate data of consciousness], Iași: Polirom Publishing House, 1998, pp. 29-122.

[20] See his note to *"Împotriva oamenilor inteligenți"* [Against intelligent people], *Discobolul* [The Discobol], no. 9, May 1933; *see Solitude and destiny*, quoted edition, pp. 205.

[21] Henri Bergson, *Gândirea și mișcarea* [Thinking and movement], quoted edition, p. 146.

[22] See „*Scrisoare din singurătate* [Letter from solitude], *see Solitude and destiny*, quoted edition, pp. 106-109.

[23] Emil Cioran, *Intuiționismul contemporan* [Contemporary intuitionism], previously unknown manuscript, page 21; see Ion Dur, *The litmus paper* (2000), quoted edition, section *"Homework"*.

[24] *Ibidem*, p. 22.

[25] *Ibidem*, p. 23.

[26] Interest for the relationship between the rational and irrational is also obvious in the cycle of conferences entitled *"The crisis of reason in European thinking"*, which the Romanian Society of Philosophy held, in the fall of 1934, in the Amphitheatre of the Carol I University Foundation. The subjects of the lecturers were significant: "Irrationalism as the basis of philosophy" (C. Rădulescu-Motru); "The irrationality of life" (C. Narly); "The origins of modern irrationalism" (Tudor Vianu); "Irrationalist scepticism in Italy" (Mircea Florian); "N. Berdyaev and the irrational prophets" (Vasile Băncilă); "Irrational knowledge" (Mihai Ralea); "The irrational in politics" (Petre Andrei).

[27] Emil Cioran, *"Noi și Hegel"* [We and Hegel], *Archive for science and social reform*, no. 1-4, 1932; *see Solitude and destiny*, quoted edition, pp. 145.

[28] Emil Cioran, *"Despre stările depressive"* [About depressive states], *Calendarul* [The Calendar], no. 210, November 5, 1932; *ibidem*, p. 123.

[29] Idem, *"Conștiință și viață"* [Consciousness and life], *Calendarul* [The Calendar], no. 220, November 15, 1932; *ibidem*, p. 127.

[30] Idem, *"Prea multă claritate!"* [Too much clarity!], *Calendarul* [The Calendar], no 294, February 12 1933; *ibidem*, pp. 162-163.

[31] See Gabriel Liiceanu, *Cearta cu filosofia* [Quarrel with philosophy], Bucharest: Humanitas Publishing House, 1992, p. 143.

[32] Cioran, *"Simbol și mit* [Symbol and myth], *Calendarul* [The Calendar], no. 256, December 25, 1932; *see Solitude and destiny*, quoted edition, pp. 135. Cioran had in mind the ecstatic experience of the East.

[33] Idem, *Entretiens*, Paris: Gallimmard, 1995, p. 20.

Chapter 8

Between *falling in time* and *falling into the temporal*

As a private thinker in the ideatic space of *the fragment*, Cioran never had a systemic and systematic vision of time. "Time is inaccessible for me. And not being able to follow its cadence, I either cling to it or I'm contemplating it, but I'm never *in it*: it is not my *element*".[1] And Cioran's thoughts or musings about time have not so much philosophical meaning, but rather express psychological, anthropological, socio-historical or even theological meanings of its reception.

Nearly always associating the existence of time with its *organic living* (since that establishes a "correlation between the deficiency of blood and its wanderings in duration: so many white blood cells, so many empty moments"), Cioran underestimated in fact the metaphysical interest in time, justifying it, somehow, by a "snobbery of the Irredeemable".[2] Time, conceptually speaking, appears to him as just an *element*, not excessively saturated by ontological order or having true philosophical consistency; a reason for which he suspects that those who, leaving aside its "positive content", make time "their main concern" can be suspected of ambiguity.[3]

In other words, time is a *"false coin* on a metaphysical scale", a plural misleading equivocation for those who take into account the features of its dubious double game and its fundamental hypocrisy, "the confusion it creates between being and non-being".[4]

In our attempt to analyse the way in which Cioran, as a thinker, refers himself to the category of philosophical time, we don't need to elude the academic context of his formative years, the *philosophical atmosphere* of decades three and four of the last century. The philosopher who expressed the spirit of the age, and who continued to be *fashionable* at the time, was Henri Bergson (Nobel prize, 1927); his essays, including *The two sources of morality and religion*, published in 1932, were bibliographic highlights, impossible to ignore for any philosophical exegesis, especially about time, which Cioran and all those who made up the generation of Mircea Eliade would produce - either during their studies or afterwards.

Not by accident, Cioran, the student, chooses as the subject of his graduation thesis (presented in October 1931),[5] *Contemporary intuitionism*, the philosophy of the French thinker being also a pretext for a few tutorial themes. In fact, Cioran starts here his endless *argument* (and: *draw*) with criticism, which he will later develop against various systems and authors; here he begins to thicken and exalt what he calls the "*personal attitude*", a dimension he believes historicism would have ignored, unless things would have been different: "the inability to have a personal attitude has led to historicism".[6]

And also starting here and now, at the turn of decades two and three of the XX-th century, Cioran's discourse will never leave a framework of theses and hypotheses which, discreetly and obsessively, will be constantly reiterated by the author in his philosophical thoughts or musings, and are built on almost always with an inimitable art of the paradox, but sometimes with a hint of quibbles or fallacious axioms. The irreconcilable *rapport* between philosophy and science; categories such as intuition, the given or the actual, the individual, intuitive knowledge, experience and its specific irrationality – are but a few of the levers which Cioran's mechanism of knowledge will reactivate and use repeatedly, in fragmentary reflections.

In the same text – about the intuitionist movement – which concludes his studies of philosophy, Cioran invokes, in a way which will prove significant for the type of discourse he will subsequently build, major affinities between intuitionism and romanticism stressing the fact that "the existential *given* can be known in its intimate structure only by philosophy".[7]

Therefore, in terms of the category of time, Cioran is now, at the end of his college years, a follower of Bergsonism, and expresses this attachment by everything he thinks and writes, and by the way in which he decodes intuitionism through the grid of a philosophy of culture. He is interested in the mechanism of intuition and the way in which *metaphysical intuition* works, by inducing *distinctions* from *aesthetic intuition* into the process of knowledge; and by the way in which, turning towards "the totality of original data", it reveals to us "the pure *given*, not falsified by conceptual elements": "By overcoming homogeneous space, thus discovering, in the place of this void form, pure duration, perceived by intuition through an inner return. Time which is counted, broken into artificial units, is a concept similar to that of space. More. Here, one achieves a kind of assimilation of time to space".[8]

He characterizes here, in a Bergsonian way, the determinations of homogeneous time and space, the pure and heterogeneous duration, in order to then invoke the sequence and simultaneity of states of consciousness, recalling also other traits from the personal file of that "fundamental ego" mentioned by Bergson.

As a student, he had read Bergson; and quotes him in French when drafting his thesis, including references to some exegetes of the French philosopher:

Réné Berthelot, *Le pragmatisme de Bergson* (1913, vol. II of *Un romantisme utilitaire*), Richard Kroner, Henri Bergson, *Logos* (1910), Georg Simmel, *Zur Philosophie der Kunst* (1922).

Uttered in such a key, reflections on time will never be too far from the influence that Nae Ionescu's metaphysics courses might have had, especially his adherence to a specific mechanism of *understanding* knowledge as *experiencing the object* and obtaining, in this way, knowledge by "co-naturality".[9]

A non-conformist attitude towards the classic discourse of philosophy and the perception of time will have, in Cioran's case, as mentioned already, ambiguous, even prolix meanings, without an epistemologically clear option put to work in a consistent approach. And even if he struggled, as he confessed, with all that was created since Adam, his exercises of thought were developed in the way of accepting metaphysics as "purely human concern of those who have missed salvation and are *trying to balance in existence,* in this human condition, through a *total and harmonic* understanding of existence".[10] Young Cioran lived, thought and wrote in a time threatened by the signs of a *crisis of the fundamentals.* Rhetorical chronicles had announced the death of tragedy and its aftermath, and after all predictions, they were going to be the death of philosophy with some authors dubitatively reflecting on religion also. Cioran himself, as we have already seen, had a special relationship with the sphere of religion and, in equal measure, with God. Even that form of time in which he believed most of all and somehow idolized was what he called "God's time", opposite in essence to the "time of the Devil".

Even at that time, Cioran seems to have understood that *history* is *the eighth day,* the day that followed the fall into sin or, in a subsequent formulation, the fall into time.

8.1 A fall in (and from) time

After he consumes other interstices of existence, which also remain as exercises of divine disobedience, Cioran attempts to imbue the *first fall of man* with some personal hermeneutics, an episode, which through Adam will mark the beginning of *history.* After all, says Cioran, it's all about "a second blow to the order of God", after Lucifer, the first protester who "attacked the original unconsciousness",[11] unsettling the original unity of the world.

The exit of the human being from what Cioran called "primordial innocence" and his entry into *time* was generated by dissatisfaction with God (who *gave him the gift of ignorance*), by knowledge, and by self-doubt. A long period of decay followed with millennia of scepticism and clear mind and with a couple of existential fundamental roles played by characters (in their essence, *puppets* – as are all beings, believes the philosopher), such as:

the barbarian, the civilized man, the demon (the carrier of *evil*, an embodiment with a semantic plethora impossible to ignore if we take into account the network of meanings created by mythology, religion and philosophy for the *daimon*'s masks).

This world, refused and denounced by Cioran, of which he himself is part, is one that seemingly wanted, and still wants to redeem his lost innocence through conjoined acting upon the human mind, of sceptical thinking, of clarity, of the way in which the human being *lives* his desire for *glory* (converted, positively, in a horror of its heyday), *disease* (metamorphosed, through the alchemy of pain, into conscience, as ascertained, before Cioran, by the author of the *underground notes*), as much as was meant, after the entry of man in history, by the challenge of *death* or some of the most important maladies of the spirit that Cioran invokes, in the section "The dangers of wisdom", in his 1964 essay about *the fall in time*.[12]

Tempted more by knowledge, and less by immortality, our prime ancestor, as Cioran likes to call him, was thus cast, just by such knowledge, into *time*, in the arcana *of destiny*, and possessed by *perversity* and *corruption* alike; man acted "as a desecrator, as a traitor, as an agent of dissolution": "Had he a however weak vocation for eternity, man would be satisfied with God, in the proximity of whom he thrived, instead of running toward the unknown, the new, the ravages to which his craving of analysis leads him . (...) After breaking into pieces the unity of Paradise, he took all the trouble to destroy that of the Earth too, introducing a principle of division what was going to destroy its order and anonymity".[13]

As "fracture and crack of being", *id est*: as *individual*, with a "deficit of existence" from the Creator because he says "I am what I am not", with the privilege of the tragic, man made an ordinary barter, changing eternity with *becoming* and maltreating life, turning, finally, into "the great defector of Being".[14] And without realizing that his ceaseless self-concern unbalanced him, instead of a fertile meeting with "his intemporal foundation", the human being "guided his faculties towards the outside, towards history".[15]

Reading the anamnesis offered by Cioran to the character who reincarnated a descendant of our first ancestor, you get the impression that the philosopher projects upon him the traits of a biography that doesn't seem so foreign. It seems we are dealing here with transcribed acts, moods, reflexes and attitudes, summed up in the experiences of a life lived and revealed to us (with all aspects of the struggle with self-preoccupation) through an overt introspection that aims to stay, rhetorically of course, incognito, and somewhat fakely-Sibylline. In addition, we cannot circumvent the fact that the philosopher Cioran is a writer and, in equal measure, an actor who performs sleight of hand tricks with the masks his ego wears, and that's why we never know whether we can believe him when he says that the mask does not serve to protect man's identity, but is used from "bashfulness" or "out of a desire to conceal one's unreality".[16]

With respect to time, we can even say – with the *feeling* of time (the stressed term comes with a load of mainly Kantian metaphysics), Cioran needs to gain access to the essential through *involvement* into it, but not through analysis or words (here, he is against any *pact* with the vocable) – a path which, as he notes somewhere, leads to a "metaphysically *superficial science*". Maybe that's why the *great trial* of his life remains the one which he circles in a note from December 16, 1970, when he had seemingly found an answer to the question posed by a television producer in connection with the meaning given by Cioran, in his early writings, to the terms "*Zerfall*" and "*Bitternis*":

"I believe the most fundamental experience that I have ever lived in my life is not the experience of poverty, but the experience of time, I mean the feeling of not *belonging to time*, of being outside it, the feeling that it's not *mine*. That was my "unhappiness", here is where all explanations must be sought for "decomposition" or "bitterness". After which, in a Platonic way, he expresses the osmotic link between being and time, telling us that he wrote about it in the last chapter of his 1964 essay (*Falling in time*):

"Any act involves a participation in time; you act because you're in time, because *you are* time; but what to do, what to attempt when you are separated from time? You can, of course, meditate and get bored, but you can't kill time, it kills you, passing *besides* you, besides meaning thousands of leagues away".[17]

Cioran lived, in his childhood, the perception of this autarchic power of time, but also the *rupture* between the latter and anything else that is not time. On the morning of November 13, 1968, he drily notes: "Hangover"; confesses that he wants to write a text about "*attention given to time*", because most days he is weighted down by its excitement and exacerbation: "This morning, as I woke up, the first sensation I had was that of the flow of the hours, hours independent of any act, of any outside reporting towards the flow as such. This extreme consciousness of time was the curse of my entire life. (...) I perfectly remember that summer afternoon – I must have been five or six years old – when everything was emptied around me and I was just feeling a *passing* without content, a rush in itself, a flow that frightened me. Time was separating from being *on my account*. There was no more *world*; there was just time. Since then, I live in the event only by chance; I only live in the absence of events, in that time which does not descend towards the event.

Inferno is nothing less than the consciousness of time".[18]

Here's a small snippet from a long and obsessive lesson on the anatomy of time. For Cioran, time was not the *curse* of his life, but his fundamental obsession, with all its dysfunctional burdens. Another confession, on January 3, 1966, reiterates the same reason:

"Last night, having not slept for a while, I came back to my obsession about the flow of time: each moment that passed, *I knew it*, passed and I was never going to see it again. This sequence of points, each painfully irreversible, is not acknowledged as long as we act or at least think about it. We perceive it only in those moments when we are outside of our existence, when we don't record inside us anything else except a great quietness which, normally, would need to become prayer instead of ruminating its own flow".[19]

To illustrate what *(non)involvement* means in the substance of time, more exactly: what is, and not only psychologically, the relationship between time and "the most ancient of terrors", Cioran (re)reads *The Death of Ivan Ilyich*. Tolstoy's text confirms that life gains *consistency* when the individual begins to think about death, or, if we take into consideration the morals induced by Ivan Ilyich: "The real life begins and ends with agony".[20]

Cioran's reflections try to offer another interpretation, not as much for the creative metabolism of the Russian writer, about whom it was said that his talent *drained* away after the age of fifty, but for the way in which a spirit who, in the modern world, had had a similar experience to that of the Ecclesiastes, ended his life in despair. Paradoxically, the one who had spoken so deeply about life seemed to be eluded by life itself, and the solutions Tolstoy proposed for the "new life" were "of a demonic or ridiculous exaggeration". Excess, lack of measure and negation, believes Cioran, were nothing more than "the vengeance of a spirit who could never learn to die with humility".[21]

Cioran's temptation was not just *the insertion of the individual into the tissue of time* and his *meditation*[22] upon such a theme, but also the *detachment* of the same individual from time. The ending pages of the 1964 essay speculatively and precisely approached this intriguing hypothesis: what does it mean to *fall in time*? Even Cioran felt "fallen in time", as his *inner writer* confesses (he thought he was boycotted by time, only to turn it into the substance *of his obsessions)*, more: he seems to have the misery of "not having the right to time", and this can happen when – and here speaks the Goethean inside the philosopher – the *moment* is leaving us and, therefore, "we are deprived of the responsibility of producing a *fact*".[23]

In such a situation, called by Cioran "negative eternity" or "*bad* eternity", time turns into something *closed*, is "untouchable", and impossible to *penetrate* by the individual.

We can enter, however, other spaces of the paradoxically specific labyrinth of Cioranian *meditation* about time, where time perception has unexpected connotations, its actual meanings being incongruous with the logic of the philosopher.[24] Life appears to Cioran as dominated by a "virtual past", devoid of present and future, which hosts an essentially dead time, and carries a rising miasma.

Thus, the danger of a *second fall* threatens Man: a fall into History (Nae Ionescu and Mircea Eliade also talked about a second fall of man, but with a somewhat different meaning), when becoming is *suspended*, when the itself is "becoming bogged down in inert and morose monotony, in absolute stagnation, where the word itself is stuck, unable to reach up towards blasphemy or supplication".[25]

What would be, however, the signs of such a future degradation, not so clearly operationalized by Cioran? First of all, an "insensitivity to one's own destiny", then indifference and even the inability to leave traces, to mark your passage through a *slipstream*, a condition that can appear as soon as the individual is in a "precarious relationship" with life, in a bad relationship with the verb *to do*. To which are added – in order to reach the brink of disaster and collapse – an exacerbation of *will*, the illegitimate human desire to overcome one's condition and become a *superman*. Such a stance, Cioran believes, belongs to the man who, smashed to *smithereens* and *crashed into himself*, goes through a slow process of extinction in the "eternity below".

8.2 The fall in the temporal. Prelude - or what history is (not)

Besides these forms of falling in and out of time, another hypostasis of the fall appears in Cioran's works, a much more pronounced degradation / decomposition of *historical time*. The essential reason: an unlawful, aggressive, malignant alliance with *politics*, a historical field (the notion of field here sends to its physical meaning) associated to a historical time in which the spirit is compromised by the hegemony of dictatorial politics. It is what we call *a fall in the temporal*, a drift that can fundamentally change the destiny of a community. With a semantic clarification: the underlined words do not clearly, but only *allusively* and by *analogy* send (as in those figures of metaphor described by Aristotle), towards distinctions operated by J. Benda in his *Betrayal of scholars*. Cioran was not a political man, but, without a doubt, we find him in a particular historical gap, in the vanguard of those who have theorized, with enthusiastic and lucid (perhaps even apocalyptic) pessimism, about politics.

Episodes of specific falls into the temporal were prepared mainly by the particular way in which Cioran understood and explained *history* (without writing the vocable in *capitals*, as the philosopher sometimes does, because it's about *a certain* history). At the same time, the fall into the temporal seems to have been fuelled by the perception of the intimate *Utopia* and, ultimately, *lucidity* with which Cioran thought that he deciphered, at some point, *the sense of history*. Let us proceed systematically.

Between the historical descriptions and formulations that could compile a glossary of the unusual, we might add the thought according to which, after Cioran, this occurs as a *revelation of experience*. Why did Cioran think, even in 1933, that history is only made by those who "didn't have any call or talent on this earth" and that the historian is "a worthless man"?[26] First of all, because positivism devitalized and modified historical research, moving away from life. The mere collection of data, their objective systematization and interpretation, rational calculations and all sorts of speculations made on account of a past – all of these did not translate, after Cioran, into genuine concerns of history.

Therefore, historicism was so damaging for the human being because it was putting subjective personal experiences between brackets. And authentic history meant exactly this: a subjective construction, based on the *revelations of experience;* "We don't like either history as science or history as process and reality, but we desperately live a sublunar tragedy".[27]

Objectivity, therefore, the long-dreamt objectivity of positivist historians, would have nothing to do with the spontaneous, *occasional* attitude, with selective experience, and with a maximum degree of subjectivity for the researcher. Whatever does not present *subjective interest* is not part – thinks Cioran – of history, and if the latter only tells us what happened, then it induces an exceeded vision of reality, which must be immediately abandoned. "From all the things created by people up to the present moment, I'm only interested in certain *facts* from which I can *start* and which are somewhat added to my being, so that they *cease* to be actually *historical*" (first italics belongs to us).[28]

In other words, everything that has the character of an exemplary lesson *is* history. Moreover, through history, one can clear his vision of the "attitudes of life seen as irrational data", as things happen, for instance, with a person who draws more profit from reading the memoirs of Casanova, than Homer's *Iliad*.

History understood as participation in the thickening of archive data without accepting reality as its reason of existence, is parallel to life, a fake discourse. There is, says Cioran, only one escape: "to sum inside ourselves a part of the past, as though it hadn't passed",[29] incorporating history into our organic restlessness foundation, the only form of questioning that engages and potentiates human subjectivity (as it happens in Pascal or Shestov) and that can cure it from the disgust of history.

But why disgust? Because, among other things, the idea of progress had been somehow compromised. It was an altered idea, says Cioran. The reason for this: in his time, a transformation altogether incomprehensible to man was going on: "Christianity is finished, and so is history. Mankind has taken a wrong turn [...] We tend to turn into a single metropolis, into a universal Père Lachaise" says Cioran later, in an interview with François Bondy.[30]

And still disgust, because when he was young, he was outraged by the times when, in order to explain the world, he would have to use dubious metaphysical concepts, such as destiny or fate. Nevertheless, with age, feeling increasingly close to his origins, Cioran will legitimize the fatalistic worldview of the Romanian space. The Romanian peasant has discovered the fundamental truths, he is right, he who "doesn't believe in anything, who thinks that man is lost, who feels crushed by history. This victim ideology has become my actual conception, my philosophy of history".[31]

Cioran's contempt for history was generated by the fact that it did not only represent a monstrous leveller, but also "the largest imaginable sample of cynicism": "All dreams, philosophies, systems or ideologies fall apart when pitted against the grotesqueness of historical development: things are happening without pity, in an irreparable way, the false and the arbitrary triumph".[32]

Thus, beginning with his youthful publications, Cioran's relationship with history is almost exclusively filled with resentment. The idea of utopia slowly appears – first vaguely, only in some texts – an idea through which he will later understand "the fragility of history, but also its great strength", because, in a way, utopia *redeems history*. Such an effect will have a deeper justification for Cioran: "The thirst for utopia is a religious thirst, a desire for the absolute".[33]

In the early years of the fourth decade of the last century, history was understood as being *destiny* on the march. Fatalism turns man into an object of history, and not into a subject, and Cioran expressed in various formulas the same sentence: "the helplessness of man". Moreover, he invariably associated history with the immense power *of evil*. "Man was doomed from the beginning. [...] Of his own volition, he put himself in the service of ruin. History, steeped in time and in movement, is doomed to self-destruct". But an evil to which man contributes, as a sorcerer's apprentice: "Man will perish through his genius. Any force that triggers it, harms him. He is an animal which has betrayed: history is his punishment. [...] Even the good is bad".[34]

Scrutinizing the situation from that place where he was not too impressed by the "beautiful melancholy eyes of Bavarian girls",[35] Cioran will be hopelessly disappointed. "Spleen, doubt and disenchantment are the cancer of our national being. The Romanian is neither a blind believer in something, nor a denying fanatic, but systematically doubts everything, making a virtue of elasticity".[36] (We seem to detect here in the mould of a scepticism and in the key of *neither-nor* the inverted way of *double-think* that Orwell spoke about in *1984*).

The most intense disappointment came, however, from intellectuals and politicians, the first being only "dilettantes and groomsmen of the spirit", a kind of *moral gel* attracted to politics, while its *natives*, the politicians, were "nobodies, conscienceless nothings, completely deprived of a troubled spirit, unable to overcome the idea of vulgar efficiency".[37]. And Cioran also noted that many Romanian intellectuals had abandoned *the spiritual* in favour of *the temporal*, of politics (to use, just formally, Julien Benda's *terms*), and all this, because of a spiritual powerlessness, and not due to the fact that "political orientation would have annihilated any spiritual possibilities". Pervaded almost entirely by politics, therefore itself political, the new generation through its political empiricism had turned the street into the only important thing.

In this largely devitalized Romania, along with "the powerful cult of the irrational", Cioran wanted to establish "the irrational cult of power". In 1934 it seemed to him that Romanians lacked the relentless will to have a destiny. Hence the absence of a "historic mark of pride" and a "Messianic vision". As in a prelude to *The Transfiguration of Romania*, which will be published in January 1937, Cioran deplores a people that "does not want to become a great nation, does not love the force and impulses of life, but lives in the restful shadow of vulgar illusions, doubting everything and not risking anything".[38]

In that anthropology which Cioran sketched in his youth, the fundamental character, man, had a peculiar physiognomy. Not a *rational animal* meaning a "mediocre, equable, balanced or with the desire *for balance*" person; but rather, in agreement with the maximalism practiced by the philosopher, "an absurd person, with dangerous fantasies, who risks everything in every moment, adventurous because of tragedy, and not because of superficiality".[39] The point is to overcome a humdrum existence, and to become a *case*, even if everyone is afraid of those who end up in such a situation.

The human – *id est*: this *case* - was judged then by Cioran in the Heideggerian terms of human becoming (of a *Dasein*), understood in the horizon of *temporality* (*Zeitlichkeit*), although the latter term will acquire, in *Falling in time*, a special meaning. Present references are but non-systematic, the language is abusive and diffuse, fit for an essay, touching sometimes on the *bavardage*. An *authentic* man is, after Cioran, one who has a destiny, meaning: "afraid of time", or "living in time with the feeling of the irreparable".[40]

Such an existence is tragic because, besides immanence and essentiality, destiny is also characterized by irreversibility. So that death may never be defeated, for it "begins with life". Hence the univocal character of destiny, which is nothing more than an "expression of our daily death".[41] Only thus, believes Cioran, does the true vitality of the human being begin, a non-simulated Quixotism, not in the least suspicious (he was talking about our *manhood*).

This was essentially the man in despair, who will eventually turn his *passion* into destiny if he wants to turn his life into something fecund. For Cioranian man, designed in such a way, there exists only the "ethics of sacrifice" and the "lust of passion";[42] suffering understood in a Dostoyevskian way will thus grow in the inner being of man, in accord with the words of Saint Teresa: "To suffer or to die".

8.3 Utopia and lucidity

Cioran lived the small tragedy of compromises which the spiritual (in whose army he was a conscript from the age of 15, dominated by the ideas of Eminescu's *fragmentarium*) has to make with the temporal.[43] A troubled and troubling experience through which he tried to find a solution for the greater good of the other, but also for salvation from his own loneliness.

Cioran's loneliness and exile – both the outer one, but especially the inner one, in whose ghettos he has lived since his early teens – are an explanation and an excuse (a supreme one) for everything. "It's dreadful to leave a world in which you never met anyone, in which nobody said anything to you, to die with no memory, with a vacuum-laden memory!"[44] These were the moments when Cioran was *on the edge* of his existence in Romania when the deforested places of another existence started to show - an existence at whose end he would say: "After all, I haven't wasted my time, I bustled here and there, like everyone else in this aberrant universe".[45]

The relationship between history and utopia would return obsessively in Cioran's writing, but it will receive a more detached treatment in *Histoire et Utopie* (Gallimard, 1960; Humanitas, 1992). Published at a time when *involvement* was *en vogue* in French academia (and not only there), this book represented, in the lexicon of Cioran's work, a two-fold attempt at explanation: first, the language *was addressed* to us, in order to bring into view the mechanism of utopia, a utopia that existed, differentiated, both in the East and in the West.[46] But, in equal measure, the book was self-referential, consciously projected, through its premises, back onto the works of his youth, in particular, *The Transfiguration of Romania*, with regard to which one must inevitably decode the 1960 essay.[47]

Published three years after the author had refused the Saint-Beuve essay award (1957), *Histoire et Utopie* had a less than enthusiastic critical reception. Syllogisms of welcome wavered between its "*très (trop?) prophétique*" character (Erica Marenco) and the impression of already "dated" noemas: "*les idées mortes du siècle dernier*" (J. Duvingnaud), while still recognising a certain sensitivity to changes taking place, as they would say, "*sous nos yeux*".

A deeply tragic thinker, from the spiritual family of those fed with "beastly sadness, somehow positioned in Job's spiritual lineage, negative and nihilist, as he himself confessed, Cioran wanted to pass, starting with *Lettre à un ami lontain* (the text with which the book opened), from the figure of an "*intolerant liberal* "to that of a "perfect moderate". But the conversion did not occur, no matter how many offerings were brought, and Cioran was left with just the dream of an ideal restraint he hoped to know, released, at some point in the future.

Cioran's discourse – the one from *Histoire et Utopie*, but also the one in *The Transfiguration of Romania* – is not one of epistemological rigour, of intentional systematization, but is sustained by a sentimental reason, refined in the depths of the biological level, transfigured, argued or exacerbated, as the case may be, by a rampant subversive heresy. Living, life, is what dominates. Both the veins of his syllogisms and the spirit of the author pulsate with the blood cells of Asia, and not with the clarity of Latin temptations. The thinker himself feels, as he tells us in *Lettre à un ami lointain*, like the "last Mongol, a Turanian soul filled with the pride and prestige of a robbery". Which *justifies* Cioran's fear, arising "not from a vision of the world, but from the pains of the flesh and the darkness of blood".

Cioran should not be taken, however, *à la lettre* in his social-political texts, particularly those which have a horizon of historical metaphysics. His delusional and overflowing linguistic production, that *verbal dementia* overflowing with Homeric voluptuousness does not need to be saved or excused, and even less justified. Likewise, Cioran is no (more) able to defend himself, and we don't know if such a gesture would still have any meaning. And if others want to do it, what he needs first of all, as Noica suggested, is to be defended against himself.

For a balanced and objective researcher, it is clear that verbal intolerance and exasperating lucidity, the circumvention of distinctions and the speculative proliferation of nuances isolated Cioran – but were not the only ones to do so – in the protective underground of an abstract universe. It is, perhaps, the only form of surety available for ideatic excess, the almost manic overvaluation of the form of expression, in fact - of the egocentric Cioranian discourse, where it coexists easily, sometimes eponymously with apocalypse and utopia, and where his writing reaches that gratuitous, even aporetic professionalism of the "pamphlet without an object", which is almost the same as the utopian pamphlet. Utopia, in one of the meanings Ricoeur conferred upon it, is "an exercise of the imagination, in order to conceive 'a social order "*different from what it is*".[48] A sense that would rigorously correspond, according to the same philosopher, to the ideological "to be so and not otherwise".

Unwittingly, the writer Cioran was deeply ideological in his utopia, even if his *solutions* had nothing to do with "transcendence, or an ideology, or a dogma".[49] However, deliberately and with a greedy complicity, he removed himself, in this figure of speech, from his own time, then from time, not through the horizon of meaning, but, paradoxically, by an "experience of nonsense",[50] and this in spite of any "*exercice d'antiutopie*" or "*défascination*" in which, sceptically, he ventured. And under that "*dandysme metaphysique*", diagnosed by Silvie Jaudeau, we discover one who accepts only the eternal present, and puts history itself between brackets: "It is not the dwelling place of being, but its absence, the denial of anything, the rupture of the living with itself: being one with history, we loathe to be partakers of its throes".[51]

Could one find here the fundamental cause of Cioran's apolitism, as explained by Jaudeau, his manifestly-organic tendency[52] to be above or beyond the events?!

For the absence of being, but also of historical being (in Blaga's sense), needs a language bearing the incessant and agonized struggle with presence: this seems to be, essentially, the Gordian knot of Cioran's discourse, contaminated involuntarily, in *The Transfiguration of Romania* and *Histoire et Utopie*, by the horizon of a social-political ideology, by contact with *the logic of the temporal*.

The language of these works, but also of publications from the interwar period, structure a type of discourse which, using a suggestion coming from Pierre Bourdieu, we could call *louche speech*: akin to people with crossed eyes, it *utters* on one side and *signifies* on the other side. A figure of speech-specific to this work as a whole in which aphorisms blatantly creep in, a kind of bodyguard for the language under whose protection the author can state with impunity, as a Pascal or Nietzsche would do, opinions about particular issues (aphorisms are both produced and producing, because "meaning neither precedes them, nor is their contemporary").[53]

Read in such a way, Cioran's discourse will be faithfully revealed in all its hidden folds, especially to those readers who do not *admire* the author (anymore). A work read, and not just cited, because the fate of Emil Cioran, placed by Saint John Perse among the world's most brilliant essayists after Valéry, somewhat resembles that of Borges, about whom the author of *Exercises in admiration* wrote: "From the moment when everyone starts quoting him, you can't quote him anymore; or, if you do, you get the impression that you are just adding to the mass of his fans, his enemies".

Cioran knew, however, from the *Mahabharata*, a verdict that he admired unconditionally: "The knot of destiny cannot be undone; nothing in this world is the consequence of our actions". And he felt that, if we are not given the chance to meet God, then we have to comfort ourselves with "the anarchy of temporality" which permits, only too often, an enthusiastic fall within the temporal.

Notes

[1] See „*Timp şi anemie*" [Time and anaemia], in Cioran, *Silogismele amărăciunii* [Syllogisms of depression], Bucharest: Humanitas Publishing House, 1996, pp. 36-45.
[2] *Ibidem*, p. 39.
[3] See Chapter. „*Să cazi din timp...*" [Falling in time...], in Cioran, *Căderea în timp* [Falling in time], Bucharest: Humanitas, Publishing House, 2008, pp. 153-162
[4] *Ibidem*.
[5] See the complete text, previously unpublished, in Ion Dur," *Hîrtia de turnesol. Cioran – inedit. Teme pentru acasă* [The litmus paper. Previously unknown Cioran. Homework], Sibiu, quoted work.
[6] *Ibidem*, p. 331.
[7] *Ibidem*, p. 338.
[8] *Ibidem*, p. 342.
[9] See the analysis of "*Scolastica, principiu dizolvant al metafizicii*" [Scholasticism, the solvent principle of metaphysics], in Nae Ionescu, *Curs de metafizică* [Course on metaphysics], Bucharest: Humanitas Publishing House, 1991, pp. 76-83.
[10] Nae Ionescu, *Tratat de metafizică* [Treaty of metaphysics], previously unknown course, in shorthand and transcribed by Dumitru Neacşu, Bucharest: Roza Vânturilor Publishing House, 1999, pp. 18-19.
[11] See Cioran, *Căderea în timp* [Falling in time], *quoted work.*, p. 76.
[12] See *ibidem*, pp. 133-149
[13] See "*Copacul vieţii*" [Tree of life], *ibidem*, pp. 10-11.
[14] *Ibidem*, p. 15.
[15] *Ibidem*, p. 19.
[16] *Ibidem*, p. 157.
[17] See Cioran, *Caiete* [Notebooks], III, 1967-1972, Bucharest: Humanitas Publishing House, 1999, pp. 272-273.
[18] Idem, *Caiete* [Notebooks], II, 1966-1968, Bucharest: Humanitas Publishing House, 1999, p.367.
[19] *Ibidem*, p. 6.
[20] see *Căderea în timp* [Falling in time], *a priori* p. 119.
[21] *Ibidem*, p. 129.
[22] In his exercises, developed in the key of the *fragment*, Cioran makes no distinction – in fact establishes an antinomy – "between *thinking* and *meditating*, between jumping from one problem to another and deepening one and the same problem" – see *ibidem*, p. 19; we note, I.D.
[23] See *Căderea în timp* [Falling in time], *quoted work.*, p. 153, we note, I.D.
[24] Cioranian discourse has, as it has been observed, a specific, self-sufficient consistency, even when we run into some voids or fractures, seemingly illogical in the carefully wrought filigree of its organization.

²⁵ See *Căderea în timp* [Falling in time], *quoted work.*, p. 159.
²⁶ Emil Cioran, "*Împotriva istoriei și a istoricilor*" [Against history and historians], *Calendarul* [The Calendar], no. 306, February 26, 1933; see *Solitude and destiny,* quoted edition, pp. 169.
²⁷ *Ibidem*, p. 170.
²⁸ *Ibidem.*
²⁹ *Ibidem*, p. 171.
³⁰ See Cioran, *Entretiens*, quoted edition, p. 14
³¹ *Ibidem*, p. 20. For Cioran, the Romanian people is "the most fatalistic in the world".
³² *Ibidem*, p. 125. Cioran recognises only technological progress.
³³ *Ibidem*, p. 27.
³⁴ *Ibidem*, p. 223. Lately, Cioran had amended his own vision on history: "There are moments in history when man rises to the dignity of subject, moments when he is truly creative" (*Ibidem*, p. 248).
³⁵ See Emil Cioran, "*Melancolii bavareze*" [Bavarian melancholia], *Vremea* [The Time], no. 341, June 10, 1934; *see Solitude and destiny*, quoted edition, pp. 266-270.
³⁶ Idem, "*Cultul puterii*" [The cult of power], *Vremea* [The Time], no. 352, August 26, 1934; in *quoted work.*, p. 271.
³⁷ Idem, "*Între spiritual și politic* [Between the spiritual and the political], *Calendarul* [The Calendar], no. 261, January 2. 1933; in *quoted work.*, p. 153
³⁸ Idem, "*Cultul puterii*" [Cult of power], *Vremea* [The Time], no. 352, August 26, 1934; in *quoted work.*, p. 274.
³⁹ Idem, "*Cultul puterii*" [Cult of power], *Vremea* [The Time], no. 352, August 26, 1934; in *quoted work.*, p. 274.
⁴⁰ Idem, "*Scrisoare din munți*" [Letter from the mountains], *Calendar* [Calendar], no. 447, August 16, 1933; in *op. cit.*, p. 222.
⁴¹ Idem, "*Omul fără destin*" [The man without a destiny], *Vremea* [The Time], no. 308, October 8 1933; *quoted work.*, p. 241.
⁴² See Emil Cioran, "*Pătimirea ca destin*" [Passion as destiny], *Vremea* [The Time], no. 332, Easter [April 8] 1934; *quoted work.*, p. 257.
⁴³ On December 10, 1926, Cioran will start to write in a notebook, stating: "For the transcription of excerpts from books". The model could not be other than Eminescu, so that his Caeite Notebooks too will be set up as true originals.
⁴⁴ Emil Cioran, "*Nu există nimeni*" [There is none], *Seara* [The Evening], no. 1713, July 13-14, 1943; text included in *Solitude and Destiny,* quoted edition, pp. 334-337
⁴⁵ Idem, *Mărturisiri și anateme* [Confessions and anathemas], Bucharest: Humanitas Publishing House, 1994, p. 174.
⁴⁶ On the occasion of the reprinting of the book *Histoire et Utopie* in 1977, R. Caillois observed that, "in his characteristic style, Cioran was often touching the deepest meaning of utopia" – see *Magazine littéraire*, no. 327, Dec. 1994, p. 36.
⁴⁷ See the parallel reading made by Sorin Alexandrescu, in *Contrapunct* [Counterpoint], no. 44, 1991.

[48] See Paul Ricoeur, *Eseuri de hermeneutică* [Hermeneutical essays], Bucharest: Humanitas Publishing House, 1995, p. 282.
[49] Silvie Jaudeau, *Cioran ou dernier homme*, José Corti, 1990, p. 14.
[50] *Ibidem*, p. 12.
[51] Emil Cioran, *Istorie și Utopie* [Histoire et Utopie], Bucharest: Humanitas Publishing House, 1992, pp. 138-139.
[52] About the organicity of young Cioran's political philosophy (more precisely: about its logic failure, and about the confusion between "organic" and "mechanical"), the essayist H.-R. Patapievici wrote an essay which is not devoid of depth: "*About intolerance: a case study*", in 22, no. 36, September 9-15, 1997.
[53] See Geneviève Léveille-Mourin, *Le langage chrétien, antichrétien de la trenscendance: Pascal*-Nietzsche, Librairie philosophique J. Vrin, 1978, p. 135.

Chapter 9

Against "national drowsiness"
– Cioran *versus* Cioran –

In the diachronies of their work, truly original and profound authors can only be contradictory, and if we investigate, in part, the great apostles of the spirit, we find that the exceptions only serve to extend the rule. Of course, there are several layers to *this self-resistance*, one that remains, we believe, *the central and touch stone of creation* in its essence and purity. This Impulse – we could write it with capital letters – harbors, in the act, those proteiform temporal hypostases that characterize an author.

We can also discover another level - perhaps the most easily discernible - of distortions: we refer to those originating from the sphere of non-theoretical interests, those which expose the "ingredients" and "impurities" in the plasma of a work. There are moments of open or discreet compromise which an author makes, states which, otherwise christened, might be called ideological partisanship. It is, in fact, the most precarious form of *dialogue with oneself*.

To a thinker like Cioran – a creator who enters, simultaneously, both into the role of Prometheus and of the eagle – *arguing with oneself* takes a very private form. Ostentatious apprentice and passionate fan of *decomposition* ("Précis de décomposition" is a syntagma with the force of *a genetic program* for the philosopher's work), which he turned into a kind of *dogma*, Cioran remains one of the finest seismographs of the *underground* of the human being. Not for nothing have the exegetes seen his books as possible primers of a therapy of the latter, where free thinking, experience and understanding coexist. With the exception – in this seemingly endless groundwork to which Cioran the *scriptor* seems so committed – of one or two books, attached to a particular context in which he has invested an ideological stake: we refer here to *The Transfiguration of Romania* or *Histoire et Utopie*.

Of books seriously weighed down by what is known as "the Cioran effect", to which those who have read the author in the last two decades seem particularly prone, the most difficult to digest seems to be *The Transfiguration of Romania* . A book that, from its initial manuscript to the present day, has had both a singular and an unprecedented biography.

The manuscript of this controversial book can be found in the archive of Relu Cioran, Sibiu, among other documents that he preserved with great care.

I don't know how many people have read those pages, or whether anyone had the curiosity to compare them with the text of the *princeps edition*. But, as stated before, perhaps it is a misnomer to talk of a manuscript in the accepted meaning of the term, for the composition in question is, in fact, a *file* with a tiled structure. It contains not only pages written by the hand of Cioran, but also parts of a dactylogram, next to which were glued – in particular in the first chapter – cuttings with fragments published in interwar magazines before the editing of the volume. (Editor Marin Diaconu would have seen yet another variant of *The Transfiguration of Romania*, with changes made by Cioran himself, at present in the possession of essayist Constantin Barbu. I wonder, however, why he did not print it until now, since the structure as such brings essential changes in the "shaping the content" of the work, to invoke a well-known phrase.)

Between the "manuscript" on which I worked and what Emil Cioran called, in 1990, the "definitive edition" of *The Transfiguration of Romania* there exist more or less nuanced differences. Some of them we will refer in the present pages. They illustrate an aspect about which much was spoken and written until now, in a way that is relatively consistent, namely: the relationship between the author and "the other", a topic discussed, long ago, in almost an entire edition of the international Cioran Colloquium, held, annually, in Sibiu.

We do not intend to research, here and now, the topic of the distinction between "*autre*" and "*autrui*", and its meaning in Cioran's work; we aim rather to draw attention to a specific *game of identity*, from an author who built his work – but also the most essential segments of his biography – in the key of productive ambiguity, one finely and carefully directed. And when we say Cioran the author we refer, almost exclusively, to the *writer* of this name, and invoke less the determinants of the *"philosopher", "essayist"* or *"publicist"*, all of them *poses* wearing the masks and the writing force of the same character.

We're interested in, to put it more exactly, the relationship – both voluntarily and involuntarily – established by the author between the successive forms taken by his works, from the stage of the manuscript to what, conventionally, is called the "definitive edition".

One can say that such a road is a natural one and that he is shouldering, inevitably, the burden of a brand of augmentation from one threshold to another, meaning all that the author finds fit to modify in his text, between two or more editions. I'm not disputing for a moment such a truth, but it is important, sometimes, to discover not just what has changed from one edition to another, but also why the author has done so, especially when the work to which we refer has many vectors of connection with the context of the preparation / reception thereof. Thus, additions and suppressions, stylistic revisions of the text and any other small or large changes become extremely significant for the author, whose writing desk or, as appropriate, computer is placed at the crossroads of at least three "ideologies": that of development, i.e. the stage of the manuscript, the "ideology" of reception (of variable size) and the "ideology" of the author himself (an entity subject to potentially variable metamorphoses) at the time of "re-development" of successive editions.

Without having to resort now to a comparative analysis between the three variants of *The Transfiguration of Romania* (the manuscript and the two editions: 1936, published by Vremea, resumed in 1941, and 1990, published by Humanitas), we will bring into discussion, not the structure of the whole volume, seriously amputated in the "authorized version" (the one from 1990), but only the beginning and the end of the manuscript, as we will also make a few remarks on the chapter on "National collectivism", completely excised in the Humanitas edition, a chapter which we restore in our present work, offering a parallel reading with the manuscript.

The first surprise and, at the same time, bewilderment produced by the manuscript comes from the title of the paper: Emil Cioran, *The Theory of Romania*, both the author name and title being, however, written with the same pen nib used for writing at the time. And on the first page of the same manuscript, the one that corresponds to the same first page in the editions, follows the title of the first chapter: "The mission of great cultures and the tragedy of small cultures", next to which is written: Romania. But here too everything is cut, all through the length and breadth of the text.

Therefore, no trace of the formulation "The Transfiguration of Romania" exists on the cover-sheet of the manuscript; while from the first chapter, only "The tragedy of small cultures" remained in the printed editions.

In relation to the end of the text written in 1936 by Cioran, it includes a statement that he subsequently abandoned: *"I do not think that I don't believe in Romania"* (my emphasis, I.D.; this double negative is also listed on page 198, row 5 as we count from top to bottom). This is actually the end of that Cioranian "pamphlet" that had, despite subsequent speculation made by exegetes, an *object*. An object upon which were converging the hurtling poisoned arrows of the critics, and which was called: *Romania*. It is thus that Cioran writes on the first two pages of the manuscript, and the name of Romania also concludes his fiery critical claims, but through an optimistically paradoxical formulation: I don't believe that I don't believe, which means: *I believe!*

We also accomplished, no doubt, a formal mirroring of the "manuscript" with corresponding texts from the 1936 and 1990 editions, to see what did not remain of the original form in the princeps edition and what Cioran suppressed for the Humanitas version. It would be ideal to anastatically print the entire "manuscript", even as patchy as it looks.

Let us do just some simple statistics on the hybrid structure of the manuscript, in the succession of its pages (we will not offer here any correspondence with the numbering in the *princeps edition*):

- on the first page, with no number, is written: Emil Cioran (underlined with two lines). *The Theory of Romania* (highlighted with a line), both cut longitudinally with a wiggly line;

- pp. 1-28 (manuscript, numbered by the author; three of the pages are mixed: manuscript and clippings from the magazine); on the first page: I ('I' meaning the first chapter), "The mission of great cultures and the tragedy of small cultures, Romania" – all cut by Cioran;

- pp. 1-14 (numbered by the author, from which pages 4, 5 and 6 are missing), II (meaning this is chapter II), "Romanian Adamism";

- pp. 1-15 (numbered by the author, one page mixed), 4-6, 13-24 (numbering done, apparently, by someone else), "The psychological and historical gaps of Romania"; part II of the chapter: pp. 1-20, 1-4 (typed); part III of the chapter: pp. 1-23 (five pages, mixed: typed, manuscript and magazine clippings);

- pp. 1-24 (manuscript), "War and revolution";

- pp. 1-19 (typescript), VI (meaning this is chapter VI);

- pp. 1-23 (manuscript), II (meaning this is part II of the "Political World", a title which does not appear in the dactylogram);

- pp. 4-11 (manuscript, the last chapter of the book, VII. "The historical spiral of Romania"; missing pages from the beginning, the equivalent of ten pages in the *princeps edition*).

We can see just a couple of examples of passages in the manuscript which are no longer found in the 1936 edition (we indicate in parentheses the place from which they are missing, in the volume): "When the Nazis revived the cult of heroes as such, they did nothing more than return to some of the trends, secrets and unconfessed secret admirations of the German people. ('Unconfessed', in the sense that this admiration occurred organically and naively and were not listed on the explicit plan of consciousness.)" (p. 15, before row 8 from the bottom up).

"The pessimism of Protestantism in general was easily neglected by the Nazis, because they were more interested in the political than in the religious situation of Luther's gesture" (p. 16, before row 15 from bottom to top).

"I am absolutely convinced that Romania, in the hands of fanatics, visionaries, ecstatic freaks and lunatics, can offer a surprise to the whole world. But the quality of these people is an absolute prerequisite. What a country could Romania become if people there were not only lucid, but also fanatics. In a few years it would become another, completely different, unrecognizable country. But it just stays the same, meaning nothing" (p. 40, before row 17 from the bottom up).

"Dostoevsky, who, of all the writers of the universe, deeply understood the Messianic problem, has shown in his political writings, unfortunately too reactionary in many points, that a nation which does not believe itself to be the only bearer of the truth, does not know what smallness is" (p. 51, before row. 13 from bottom to top; row cut from a text originally published by Cioran in a magazine, cut-out pasted by the author in the "manuscript").

"Religion stopped humanity in its tracks, not because it is inferior, but because it is *too much* for man. What's the point of celestial visions in such low beings? Because man didn't deserve religion, because he is not capable of it, religion has paralyzed him. A religion of things down here, especially tailored for us, will have to be born. Really, God is too far away" (p. 74, before row 4 from bottom to top).

"Romanians have always felt God to be too far away, and therefore never tried to oppose Him in any way" (p. 82, before row 2 from the bottom up, as: "... it is not good to get away from.").

"Utopia stems from a practical theoretical cowardice and a theoretical indifference. It is the easiest way of defection in the face of realities. Rousseau and Plato were no Utopians" (p. 96, after row 13 from top to bottom).

And the whole "manuscript" can be appropriately taken as a witness for the many deletions that occur in the Humanitas text, especially because, I don't know whether by his own initiative or at somebody's suggestion, Cioran removed from the book a full chapter: "National collectivism"; and from "Romania's historical spiral" (a simply butchered chapter) he excluded almost all the passages relating to the Hungarians, although the judgment against this ethnic group comes through, loud and clear, from other parts of the work, not to speak of the fragments of *Histoire et Utopie*, left untouched in the Romanian version. It is surprising how a kind of exaggerated caution or self-suspicion of an ideological nature force Cioran to omit, in the text of the *princeps edition*, sentences and phrases previously published in various journals; such a *directing of the context* only attracts our attention towards the *subjectivity* of the author.

Believing he obscures, through the exclusion of the "National collectivism" chapter, what we could call "the Jewish issue" or "the issue of foreigners", Cioran managed, in fact, to emphasize, not just by the *presence* of an absence, his ideologically loaded approach.

With all the obstinacy of concealing "ideologisms", with various underground connections, sufficient references to the Jewish space and mind were left in the rest of the book (let us not elude the "object" which Cioran puts under the magnifying glass: "I was criticizing in particular the *post-war Jews*"). In the manuscript, the chapter mentioned above was titled, originally, "Nationalism, Socialism, Judaism", over which Cioran wrote, in pencil, "Nationalism and social problems, and then, starting with the first edition of *The Transfiguration of Romania*, we find the formulation: "National collectivism".

This chapter is truly incendiary with assumptions hard to accept for an objective spirit. A parallel reading – manuscript-*princeps edition* – reveals some terminological or stylistic nuances. Here we will identify some of them.

For instance, speaking of nationalism, Cioran says: "The nationalism we need has to stem from a desire to avenge the sleep (in *manuscript*: the base, the word being cut with a Messianic thought following), with the will to make history".

Or: "I can't conceive and I refuse to believe that (followed by "the generation of which I am a part", cut in manuscript) we could make a national revolution which, by destroying Jewish capitalists, would spare the Romanian ones. A national revolution which would try to save the Romanian capitalists seems to me something horrible (followed by: "to take political force away from the liberals in order to strengthen [their] economic one!", cut in *manuscript*).

Or: "We Romanians can only be saved by a different political form. The Jews have resisted with all the means available to their underground imperialism, cynicism and centuries-old experience. The democratic regime (in *manuscript*: political, the word being cut out) of Romania had no other mission than to defend the Jews and Judaeo-Romanian capitalism. We need to get it in our heads, once and for all: Jews have no interest in living in a consolidated and self-aware Romania. We, as Romanians, have only got one interest: a strong Romania with a will to power (in *manuscript*. This follows: "Only now Romania has started to become conscious of itself. The actual historical moment is so important that, if we lose it, we will have definitively missed our mission", subsequently cut).

Or: "For our destiny, the problem of uprooting (it's about the role that intellectuals and literature had) is a bad sign and (followed by "compromising", the word being cut out) a compromising memory (in the *manuscript* it continues with: "*Fear of history* was the substrate of uprooting", the sentence being subsequently cut out).

Or: "No Saxon has a leading role (followed by: "in our country", subsequently cut) and none of them ever tried to interfere in Romania's problems. Even if, in the past, they exploited us, from them we could only learn. Representing an isolated minority, which follows its own autonomous law of evolution, either integrated or misaligned in Romania, they do not represent any danger. Ten million Saxons would be less lethal (in manuscript it's formulated differently: "are less *threatening than fatal*"; the italicized words are cut) than a million and a half Jews."

Or: *If the ideals for which communism struggles were to be founded on another Weltanschauung, the religion of the future would already be established, and Christianity - only a memory.*

One does not fight communism by nationalism, but by addressing social issues" (passage underlined in the *manuscript*.).

Or: "The gross tears of the Jew shine like the stars of an inverted sky (after: "An upside-down sky wept for its fate in the sewage sludge of our times. There is no salvation for them", sentence cut). These people will never reap the fruit of its tears. That's why it doth suffer from the obsession of paradise (initially it was written: "salvation and heaven", then cut) that other people's taste (after: "unconsciously", the word being cut), just looking at the earth".

9.1 The solution of "national collectivism"

The Transfiguration of Romania was, says Z. Ornea, *the most important "document"*[1] of the 30's generation. It is for that reason that we can't ignore that which Emil Cioran wanted to exclude from the Humanitas edition.

Cioran's changes are both unnecessary and hilarious. As I said already, he removes, sometimes with a change of meaning, sometimes without, sentences and phrases that don't always carry a symbolic load. To give some examples of what text deletions mean:

"Force is either ethical or beyond ethics. Strictly speaking they don't need to support or to condition one another".[2]

"Perhaps history is, in fact, the only excuse for time. What does Soloviev do in the face of history? He deserts into the mystical" (p. 35).

"As people we want, if not the right, at least the freedom to have many hopes. As Romanians, we can only have one: hope in a different Romania" (p. 47).

"I want another nation!" (p. 64)

"Lenin, Hitler, Mussolini remain in history not only through the mark of their personality, but also by the ideological and moral crises they caused in mankind. A political idea, if it does not overlap its circle of validity and application, if it does not exceed the space for which it was created, has no historical value. Hitlerism, if it had not put the Jewish issue in such categorical terms, if it had not brought the solution to a universal problem, would have been of little interest to the world. The same can be said for its attitude, hostile to both Christianity and Bolshevism" (p. 188).

"Ah! If only I were Saint Elijah, to throw lightning and thunder over this country, every time it refuses to be different!" (p. 194).

"The existence of myths is a proof of the insignificance of the human being" (p.196).

"Hungarians no longer have any meaning in the universe, and if you take away Hungarian women and the music of the gypsies, they never had any. Bulgarians will be satisfied by the memory of the occasional heights achieved by their cruelty, Serbs will be happy to remain Serbs, and the Greeks will know that any grandeur is irreversible" (p. 221).

"The Hungarians are a people of conquistadors, who ended up fattening pigs. A bunch of peerless losers.

Despite a very national and natural hatred of Hungarians, I have a faint fondness for this unrealized people. Totally devoid of political sense, it created the most artificial state settlement. They collaborated with the Austrians because the latter did not represent a sense of values in the world either.

Hungary deserves its fate. Having lost territory and more, it deserved to lose so much, only to be able to give birth to those irredentist songs, of a heart-breaking infinity, and with which they will never conquer anything - ever again.

The existence of Hungary is a historical adventure and a matter of the picturesque. Was it not left as the only structurally feudal country in Europe, in order to extend an anachronism in the historical landscape from an aesthetic need for diversity? Hungary has now just an aesthetic justification. Even when it was persecuting us, it was nothing more. Their tyranny is a shame for us, not for them. What did Hungary spread in the world? Gypsies and women. And Romanians who are afraid of the Hungarians" (p. 225).

"Hitlerism seems to me to be a serious movement, as it knew how to directly associate problems inherent in social justice to a consciousness of the historical mission of a nation. And Bolshevism, even if it means a barbarism unique in the world through the assertion of absolute social justice, is no less a unique triumph of ethics" (p. 229).

This is the content of the cuts made by Cioran on the body of the *princeps text* of *The Transfiguration of Romania*. Why was Cioran so afraid of the "National collectivism" chapter, enough to eliminate it completely from the Humanitas edition? Especially because here he discusses the "only solution", "only exit" of Romania from the state in which it was then, by bringing to the fore what he called, somewhat improperly, the actuality of the national.[3]

Cioran was passionately interested, in the chapter in question, in nationalism and its vitality, in the space of a nation whose forms of life revolved around labor and social justice. Lenin appeared to him as a downright providential personality. He "saved nationalism" (thus it would be turned into a "reactionary" kind, unable to solve conflicts and social inequalities), and, "with Klausewitz at his bedside" and giving proof of "sublime fanaticism", he became "the prototype of a politician of the future".[4]

Romanian nationalism was, for Cioran, a relatively narrow vision, one of the reasons being its centering on a matter which should have been peripheral: "rebellion against foreigners", especially the Jews. There is a historical reason for this attitude: "A thousand years ago we all lived under the yoke of strangers; it is a lack of national instinct not to hate or eliminate them". Only that the Jews "at most, delayed the solemn hour of Romania; they are not, in any case, the cause of our misery, of our eternal misery".[5] So anti-Semitism could not constitute "a way of entry into history", and Romanian nationalism had to be based on "the desire of vengeance for our historical sleep", on a "messianic thought", on the "will to make history".

And yet, citing partisan theories, "the Jewish question" remained "absolutely intractable" from the perspective of universal history, but not in that of national history (could what Germany was doing with the Jews represent a "solution"?) Between Jews and Gentiles there was a gulf, which could never disappear. "Humanly we can't get close to them, because the Jew is first a Jew and then a man".[6] For, characterologically speaking, the Jews are traitors in certain "historical moments", they meddle in the destiny of communities through false attitudes ("In all national defeats, the only ones who don't lose their temper are the Jews"), they accept persecution and exile with cynicism and prove themselves, therefore, to be insensitive.

Cioran believed that all the vicissitudes which had befallen the Jews had not managed to make them suffer a tragedy of alienation. A hypothesis, let's face it, which is hard to admit even with a smattering of serious arguments, which is missing from the sequences specific to the Cioranian discourse. "The Jews are the only people who don't feel tied to the landscape (view would have been more appropriate – I.D.). No corner of the world has ever shaped their soul; therefore, they are the same regardless of country or content. Cosmic sensitivity is alien to them. The gypsies, who have etched a living on the edge of villages and towns, with so many dusks and dawns in their soul, are infinitely closer to nature than the Jews, who drag throughout their history the obscurities of the ghetto, with its nauseating sorrows and its disgusting ironies, that have removed the Jews far from nature and reprovingly keep them in history".[7]

With all that the Jews make up the "most intelligent, most gifted and most wicked people", Cioran would have never wished for such an origin: "If I were a Jew, I would kill myself on the spot". It's all about the post-war Jews, those who resisted any attempts at Romanian national and political consolidation (paradoxically, however, the country's political regime protected them).

The Jews were also guilty of contaminating socialism with their "material outlook" and with internationalism, thereby distorting "the idea of collectivism" with their Marxism. The kind of communism they wanted included "items that could justify them and ease their wanderings through the world".[8]

The anthropological conception of communism appeared to Cioran as precarious as that of Christianity, which "did not give man his daily bread; for two thousand years, mankind has been starved in the delusion of eternity. Because, unfortunately, Christianity was not only a precept for poor people, but also a factory of poor people".[9] We recognize in these sophisms, as well as in others relating to the Jews, the influence which Nietzsche's thinking exercised over Cioran (whole pages of *Antichrist* underpin the claims of this chapter).

Cioran's sarcastic language does not spare the Romanian, especially the intellectual - not even here. "There is no human being more inclined to failure than the Romanian. Besides other causes, the absence of a strong national consciousness was crucial. [...] The Romanian's approximate nihilism finds in failure its natural implication. It is the nihilism of a people that has no history and just endures, until it becomes a nation". And the Romanian intellectual, at age 30, "becomes matter again", has "a rotten inner pit", "is uprooted and has lost contact with the people." He reaches – in contrast with the peasant, who is full of virtue, because culture "doesn't agree with him so much" – a "spiritual nothingness".

Treated sometimes with passion in literature, the problem of uprooting continued, says Cioran, "to smolder in a national inclination towards losing". The conclusion was catastrophic: "Romania always lacked an interior shape. Either too rigid or too gelatinous, it was looking for a way of life through the thickets of its own shortcomings".[10]

In terms of xenophobia specific to Romania, it would have been facilitated, thought Cioran, by an inequality of "historical level" between Romanians and minorities, against the backdrop of a yet-unformed nation.

What accounted for these differences, which he restated for the umpteenth time? One must note, first, an almost completely distorted logic, one willfully deranged (we may recall Blaga's aphorism, where he says that a frog in a well believes the celestial vault is only as large as the mouth of the well!?). "The Saxons feel tied to Romania only through the landscape." Without being, however, dangerous, being rather "a moral oasis in the Balkans" (ten million Saxons would be a smaller danger than a million and a half Jews), they "isolate themselves and they despise us" (?!). Moreover, even if the Saxon nature is enterprising, with constructive "vision", they have always had a "centrifugal" existence (?!).

With the Jews, something else occurred. "The vitality of the Jews is so aggressive and their will towards enrichment so persistent that any tolerance towards this worker and wandering people would mean our bankruptcy for sure." A "cerebral" people, "the pariah and the equivocal halo of history", the Jews should understand anti-Semitism as being "the highest commendation"[11] ever offered them.

The Hungarians? Well, they "are content with being honest and hating us" and "there's too much blood in the Hungarian spirit, for Hungary to be anything else but soul" (the ethnic Hungarian will be put under the magnifying glass of deforming diopters in the chapter "Romania's historical spiral" – see pp. 219-234). Cioran's opinions reach, in these pages, the outer limits of inadequacy. Judgment falls into sterile speculation, disarray, cheap tropes. The Hungarians would have come in the Pannonian plain to drink and to sing. And then, ask Cioran, what can one say that "will endure, from the Hungarians"? Only Hungarian women and their music. "At the last judgment, the Hungarians only need to send a band of gypsies, and they will be received into paradise without any comment". Also deprived of "political sense" and with "the instincts of the nomad", they spread into the world gypsies, women and "Romanians who are afraid of the Hungarians".[12]

In the face of these inequalities, of the disaster that threatened Romania, Cioran's solution was that of "national collectivism". Which meant breaking all the patterns of mediocrity, developing a political mood akin to cynicism and the use of force. In such a mechanism, power becomes the "criterion of value", and the transformation of politics into a vision of the world (*Weltanschauung*) converts force into an "axis of history".

This heralds an unusual social logic: "From a political point of view, a street sergeant has a greater reality than a wise man. So, for a state in time of peace, a watchman is more useful than a general".[13] Politics gets, on this path, "to ride history", for *everything becomes political.* As, says Cioran, *everything becomes mystical,* that mystical through which history is saved from itself.

The first step to salvation was supposed to be the achievement of the spiritual and political rule of Romania in this part of Europe. Such a political obsession would outline, perhaps, a political destiny for Romania, through which, with the help of the force, it would also beget a historic destiny. "National collectivism – said, in 1936, Cioran – is the only solution for Romania, the only way out".[14]

Bounded ideologically by Germany and Russia, our country had to go beyond Hitlerism and Bolshevism in order to fulfill its destiny. Neither the passivity of the first nor the vision of life and pretentious universalism of the other were desirable ways forward, but the "conscious cult of force, the obsession with unlimited power, organized megalomania" (the influence of Germany) and "the frenzy of industrialization, the mystique of the urban world, the absolute will to make a historic jump, with discontinuity through revolution as a vital manifestation"[15] (Russian influence). All of these would have structured the figure of Romanian nationalism (by which Romania would individualize itself), but not one resembling what Daudet and Maurras promoted because it would have meant to stick, like the French, to a kind of "aesthetic delight" in solving fundamental political issues.

Engaged in a hegemonic process in South-Eastern Europe, our country had to face, potentially, a very difficult task: "will Romania be the unifying country of the Balkan, will Bucharest be the new Constantinople?".[16]

As discourse, the formulations of *The Transfiguration of Romania* were nothing more, says the author, than "suggestions for the grandeur of Romania", "the great lines of our destiny", without recourse to "details" and "immediate solutions". Which does not mean that "practical and special implications" could not be detached from them, as Cioran's rhetoric does not leave his emergency kit in the wardrobe of reasoning, nor does he abandon the dexterity of a (sometimes amateur) conjurer of paradox. The corollary of his "suggestions" addressed, in context, a form in which they could pose as radical "solutions".

9.2 Reception and contextual ideological comfort

In an anthology covering the reception (up to 1989) of Cioran's work, we can easily see that *The Transfiguration of Romania* is clearly his most passionately commented on and most controversial book.[17]

Analyses of the most sophisticated kind about this work have appeared not only in Romania but also in France, where criticizing Cioran took the form of a media performance, appetizing and intensely spicy. And the main the accusation was Cioran's concealed ideological past from the fourth decade of the XX-th century.

We will briefly bring to the attention of the reader a few items of data that have already become common places, in the Aristotelian sense of the phrase. Previously published in two editions, Cioran's book is, in its 1990 form published by Humanitas, "the only authorized version", as specified on the cover page of volume – a variant, reviewed and deemed "final", according to the imperative statement of liminary ranks drafted and added to the work by Cioran himself, on February 22, 1990 (Paris).

Cioran does not rewrite *The Transfiguration of Romania*, but (self)censors it; he suppresses himself. Of course, Cioran is the master of his creation, and no one can stand against him. He is not, however, master of the interpretations, more or less speculative, which can occur when faced with his actions. "I thought it my duty to eliminate a few pretentious and stupid pages" – he says in the same "supporting" note.

The phrases with which Cioran opened, in 1990, *The Transfiguration of Romania* should be read and re-read. We saw how an interpreter and exegete such as Pierre-Yves Boissau judged it. After successive readings, a question still remains: what should the motivations of this change of "physiognomy" be, of resizing "the shape of content"? Especially because, coming from a "bricoleur" such as Cioran, these words – seemingly neutral, detached – hide the same rhetoric, the same temptation of the paradox, as well as a histrionic symmetry of the word.

Cioran does not commit – as one might think – any poietic act, but ensures an *ideological contextual comfort* for his work, through "adjustment". He calls the pages of the first editions "disorganized speech," written at age 24 with "passion and pride". It's so broken from the placenta of its genesis that the book constitutes the text of "a total stranger". And then he continues: "I'm not found in him, though *I'm obviously in the presence of my hysteria, that was of those times*" (Cioran had a similar reaction towards the anthology of published texts *Revelațiile durerii* [*The revelations of pain*] Echinox, 1990, when he replied to Dan C. Mihăilescu, author of the *Preface*: "You will never know what despair some of your observations concerning me made me feel. I think I deserved something better. *My past deserved, I think, a little bit of oblivion*" – see *Letters, arts, ideas*, no. 23 of June 26, 1995; my emphasis).

In other words, a composition in which the originator no longer validly sees himself, even if "the hysteria" of "back then" seems "obvious". And to restore a different relationship with his creation, which he could not throw into the void, the same author, becoming over time another, felt the "duty" to "delete" those "pretentious and stupid pages", warning at the same time about its new structure, almost manufactured, that: "No one has the right to modify it".

We asked ourselves – who can this "Mr. Nobody" be? and then let our thoughts fly, all in vain, to this sample of faked naivety particular to Cioran: who would want to "amend" the text of *The Transfiguration of Romania* more than he did himself? What we can do – for those interested in the anamorphic route of the book – is to (de)construct that road starting with a laboratory of the work, more exactly with the manuscript, and to study the many facets of Cioran's sentences.

For anyone comparing the two editions of *The Transfiguration of Romania*, it is clear that Cioran's reading was not so much psychological, as was usual for him, but was assisted by a rather urgent *ideological concern*.

No doubt that detachment from the text of the book did not occur in the last part of Cioran's life. This discourse already appeared as "the strangest" for him in France, in '47, when he said that he changed his point of view "in all that concerns 'historical' realities". But Cioran was right, and he knew what he said: *The Transfiguration of Romania* is his most "phenomenal", most detailed and circumstanced book. Written largely on the epidermis of history, with the ink and the wilderness of emotions. Written even with the despair that takes the form of pure lucidity, a lucidity corroded, as in Eminescu, by the barbaric, bestial layer of our being. (The text *Mon Pays*, written in the '50s, a really disturbing document, qualifying, among other things, the violence of language in *The Transfiguration of Romania* as the fruit of an "upside down love", of a "toppled idolatry".)

If a "systematics of desperation" were ever designed, this book of Cioran's would necessarily have to be part of it. Writing the most profound, but also the most passionate pages about *Romanian inertia*, about coming out of anonymity, and about revealing individuality, the essayist risked, with the ease of a juvenile metaphysics, offering a discourse enormously dilated in the void, in the negative. It was a risk he had fully felt since 1947, when, in the same letter sent to his brother, he sneaked in a small self-comment: "A man, if he wants to keep his spiritual dignity, needs to forget his contemporary quality. How far ahead I would be now, had I only known this when I was twenty. Every person is a *victim of his own temperament*. I think *I eliminated many errors and many misleading hopes*". After which, he even gave him a tip: "Try, through any means, to keep yourself apart from any temporal passions and superstitions that uselessly poison the soul and the impulses of the spirit. That's the only way you can suppress *fruitless regrets and ineffective hopes*".[18] (My emphasis, I.D.).

We don't know if the editorial option made by Humanitas in a somewhat confused context of values, in a misleading political background not at all favorable to an equilibrium of ideas, has been the most appropriate. For works such as *The Transfiguration of Romania* or *Histoire et Utopie* cannot be permitted, however, to leave again for the world without being accompanied by critical guides. As long as no fundamental studies have been published in Romania which would conceptually situate the work of Cioran, then simply sending his books onto the cultural market is a risky and somewhat suicidal venture.

There are plenty of reasons. First, because we don't know, even now, what is the apperceptive foundation of many readers approaching, more or less "disinterestedly", the work of Cioran. Then, because – in the post-communist period, of poorly understood freedom countless factors interfered to unsettle our axiological North. And, last but not least, because *The Transfiguration of Romania* was and is violently contested, by taking from it, time and again, "evidence" which is damaging and accusatory in the highest degree. It's enough to remind us of the negative reactions of its time, or to consult "treatises" of the history of Romanian philosophy, whence the tweezers of zealous minds extracted everything which could serve, in a Machiavellian way, for demonstrating theses and legitimizing convictions made with the censorship of "revolutionary" ideology. (Rather oddly, it was literary criticism which actually offered pertinent and balanced comments on this Cioranian essay.)[19]

It's true that nothing written in *The Transfiguration of Romania*, in spite of any withdrawal made by the author himself, is foreign to Cioran's nature. G. Călinescu issued a literary-psychological diagnosis when he "regimented" the author inside "the philosophy of anxiety and adventure", a producer of "vaporous philosophical essays" and aphorisms which were "a little childish", built on paradox and exclamation, "pastiches" after Kierkegaard.[20] The theory of adventure and of the duck which never misses – coming from Nae Ionescu – was illustrated, believed the critic, by a "passion for the absurd" and through a grain of "madness inside". Printed after a juvenile "workshop exercise" (by this we mean *On the Heights of Despair*), *The Transfiguration of Romania* seemed to Călinescu a kind of "speech to the Romanian nation" specifically aimed at young people in the new Romania.

Agnosticism and pessimism will be "lesions" frequently detected from now on, and one of the risks Cioran proposed for our country, that of imperialism, as well as the language he used, will come from the same teacher of metaphysics become in a way the idol – in the sense of Bacon – of his generation. Călinescu also accused him of a lack of information and documentation, vagueness of concepts, as (evading, in his analysis, both *The Book of Deceptions* and *Tears and Saints*) he was accused, perhaps most of all, of rejecting the culture of the peasant and the national spirit, of approving liberalism, and of raising a bill of indictment against *Junimea*.

But these were not the only anathemas hurled upon Cioran's book. In its time, after being published, *The Transfiguration of Romania* generated many other reactions. Nichifor Crainic, for example, expressed tempered reserve, characterizing the author as "a representative type of the youth of today" (youth who "calls itself heroic from a horror of suicide"); and the book – "with an Orthodox title and an anti-Orthodox spirit" – was nothing more than "a bloody pitiless massacre of today's Romania, without even a shadow of remorse for the matricidal and the sacrilegious".[21]

Another columnist who identified himself only as "R" – and under this letter was hiding none other than Mihai Ralea – proposed a reading of the book starting from a dichotomy: *man of the Right* (in which he identified Cioran, the author)/ *man of the Left* (in which we suspect the presence of the reviewer).

What were, after Ralea, the major differences between the two human types for which he wanted to draw an ideological "clinical chart"? Besides some trifling differences of detail, the concept conferring upon them a particular flavor consisted in the idea that the man of the Right is "sensitive to *the idea of order and hierarchy*, while the latter predominantly accepts *the idea of justice*".[22]

We would have expected Ralea's observations, beyond his usually suspected *parti-pris*, to overcome any generalizing-doctrinal cut-outs copied from a type of right/left Manichaeism, operating in particular in the context, and to try instead a vivisection on the "ideas" of Cioran's book. Ralea's sentences are not as incisive as one might think. They follow the "equation" in which texts with such a psychological formulation were usually entered. Conservative, even if he desired a "heroic revolution", "kneaded and tormented, often in a pathetic guise, without any hope of clearing and calm", Cioran expressed, in his writing, a Dionysian temperament: since that "endocrinological confession" called *On the Heights of Despair*, a book "belonging to physiology" (here the diagnosis falls exactly in the "center point": akin to Nietzsche, Cioran tries to introduce the physiological into metaphysics), the evolution of his writings showed the good signs of some balance.

But *The Transfiguration of Romania* also had a "psychic meaning" in itself. Cioran and his book were not, for Ralea, an author and a reading to be recommended. On the contrary, he found that there were "so many differences that should distance us from Mr. Cioran", even if the intellectual endowment of the essayist could not be so easily ignored. Which leads him to recognize, at the end of his chronicle, the talent - "full of promise", the force and ingenuity of intuitions, the "almost always happy", phrasing - qualities which, with some temperamental adjustments, could transform Cioran into an author of "real contributions to subjective and literary philosophy, in the genre of Kierkegaard, Ammiel or Nietzsche". Except for some asperities or formulations with the flavor of a pamphleteer, Ralea's review was a eulogy to Cioran's *writing* bringing to attention potentialities that, paradoxically, the author would later grace with over-measure.

The Transfiguration of Romania had managed to unsettle even the judgment of Cioran's generation. Eugen Ionescu had sharp and ironic reactions to it since 1933: he had talked about Cioran as being "this yellow edition of Rozanov and others," he had indexed "inevitable frenzies" when he spoke of the literary year 1936 (when Cioran had published *The Book of Deceptions* and *The Transfiguration of Romania*), and in *No!*, the volume of his editorial debut, he produced a significant letter. Arşavir Acterian published a glum indictment about a "book as revolutionary as it is heretical",[23] this being not the last of its "welcoming notes"; seemingly in response to Ralea, some notes by Pompiliu Constantinescu rightly observe that if someone sees in Cioran's ideological literature "a theoretician of 'the Left' or 'the Right', he can be deceived with the same certainty with which this fanatic lives in one sense or another".[24]

Many scholars commented upon Cioranian sentences or phrases that violated common meanings and produced a sense of shock: "I would like a Romania with the population of China and the destiny of France," "I can only love a Romania in delirium" or "that poetic and national curse called *Miorița* ", to mention just a few of the ideas making Cioran an author fit to be impaled, as Arşavir Acterian maliciously said. We offer the reader other characterizations of *The Transfiguration of Romania* : "gratuitous dramatism" (with roots in Shestov and Nietzsche), "factitious vehemence", "artificial processes" and "platitudes" (Miron Radu).

Paraschivescu, in *Azi* [Today], Jan. 1937; "a prophetic book", "a symphonic thinker" and "a lyrical philosopher" (Dragoş Protopopescu, in *Buna Vestire* [The Annunciation], March 1937); "the first alpenhorn signal of our awakening", not at all cerebral, but a "poem" which must not be understood, but felt (Toma Macovei, in *Vremea* [The Time], March 1937); Cioran studies Romania too much through the focus of politics, renouncing the spiritual, although the destiny of our country is carried out not on the mystic, Orthodox plan, but on that of Western policy, meaning: by leaps and bounds (Dan Petraşincu, in *Viața literară* [Literary life], April–May 1937); "one of the best books of the century" (Nicolae Ciuceanu, in *Primăvara literară* [Literary Spring], May 1937); "jerky, discursive lyricism, worrying through the very validity of its axiom" (Stelian Tecuceanu, in *Semne* [Signs], June 1937); the author "prefers error to evidence", has "a passion for the absurd", is an "unsurpassed paradoxeur" (Ionel Neamtzu, in *Pământ şi vrajă ardeleană* [Transylvanian earth and its spell], December 1937); it's not a "book of program and doctrine, but one of vision and prophecy" (Bucur Țincu, in *Linia dreaptă* [The straight line], March 1938); "the exercise of language"

(Dragos Vrînceanu, in *Curentul* – the literary magazine Current, Feb.1940); "a romantic thinker" (Victor Isaac, who writes a more extensive but superficial study, also in *Curentul* [Current], Oct. 1940); there is even talk of a plot against Cioran's book, an "exactly orchestrated silence" a "mute conspiracy" (Grigore Popa, Dan Petrașincu, in *Viața literară* [Literary life], Apr. – May 1937 and *Sfarmă piatră* [Stone Breaker], May 1940).

Almost all reviews of *The Transfiguration of Romania* suffer, however, from a common excess: their inflated use of adjectives, as does Cioran's text. Affinities or ideological affiliations of ideas are established, and in very few cases do the rays of a persistent study of the work itself shine through.[25]

In the '70s, reminiscing about *The Transfiguration of Romania* ("a delusional work" as diagnosed even by its author), Emil Cioran wrote to his brother, Relu: "I read the article that you sent me. Here, our old friends attack me for exactly the opposite. What fools can people be! For me, the era in which I was writing *The Transfiguration* seems incredibly distant. Sometimes I get to wonder if I even wrote those evasions that keep getting quoted. In any case, I'd better be walking *under the Alders...* Enthusiasm is a form of delirium. We have suffered from this disease and no one wants to believe that we are healed" (Paris, Nov. 2, 1973).[26]

Any shortcomings detected in the discourse of *The Transfiguration of Romania* were, from then on, reiterated. Whoever reads the second volume of *The History of Romanian Philosophy* can find out that, together with Crainic and Nae Ionescu, the author of the *Fall in time* was, in politics, an active, relentless militant of Legionarism (an analysis of this dimension, in other terms, is also performed by Z. Ornea in *Anii treizeci. Extrema dreaptă românească* [The thirties. The Romanian extreme Right]); a partisan of that regime based on authority and the cult of force, justifying – by its appurtenance to the "new Legionary aristocracy" – both the war and fascist barbarism. The final judgments of this "treaty" with ambitions of "philosophical research" are, to use a modern barbarism, *irrefutable* and, therefore, unassailable: Cioran's total negativity led inexorably to anti-intellectualism, agnosticism and subjectivity, irrationality and aggression. In this way, one of the theorists of the extreme Right was born; by his attitude, he would have opened "the way for the arbitrariness of fascist policy".

But – one should not forget so easily that the same Cioran and none other, would have blamed, in equal measure, communism, democracy (of course, the totalitarian variety), historical materialism and, believe it or not, even the working class. This would have happened, as another exegete said because the author of *Histoire et Utopie* didn't understand socio-political phenomena such as fascism and communism. It's hard to explain how a political scientist such as Vladimir Tismăneanu, a modern spirit in the substance of his ideas and style, discovers in the same Cioran not a slouch but, on the contrary, a specialist of the avant-garde. The proof is located in the same *The Transfiguration of Romania*, "one of the most important manifestos of European fascism in its "national-Bolshevik variation", a book which belongs to "that clan which facilitated the establishment of the fascist dictatorship in Romania, a bloody prelude to the no less odious communist tyranny".[27]

Such attitudes towards the work of Cioran were a kind of natural continuity of anathemas that, since the '50s, will be blatantly run by the "critical" mixer of communist ideology. For "the 'usual' interpreters", hopelessly vexed, Cioran was part – what a joy for one who, at the time, was wandering through France on a bike – of the "philosophy of the bourgeoisie" and was, along with Mircea Eliade, "the deadly enemy of the new, socialist forms of life", enjoying, however, "the protection of reactionary forces in France".[28]

After 1956, when *The Temptation to Exist* appeared (a book, some have said, in which the blaming of Romanians exceeded all limits), Cioran becomes a "mystifying disciple of Heidegger", but also an author who emits fabrications about the place and people of his origin.

However, Cioran was not judged so unfairly for the harsh words he uttered about Romanians: "The 'selected' ethics of Mr. Cioran is an ethics of being stateless, the ethics of a renegade".[29] The deliberately paradoxical script that some critics pretend not to note in *The Temptation to Exist* (see the section "A little theory of destiny"), is almost the only thing by which others feel that Cioran is still connected to a past he threw, perhaps too soon, in the closet of his own history. D. D. Rosca is disgusted and outraged by *The Temptation to Exist* and writes a long text, devoid of even minimal understanding of the author, in whom he sees, however, "a remarkable literary talent"; but with his thinking still stationary after a quarter of a century, and becoming what Cioran himself had wanted: "*a case*".[30]

For the work of Cioran, the years 1957-1959 are those in which, by ideological orders, orchestrated critique will target his works. To the names already mentioned (N. Bolboașă, Dinu Lipatti, D.D. Roșca) are added others (Radu Popescu, G. Călinescu, Șerban Cioculescu, Nichifor Crainic and Lucian Blaga), and the critical "instances" will bear names such as *Gazeta Literară* [The literary gazette], *Contemporanul* [The contemporary], *Glasul Patriei* [The voice of the fatherland], to remember only some pieces of the artillery of the party. All the "contra" texts that appeared at the time might be subsumed to the title of lines written by Blaga: "The farce of originality".

The article published by the author of *Eonul dogmatic* [The dogmatic Aeon] raises many question marks, being perhaps the most unexpected Romanian reaction against Cioran. Written in 1959, for the magazine *Tribuna* (on request), the text was published after Blaga's death in *Contemporanul* [The contemporary] (no. 45, November 9, 1962) and then included in the volume *Isvoade* [Origins] (Bucharest: Minerva Publishing House, 1972). There are oral testimonies about the "authenticity" of Blaga's attitude, in large part not so different from that of other pamphlets which, undoubtedly, belong to Blaga (we take into account, for example, the relationship of the philosopher with C.R. Motru). But, beyond any interference of "extra-aesthetic" factors, the text about Cioran needs to be properly judged through the paternity signs of the signature that accompanies it.[31]

The thesis from which Blaga was feeling "tempted" to depart in his commentary on the book L*a tentation d'exister (The tendency to exist,* as he translated it) was one that belonged, in a way, to the mythology of creation: "Whoever forces originality, usurps the prerogatives of the Muses". Cioran appeared to him as the author of works "created in the surrealist spirit", able to write, realistically though, yet another one about "The technique of literary success"; temperamentally, he considered him "a grandiloquent depressive who indulges in a Universe tainted by chaos". Readings from German authors with whom he came in contact while still in his teens, would influence him so much, that Cioran came to suffer from the "amnesia of quotation marks".

Being "always prohibited, on the verge of his 'roots' and turning all into a meaningless "secondary game", Cioran's originality, concluded Blaga, is, in its essential points, "mimicked". He has a "phobia of stale words" and remains, hopelessly, at the "adoptive age" of a "teenager", one with "publishing talent", who always plays "the farce of originality" (the first act of this piece happened when he mimicked Kierkegaard in his first book: *On the Heights of Despair*).

But what seems to have irritated Blaga most was *The Temptation to* Exist, where the "misdirected and lost" (Emil Cioran) had resorted to the "stunt" of defaming the people of his origins, his very sources. "We find it very hard to transcribe all the shameful exhortations, cadenced for the delight of foreign ears", said Blaga, putting Cioran in the service of the dark forces of the diaspora. More, after having learned, *in extremis*, just when he wanted to wrap up the pamphlet, that Emil Cioran had published, a little while ago, in *Nouvelle Revue Française*, the essay "My Friends, the tyrants", Blaga, outraged beyond measure, gives the final diagnosis. Cioran becomes a "hopeless case" and, devoid of originality, he continues to play "only the role of a mumbling buffoon". His "ravings" from the Parisian magazine and mimetic enthusiasm for Nietzsche could have reminded the German philosopher, says Blaga, of his last words: "Take him away from here. He is not a dragon, he's a monkey!"

You read and reread the text of the philosopher Blaga and you almost can't believe your eyes. Oppressive words, spoken by someone who knew like no other their weight and effect. A creator whose works fascinated Cioran in his youth, when he spoke of the "inner style" of Blaga's philosophy, "the most complete personality in Romania"[32] at the time. And even when "lost and misdirected", in Paris, Cioran will not give up his readings of Blaga's poems (his brother, Aurel, would send him a volume in 1967) or his anthology of popular poetry.

Cioran was, however, disappointed when he read the pamphlet in *Contemporanul*: "You don't need to send Blaga's text about me. I read it and it does not honor either me or him. Poor fellow! I'm glad he gave me the opportunity to get rid of the respect that his books had inspired in me, substantial but boring".[33] However, Cioran's resentment seems superficial, for it did not touch the respect that, discreetly, he still preserved: "I read this morning, with some excitement, a few poems by Blaga. I had a gripe against him, for petty reasons. I have to admit that he was awesome".[34] And, not to refute his paradoxical style, a month after these lines, Cioran wrote to another friend: "And, sticking to indigenous values – how artificial, slow, irritated is Blaga when compared with Him!"[35] ("Him" was none other than Eminescu).

We know Lucian Blaga the polemicist from "Săpunul filosofic – The philosophical soap" (*Saeculum Magazine*, 4-1943) and other "cosmetics", but none of them rises to the corrosive altitude of "Farsa originalității – The hoax of originality". What *prerequisites* could have been responsible for the detonation of this pamphlet? Did Blaga have some personal gripe against Cioran, was he somewhat jealous of the latter's French fame, was he trying to redeem a sin or to avail himself of any axiological privilege he would thus get?

Maybe a little of all these; or it's possible that the springs of this behavior could belong to an unavowed logic of our *nationality* and the *prestige* of our culture. Blaga's text is written about three years after Cioran's book appeared, in the middle of the *haunting decade*, to use the words of Marin Preda. And it is also true that the philosopher from Rășinari was not good at quietly sitting in his place either. His ideas which had targeted, without too many reservations, both Romanians and Romania – but other ethnic groups such as Russians, Hungarians or Jews were not forgiven either.

Hence, what could have been the inherent reason for Blaga's text, stuffed with so many envenomed reproaches?

Two other possible sources for the biography of the pamphlet in question have been put forward: it could have been *demanded* by historian Constantin Daicoviciu; and Danielo, the not at all discreet mistress, girlfriend or muse of the Lancrăm philosopher, could have had a small role in the matter too (Blaga's wife would have knowingly *allowed* such a love affair, because it was a fertile spring of inspiration for Blaga).

If the article had been requested, this means it was a command dictated by someone, a someone whose identity is easily guessed but is of no importance to us at all. What is important is the process of writing *according to commandments* coming from "higher up" (the sphere of transcendence being excluded). I'm not surprised, if it's true, by the assumption that Blaga wrote what he wrote, as it's a text-exercise intoxicated with high blood pressure; but I'm surprised that the same Blaga was able to obey an *ideological diktat* or even the value choices of a historian - options that, if the assumption is factual, he can also claim for himself. I'm surprised, and I have to ask yet again, maybe even rhetorically: what was at issue in such a gesture?

9.3 A pamphlet on Romanian inertia

Like few others, Cioran wants to throw light upon the darkest parts of our selves. Thus, he finds out that the barbarity of life is congruent, i.e., compatible, with our personal barbarity. And this, when the "disease" has specific ontological status: *it's our way of being* (a wind blows, here, from Foucault's direction).

The Transfiguration of Romania is thus an *essayistic* attempt to undertake, in a personal manner, the critique of historical reason, through a survey of the past and present of Romania at that time (1936). Cioran is similar to a surgeon who's never heard of anesthesia or painkillers and does not want to hear about the dangers of heart attack or stroke. Romanian grief was transmuted in him, as in Eminescu, into lucid pessimism. The logic of history, which he judges in such an unforgiving manner, fits in a few parameters of Simmel's doctrine: *almost full relativism, psychological transposition of concepts, and extension of critical subjectivity to the field of history.*

The language of Cioran – in *The Transfiguration of Romania*, in particular – *is not at all specialized*. We would be exaggerating if we supported the view that the author uses categories because there is more of a categorical fuzziness in his approach. Even if concepts are invoked in a specific manner, soaked in excessive lyricism and hence far from the rigor and coldness of research marked by accuracy, the discourse remains, in its essence, *psychological-adjectival*.

Judgments are made in terms of the current language. In the language used by Cioran, one can discern traits that a Blanchot – when speaking of the "ontological" status of literature – included in his analyses, in the '40s: "I don't know what he expresses or represents, whether it is a thing or a meaning; if it is here to be forgotten, or if it's only forgotten in order to be seen; if it is transparent because of the too-little meaning of what it says, or clear by the accuracy with which it says it, obscure because it says too much, opaque because it says nothing...".[36] Cioran writes, therefore, not science, but *casual essayistics*, which is not foreign to a certain imaginary.

The text *of The Transfiguration of Romania* is trying, sometimes unwillingly, to express a tautology. One of the "shape of content". "The myth" is one of inculcating ideas by proteiform expressions, through the successive forms which the idea – the same idea - takes. The purpose, unreported, is nevertheless reached: the obsession of a transvestite reiteration makes the idea take residence in our minds. Here, perhaps, is another way of "digressing".

Therefore, the social or political Cioranian discourse is, ultimately, all *literature*, one that builds dark havens populated with the ghosts and fanaticism engendered by an absolutely contradictory state: the identification of the thinker with existence, but also with a fearsome recoil in front of it. This is how despair incidentally occurs; this is how, in the case of Cioran, an obsession with death is born. Salvation from death – in the case of our author: from suicide – is accomplished (let's not forget that we are in lands haunted by the ghost of literature) through language, which, in terms of the French exegete cited above, is a "murder deferred".

Penance does not disappear, however; it is only transferred. Speech – concluded the same Blanchot - is "the warning" that death is "launched into the world", shooting out suddenly between the one who speaks and the person being addressed. "Only death allows me to bring to the fore what I want to achieve: it is, in words, the only possibility of their meaning. Without death, everything would collapse into absurdity and nothingness" – here's the sentence that might have an axiomatic value for the metabolism of Cioran's creation.

In this "usual sceptic" of the universe, a battle between *language* and *presence* is thus revealed, the latter being osmotically related to a plasticity that proliferates in a Homeric manner. But such a struggle is also perceived in the transition of language from a being without limits (see the text written "in cursive", meaning "continuously") to one with limits (see the pages in which gnomic aphorism is practiced). Targeting the fragment or fragmentary illustrates, this time, the battle between language and presence, an opposition mediated not by sense, but by *feeling*. But Cioran's writing is also "sentimental" because it exhausts all the supplies stored in the pantry of the psyche and does that – paradoxically –because he doesn't like "preserved" life. That's exactly why he wants to exhaust the store.

Without being neglected, in no other thinker does the issue of *language* become as essential as in Cioran – for at least two reasons: 1) it clearly expresses his vision about what philosophy meant at the time; 2) it explains the auctorial *parti-pris* and the interference between ideology and discourse. Here's why, with the printing of the works of Cioran, the publisher Humanitas should have undertaken the labor of decoding, of unbinding, of interpretation - at least for some of them. In addition to minimal bibliographic notes and some "actualized" spelling revisions, Cioran's works appeared *tale quale*, i.e., unchanged and unaccompanied by any explanation or introductory study.

It was said that there is, in Cioran, an "excess of expression", a "style of death", which only his native language could reproduce. Overwhelmed by the boundless futility of Ecclesiastes, the Romanian philosopher transforms the *invective* into something extremely trivial. With such a legacy left, for instance, by a Caragiale – who, spiritually speaking, seems to be his blood relative – Cioran could not achieve any rigorous research. He remains only an *essayeur – essayist* on a theme with variations, transmuting anger and sadness into protective substances for the fiber of his being by transforming language into a sickly structure that struggles "between the curse and the slum".[37]

He has mastered language to its utmost limit, where the humors coexist in overflowing luxuriance. A language that likes to play with the windmills of superlative adjectives and, sometimes, absolute negations. Thus said, a writer of humoral tensions, a peculiar nihilist in whose works *the will to power of the language* is struggling with *the will to destruction* dictated by his affects. Even if he masters the imperceptibly fine hue of the word, sometimes he just dives into generalizations. Terms of quantification become then a kind of juggling with swallowed swords or with the flames miraculously consumed by a circus actor. Through his structurally poetic nature, Cioran reaches – as Noica rhetorically notes – a kind of pamphlet without object. A sign, of course, that he is exclusively stuck inside the imaginary and makes *pro tanto* literature.

His self-referential claims, made both then and later, support the hypothesis: "My good luck, and Romania's too – is that I didn't know this country well when I wrote about it, because otherwise the worst book that was ever conceived about a human community would have been written".[38] Or: "*Change* is for me something distant, prehistoric, a time of wonder, a product of delirium, in the end - a digression. I don't think it can be brought into discussion at this point. Never mind! – The truth is that we are old and have to live with the consequences".[39] And, as he wrote to Arșavir Acterian in 1975: "In our youth we were tormented by a taste for scandal, for history. *The Transfiguration* is a testimony in this regard";[40] "As for the incredible allegations that you discover in *The Transfiguration*, the truth is that Jenny told me so since 1936. I find that it's absurd and ridiculous to make such a case of History – my divinity at that time. She was right, but I was young, vain and crazy, swept like so many others into a kind of delirium. The idea that I made History put me in a trance. What morons we were!".[41]

But he will confess - a partial retraction - in a 1947 letter to his brother, Relu: "I somehow changed my point of view in all that concerns 'historical' realities. Sometimes it seems downright comic that I have been able to write *The

Transfiguration; [...] Any participation in the unrest of the time is wasted time and unnecessary waste. These things I only understood too late, unfortunately, but I console myself with the thought that I understood them at long last".[42] And he would write, much later, also to Relu Cioran: "In terms of our nation I believe that no illusion is permitted, now more than ever. I feel a sort of desperate disdain for it. The vision of *The* Transfiguration seems today unacceptable to me, with the exception of the negative parts. I have to admit, however, that the fatalism of the Wallachian marked me, in the same way one is marked by a disease or ... an illumination. You can't get rid of your own origins and, above all - of ours".[43]

Therefore, in *The Transfiguration of Romania*, there is a lot of literature. To which I add the fact that the essayist is always judging history through *the master-slave duality*, or through the roles of *victim* and *executioner* (which he transforms into so-called ontological prerequisites for the existence of a people). Hence the defeatism and fatalism, the cultivation of fanaticism, intolerance and vengeance. History demands the Leader, the Ruler, or the Tyrant.

(By April 1991, when I invited him, by phone, to participate in the first Cioran symposium that I organized in Sibiu, the critic Adrian Marino, after he somewhat stylishly refused to come, warned me that, in the West, an anti-Cioran movement was underway, that Cioran made imprudent statements and that he was unable to figure out what was going on in Romania at the time; not surprising, from an author who wrote an apology for dictatorship and fascism – the reference being: *The Transfiguration of Romania*).

Such writing occupies a special place in the work of an author who wanted to be mystical, but, as he himself observed, could never achieve this *(n'est pas mystique que veut!)*. Cioran was under the rule of a "negative mystique", as we also find in him a mysticism which transformed the religious sentiment into the experience of an almost religious style. He transmuted - do we need to repeat it? – his style into his personal religion. Only that explains that frantic sensualism which generates a psychological attraction for writing, as it also offers reason enough for that trend, temptation even, to be confused with, and to immerse oneself with/in reality(ies). (Those exercises of thinking in which the bet is always the "discovery" of the gnomic fragment, occur in Cioran at the edges of *a psychological real* perceived in its aggressive anomia, and not at all on the surfaces of a "metaphysical" reality.)

Almost any work can, even posthumously, take revenge on its author. Believing that it is stupid to write "a book of facts without a vision for reform", Cioran arrived, against his will, exactly at the opposite pole: a theoretical approach in which the ways of recovery were all Utopian.

Whatever the reading code of *The Transfiguration of Romania* might be, we repeat: a not so systematic book, a test of agonized reflection on political and social-cultural themes, necessarily needs to acknowledge, first of all, the great coefficient of "*poetry*" of its *language*; on the other hand, we cannot circumvent a possible relation between the Utopian vision reached by an exacerbation of lucidity (lucidity as a form of desperation: "I like, in moments of sadness, to increase their intensity..."; "the lucid and bitter vision of the past must be lived until the last consequences..."), on the one hand; and ideology and politics immanent to the context, on the other hand.[44]

The first suggestion, which I tried to expound in the present pages, might seem superfluous. Interpreters have noticed, however, in meditative prose but also, incidentally, in the essays, Cioran's performance in achieving "the equivalent of what poetic perfection means" (Jean François Revel). Hence, probably, the trap which befalls any interpreter of his work, or the consequences that arise from an inadequate use of the quote. *Under this aspect*, Cioran's essay is an offhand and idea-phagous, stylish exercise by a thinker-artist.

But Cioran's book might also speak about something else. A few years before *The Transfiguration of Romania* was published, in 1932, Aldous Huxley published the novel *Brave New World*. It presented a future world in which people could be programmed, before birth, to respond to social needs. The five types – Alpha, Beta, Gamma, Delta and Epsilon – intended for management and control - the first, and for manual labor - the last two, lived in unimaginable happiness. Not missing anything, they even had electronic golf games or "*Electronic Bumble-Puppy*". As in a paradise regained, there was no sadness or illness, shortcoming or inconvenience; people were all happy, lived an average of sixty years, after which they fell asleep serenely – that was death! – for all eternity. And if, however, little troubles arose, a drug or a sleeping pill relieved them, harmlessly, of any negative consequences. In Huxley's society, there is no *opposition to something*, because everyone was in perfect agreement with what there is.

It was said that, apart from one or two exceptions, the determinations of Huxley's societal struggle can be found today, *tale quale*, in the space of Western Europe or of North America. The thirties were, therefore, an extremely fertile time for the fabrication of utopias. In the continuation of a vigorous Utopian vein, the social imaginary enriched its sphere through Romanian constructions, through socio-political theories, through essays developed at the level of intersection between the historical, political, ethical and cultural.

Comparing *The Transfiguration of Romania* with *Brave New World*, without forgetting for a moment that we are comparing an essay and a novel, we see both the inadequacy of the real and the ways of escaping it proposed by both.

But if Huxley wanted to provide some sort of serene compensation in an undefined future, Cioran's book advocated the violent substitution of one reality with another. Or, more radically put, Huxley's novel produced, willy-nilly, a palliative romantic remedy for the immediately real, while Cioran's essay expressed, as Karl Mannheim, quoted by Paul Ricoeur, would say, another "Utopian mentality", namely: "the absence of any reflections of a practical and political character on the support which Utopia can eventually depend in existing reality, in its institutions and in what I call the available credibility of an era".[45]

An unwanted romance with a not at all tempered vehemence of the vocable in a wintry scroll of syllogisms transformed, not infrequently, into sophism and fed with a skepticism pushed into its ontological abyss, here's what characterized, in large part, the Utopian Cioranian discourse, a construction that, as it advanced, increased the censorship between the imaginary and the real.

An exercise of style with a thickened touch, *The Transfiguration of Romania* risks becoming a sanguinary "story" about the "destiny" of a country, coincidentally called Romania, a destiny surprised not only in that segment of history between decay and a will of grandeur, but also through a peephole in the steamed visor of the relationship between *history and utopia*, a binomial that would return, in Cioran's creation, in an approach that is more detached and more "systematized".[46]

We will not doubt, not even for a moment, Cioran's honesty, or the fact that Romania was, for him a pretext of "theoretical sadness". Neither will we say that he had, *at that very moment*, other interests than "the ascendant momentum" of our country, its "historical spiral". Hence, probably, this book which listed Romania's flaws, "with the passion and the regrets of a desperate love". And probably the same stake of Cioranian reflection will also issue those phrases, placed at the end of the book, which we cite here, at the risk of a certain redundancy: "Does no trace of the heroic, convulsed ethos of Spain and Russia flicker in us? Might the excesses and the paroxysms of the Germanic soul remain forever alien to us? I don't want a logical, orderly, seated and quiet Romania, but a hectic, contradictory, angry and menacing one. I'm too much of a patriot to wish happiness for my country.

Until now we have been reptiles; from here on we will rise in the face of the world, and it will find out not only that Romania is in the world, but that the world is in Romania too. If we do not live the apocalyptic destiny of this country, if we do not put the fever and passion of the end in our beginnings, we are already lost and nothing remains for us than to regain the shadows of our past".[47]

We reproduce this ending, to emphasize that the final line of the manuscript, circumvented by Cioran in the first edition of the book, was not at all redundant, but signified a productive tautology: "*I don't believe that I don't believe in Romania.*" (My emphasis, I.D.)

Notes

[1] See Z. Ornea, *Anii treizeci. Extrema dreaptă românească* [The thirties. The Romanian extreme right], Bucharest: Romanian Cultural Foundation Publishing House, 1995, pp. 50 to 52, 136-145, 190-200 and *passim*.

[2] As per Emil Cioran, *The Transfiguration of Romania*, Bucharest: Vremea Publishing House, 1936, p. 35; starting from here we will quote, in the text, only the pages of this edition.

[3] To facilitate a better understanding of Cioran's approach, we reproduce in *Restituiri* [Refunds], in its entirety and after the manuscript, the chapter he excluded from the 1990 Humanitas edition: "Nationalism, Socialism, Judaism".

[4] *Ibidem*, p. 127

[5] *Ibidem*, pp. 128-129.

[6] *Ibidem*, p. 130.

[7] *Ibidem*, p. 131.

[8] *Ibidem*, p. 135.

[9] *Ibidem*, p. 137.

[10] *Ibidem*, pp. 140, 142.

[11] *Ibidem*, p. 144.

[12] *Ibidem*, pp. 223, 225.

[13] *Ibidem*, p. 147.

[14] *Ibidem*, p. 229.

[15] *Ibidem*, p. 228.

[16] *Ibidem*, p. 230.

[17] See *Pro și contra Emil Cioran. Între idolatrie și pamflet* [Pros and cons of Emil Cioran. Between idolatry and pamphlet], Bucharest: Humanitas Publishing House, Edition by Marin Diaconu, 1998.

[18] See the letter "Către Aurel Cioran" [To Aurel Cioran], 1947, in *Scrisori către cei de-acasă* [Letters to the folks back home], quoted edition, p. 43.

[19] See, among others, Eugen Simion, "Frenezia negației" [The Frenzy of negation], in Azi [Today] – weekly supplement, no. 932, July 17, 1995.

[20] G. Călinescu, *Istoria literaturii române de la origini până în prezent* [The history of Romanian literature from its origins to the present], Italy: Nagard Publishing House, 1980, p. 861 etc.

[21] Nichifor Crainic, "The Transfiguration of Romania", in *Gândirea* [Thought], no. 2, February 1937, pp. 93-95.

[22] Mihai Ralea, "Emil Cioran, Schimbarea la față a României" [Emil Cioran, The transfiguration of Romania], in *Viața Românească* [Romanian Life], no. 10, October 1937, pp. 130-131.

[23] Arșavir Acterian, „Emil Cioran, Schimbarea la față a României" [The Transfiguration of Romania], in *Vremea* [The Time], no. 471, January 17, 1937, p. 4.

²⁴ Pompiliu Constantinescu, *"Anul literar"* [1937] [The literary year] [1937], in *Vremea* [The Time], no. 519, Jan.2 1938.
²⁵ See above, *Pro şi contra Emil Cioran. Între idolatrie şi pamflet* [Pros and cons of Emil Cioran. Between idolatry and pamphlet], quoted edition, pp. 75-122; 155-163.
²⁶ See above, Cioran, *Scrisori către cei de-acasă* [Letters to the folks back home], quoted edition, pp. 114.
²⁷ See Vladimir Tismăneanu, "Revoluţionarii mistici ai României" [Revolutionaries and mystics of Romania], in *Cuvântul* [The Word], no. 7, July 1997.
²⁸ See N. Bolboaşă, "Filosofia burgheză din România dintre cele două războaie mondiale, duşmana ştiinţei şi materialismului" [Bourgeois philosophy in Romania between the two World Wars, enemy of science and materialism], in the collective volume *Din istoria filosofiei în România* [From the history of philosophy in Romania], vol. I, Bucharest: Academy R. P. R. Publishing House, 1955, pp. 255-256.
²⁹ Valentin Lipatti, "Un filosof al minciunii" [A philosopher of lies], in *Gazeta literară* [The Literary Gazette], no. 13, March 28, 1957. What are we to make of the end of the text, where it says: "and we promise you we'll translate your complete works..."?!
³⁰ D.D. Roşca, "Ispita de-a exista... a domnului Cioran" [The Temptation to Exist... of Mr. Cioran], in *Contemporanul* [The Contemporary], no. 18, May 1, 1957.
³¹ And Blaga's text was included by Marin Diaconu in the anthology *Pro şi contra Emil Cioran. Între idolatrie şi pamflet* [Pros and cons of Emil Cioran. Between idolatry and pamphlet], quoted edition, pp. 215-219. Our quotes send, without notes, to this edition.
³² See "Stilul interior al lui Lucian Blaga" [The inner style of Lucian Blaga]S, in *Gândirea* [Thinking], no. 8, December 1934; text included in the anthology *Solitude and Destiny*, quoted edition, pp. 275-280.
³³ "To Arşavir Acterian", Feb. 27. 1973; in Cioran, *Scrisori către cei de-acasă* [Letters to the folks back home], quoted edition, pp. 208.
³⁴ "To Arşavir Acterian", June 23, 1975, *ibidem*, p. 219.
³⁵ „Către Constantin Noica" [To Constantin Noica], July 27, *ibidem*, p. 306.
³⁶ See Moris Blanchot, *La littérature et le droit à la mort*, 1948.
³⁷ Cioran used these terms when writing to poet Wolf Aichelburg on June 16, 1970, when he rebuked his compatriots (he used the German word Landsleute) – see *Scrisori către cei de-acasă* [Letters to the folks back home], quoted edition, p. 240.
³⁸ "Către Mircea Eliade" [To Mircea Eliade], May 7, *ibidem*, 1937, p. 275.
³⁹ „Către Arşavir Acterian" [To Arşavir Acterian], March 15, 1981, *quoted work.*, p. 231.
⁴⁰ „Către Arşavir Acterian" [To Arşavir Acterian], August 24, *ibidem*, p. 219.
⁴¹ „Către Arşavir Acterian" [To Arşavir Acterian], Oct. 5, 1971, *ibidem*, p. 203.
⁴² „Către Aurel Cioran" [To Aurel Cioran], 1947, *ibidem*, p. 43.
⁴³ „Către Aurel Cioran" [To Aurel Cioran], August 30, 1979, *ibidem*, p 173.
⁴⁴ Very productive, for this relationship, are the assumptions made by Paul Ricoeur in *Eseuri de hermeneutică* [Essays on hermeneutics], Bucharest: Humanitas Publishing House, 1995, p. 274-300.
⁴⁵ *Ibidem*, p. 284.

[46] See *Histoire et Utopie*, Paris: Gallimard Publishing House, 1960; on the occasion of the book's reprinting in 1977, R. Caillois observed that, "in his characteristic style, Cioran is often touching the deepest meaning of utopia" – see the magazine *littéraire*, no. 327, Dec. 1994, p. 36.

[47] As per Emil Cioran, *The Transfiguration of Romania*, Bucharest: Vremea Publishing House, 1936, p. 234.

Chapter 10

Waiting for Cioran's *reply*

With this feeling, perhaps both exaggerated and Utopian, I have lived since the death of Cioran, whenever I thought about the *trial*, in a unilateral way, that posterity was submitting his texts to. For as long as he is still alive, a dialogue with a creator involves not only the surface and depth of the work but also a man of flesh and blood. Because after death, such a dialogue will be reduced to a dialogue between the critic and the creation, which remains as a witness; the irreplaceable reply of the author becoming, alas, impossible. And Cioran was, undoubtedly, an author who had a response: original, robust, and indelible.

It will be said, however, that the posthumous instance of such a critical relationship is the one that ensures a more pronounced objectivity for the judgment of value. And yet, on its own, the work cannot fully support a right to reply in the face of that tribunal of criticism, the critics, and needs the confusing exponentiation of an author's physical (and metaphysical, in equal measure) presence.

It happened with the work of Cioran too, immediately after his death, the first episode being engineered by the French press, promptly and with barely disguised enthusiasm; "*Le mauvais procès prosthume*". Thus, under a justifying cover title (to be read, in the subtext, as "vigilante") such as "*Débat*", the analyses of various commentators have tried to find (in the key of a discreet sensationalism) the reasons for the young Cioran's adherence to the Extreme Right, a few of his ideological options piercing the rhetoric of his speech in The Transfiguration of Romania .

The onset of these re-examinations – in fact: the eruption of a volcano that smoldered – was produced by an article written by Pierre-Yves Boissau and entitled "La transfiguration du passé" ("The transfiguration of the past"), appearing in *Le Monde des livres* (July 28, 1995) only a month after the death of Cioran.[1] The well-known French newspaper made, in this way, a gesture which was, at the very least, unusual, "a strange exception", as Alain Finkielkraut will later call it, in which it offered, "in the guise of obituary, a debate about Cioran's obscure nationalist past".

P.-Y Boissau's text violated the "grand truce" required by the customary practice of mourning. A researcher of Romanian literature and culture, preparing at that time a *translation with commentary* of The Transfiguration of Romania (he actually published comments on fragments from Cioran's book), the French critic, after he had discovered Cioran's other Romanian writings, considered the work of the Rășinari philosopher to be nothing but "a huge disguise". He was annoyed, first of all, and rightly so, by the changes that Cioran had made to the Humanitas edition (1990), as his retraction from the warning prefacing the "definitive edition" seemed to be the staging of a superfluous test: the book was not changed because the author now offered a "key" to make it more "readable". As Boissau will put it, a year later, in "Writing to disband", that "amputated" republishing (without telling the reader what was removed) was akin to a "rehabilitation perestroika (or a softened reconstruction) of Romanian political thought in the interwar period".[2]

Erroneously placing its chronology after *Tears and Saints*, a book that would have outraged (!) a country of believers, *The Transfiguration of Romania* appeared to Boissau as a *paradoxically more acceptable discourse*, because the national collectivism that it advocated had "nothing "aggressive" in it, as no Romanian was targeted by its tropes, only "foreigners".[3] Put in the service of a "secret logics of exhibition, of a rehabilitation of the "self" and not in the service of any party, Cioran's book contained numerous challenges, mixed with common places, all "protected by a theme (much appreciated in a "small" country) exalting the "we".[4]

The French exegete also blamed Gabriel Liiceanu, not only for publishing, in the same year (1995) *Itinéraires d'une vie: E. M. Cioran*,[5] where he had not revealed the author in his entirety, but also because he endorsed the Humanitas reprint of Cioran's book, being in a way an accessory to a mystification of the truth.

What P.-Y. Boissau found most irritating was Cioran's sincerity, especially the strange directness of the Note with which he opened the Humanitas edition of *The Transfiguration of Romania*, as well as the "loyalty" of removals from the text of the book. But he also considered Cioran's connection to his own past as exceedingly strange. A valid issue even in 1936, when the Cioranian "ego" "wanted at any price to be free of the obstacles of tradition, of the proverb – eternal word, and to impose upon us a new man, a rare verb: to no longer belong to the past, which is the deed of another"[6] (we will quote further from this text, without giving specific references). A "rupture" that Cioran accomplished "by the book", but without being limited to it.

Only that the ("discreditable") past still obsessed him in the 1990s (and even before then); a past of which Cioran wanted to be free. That's why, says Boissau, his French texts "must be read as signs obstructing an (almost) native sin". "'*The Ego*' reinterprets its own sentences almost without warning us, superimposing upon them not only another language (French), but also a more convenient script, closer to the new public". The exegete cites, in this sense, comparative passages about the Jews.

Two of Boissau's conclusions: "The work of Cioran is a palimpsest. A disguise or atonement, mea culpa or repeated bad faith – who can decide..." "Beyond good and evil, discourse depends, in a disturbing manner, upon the place where the self speaks from. (...) The spirit of the time makes the writer irresponsible. This is the way in which Cioran justifies himself, and thus we explain him too, without justifying him ...".[7]

In this tone and with such an idea Pierre-Yves Boissau concludes his article, which also included contributions by Edgar Reichmann ("Le funambule du desespoir") and François Fejtö ("*Je doute, donc je suis*"), but also a note, unsigned, that "transcribed", from the book written by Zigu Ornea (*Anii treizeci. Extrema dreaptă românească* [The thirties. The Romanian extreme right], quoted work), the passage concerning Cioran's return to his country between November 1940 and January 1941, reminiscing about his position as cultural attaché of the Romanian Legation of the French Vichy government (a place where Eugene Ionesco will work too, starting in 1942).

Less than four months after "La transfiguration du passé", Radio France Culture organized a debate in the "Répliques"[8] program, attended, along with Pierre-Yves Boissau, by Alain Finkielkraut (moderator of the discussion), and Gabriel Liiceanu, invited not only as a philosopher and the editor of Cioran in Romania, but also as the author of the essay *Itinerariile unei vieți - Itineraries of a life* (Publisher Michalon, Paris).

The person who had disturbed Cioran's posthumous life with his texts, Pierre-Yves Boissau, reiterated already well-known themes, but began initially with the "theme of the Jew". Comparing *The Transfiguration of Romania* with *The Temptation to Exist*, he discovered a contradictory Cioran, with the relaxed transition from "energetic anti-Semitism" to "filo-Semitism" (the subhuman became a Super-man"). The hypothesis was illustrating, again, the fact that the Romanian philosopher would have been obsessed with a certain "scheme of the liquidation of the past, of any past" (symbolically speaking, Boissau associated his response to the past with a "hatred against the father" or with an accusation against ancestors in general). Synthetically said, Cioran did not have a "constructive vision on the past", but he tried to prove it "by only denying, denying everything he did before", wanting to make *a tabula rasa* of all that had been and to start, permanently, from zero.[9]

Cioran's essential fault is, however, according to Pierre-Yves Boissau, his unchanging "lack of sincerity" that was hiding not so much an "aesthetic of the fugue", which would agree with Cioran, as an "ethical attitude of running", as, some other times, the same Cioran resorts to "lies by omission" (in particular in connection with Codreanu and the Iron Guard). All these, suggests the French commentator, made Cioran an author who, paradoxically, gave the world remarkable texts just because of that permanent turning upon himself.

Characterizing most of Boissau's hypotheses as "processes of intention" "fueling a post-mortem iconoclasm", complaining about the use of anti-Semitism as a unique and permanent grid for reading Cioran, G. Liiceanu offered, in the *Radio France Culture* debate, some reservations about the way in which the philosopher's "political shipwreck" was judged (sometimes even seeing him as an "unconditional apologist of the hangman").

The passion with which French critics attacked Cioran for his confessions regarding the political sympathies of his youth – even though his work, written in France, contained similar disclosures in a not always symbolical form – finally managed, observed Liiceanu, to deny the Romanian philosopher his "right to regret". In addition, it circumvented a fundamental truth: "the widespread excess" customary for young Cioran, "was as 'anti-Semitic' as he was anti-Romanian, as he was against almighty God, against the saints, against the human condition, against all and everything. It was about the anger of a negation that swallowed everything in its path. Cioran had reviled everyone: the Hungarians, the Russians, the French and, above all, his own people, the Romanians".[10]

If the debate caused by *Radio France Culture* suggested a conclusion – beyond the insistence with which Boissau returned to the thesis that Cioran's French works were just a "rewriting" of his previous ones, this could only be linked to Cioran's *condition – that of writer and thinker* (having to face politics both in the interwar period, and after). If we "suspect" him of insincerity, the suspect is a philosopher, not an ideologue; and "the shipwreck of thinkers must not lead us to the conclusion that their whole system of thinking flounders"[11] if we could invoke here Alain Finkielkraut.

Other moments in the dialogue between posthumous contemporaries and the work of Cioran were generated by the book written by Patrice Bollon, *Cioran, l'hérétique* (Gallimard Publishing House, 1997). It jumpstarted again the dispute or quarrel around the "fascist past of the Franco-Romanian moralist", as Philippe Cusin said in an article summarizing the *pro* polemics around this theme.[12] The most caustic text was that of Jean-Paul Enthoven, who stigmatized in Cioran the absence of remorse and the technique of dissimulation, heralding a "great loneliness" of the remaining "orphans" after the second death of Cioran.[13] Also in *Le Point*, where Enthoven's criticism appeared, Bernard-Henry Lévy related the story of a meeting with Cioran, in 1989, when the philosopher was concerned with avoiding this subject, which would have made considerable difficulties for him.

It was said that the series of controversies around the work of Cioran reloaded, in fact, the terms of the lawsuit filed against Heidegger. Parisian intellectuals were divided by the way in which, after Philippe Cusin, they addressed some questions, such as: "Can an ideological commitment involve a work and its author in a post-mortem trial / lawsuit? Are there some excusable errors of youth, and others - which are unforgivable?".[14]

The Manichaeism of these formulations was the first to be filled out, as some French thinkers did not join the shady game. "You can't lock someone into his past and into his youth, when he evolved", stated Edgar Morin, sociologist and philosopher, who, in the volume *Autocritică* [Self-accusation], talked about his Stalinist years: "I've analyzed the errors of my youth, and Cioran did the same thing. Are there two weights and two measures: if someone was a Stalinist, we neglect such a thing; but if someone else was a Fascist, we are not allowed to forget his past?".[15]

Philippe Cusin, who collated the positions of "witnesses" in the posthumous trial of Cioran, claimed "measure" as a criterion of judgment: *"De la mesure avant toutes choses!"* And that's because, as Julien Benda demonstrated, history has often illustrated the betrayal of intellectuals, he himself becoming a Stalinist after he had been friends with Péguy.

The judgment with the greatest impact in such a context was coming, it seems, from historian François Furet, author of a work that cannot be ignored: *The passing of an illusion The idea of communism in the twentieth century.* For him, boundaries are clear: "The works of the spirit – literature, art, philosophy or science – are located at a different level from political opinions".[16] The great spirits or famous artists, stated the French historian, expressed "questionable political views", but many changed them before the end of their life. Of the many examples, he chose, for the XIX-th century, Lamennais, who "went from the far Right to the far Left"; Hugo and Lamartine, who slid "from the legitimist Right to Republican progressivism"; or Péguy who, orienting himself backwards, changed "Dreyfusism" for "nationalism". "Who would use this pretext, asked Furet, in order to discredit their ideas or works?"

What happened in the XX-th century had, says Furet, a totally particular significance. There was a time when "hatred of bourgeois capitalist society led to regimes that were guilty of crimes unprecedented in History". Hitler and Stalin were the authors of an unrepeatable genocide. But it is strange that especially Germany and Nazism – or Fascism – was anathematized, and intellectuals and artists found themselves subjected to the sanction of the public for their political sympathies towards such ideology.

Furet's judgment remains, again, a reference point: and here, for interpretation, "this way is wrong" because "it means assuming that people in the '20s or '30s would have already known what was going to become of Fascism or Nazism, which, by definition, was impossible. It means forgetting that Fascism represented a hope for millions of deceived people, it means to give it back its confused history, which cannot be done. Cioran is a great writer and even a great moralist, regardless of his ephemeral adhesion to the Iron Guard".

Beyond their opposite opinions and political preferences, those thinkers that Philippe Cusin invoked as "witnesses" in that ugly "procès posthume" had one thought in common: they didn't want to start a "new "*guerre picrocholine* – a petty wrangling war – in connection with Cioran, who is no longer here to defend, amend or justify himself".[17]

In addition, in spite of the fact that Cioran never explicitly returned to the errors of his youth, everything that he wrote after leaving the country may appear as an "underground denial" (Patrice Bollon) of his past in Romania. And the most significant confession in this regard is the letter sent to his parents on the 17th of April, 1946, from which we reproduce an excerpt: "In fact, all ideas are absurd and false; we are only left with people as they are, regardless of origin and beliefs. In this regard, I've changed a lot. I think I will never embrace any ideology again".[18]

We have here, I think, *the reply* that Cioran would have reiterated for those who have waited, in vain, *for the confession of one who was defeated.*

Notes

[1] The French essayist justified himself by saying that, knowing of Cioran's illness, he had sent the article at the end of April and insisted it be published in the May issue, which was dedicated to the philosopher. The text was published – through it is not known in what circumstances – at the end of July

[2] See Pierre-Yves Boissau, "*A scrie pentru a desființa*" [Writing to disband], in *Cioran, Țara mea* [My Country], Bucharest: Humanitas Publishing House, 1996, pp. 79-87. This text is slightly modified from the one that appeared *in Le Monde des livres*, on July 28, 1995.

[3] Idem, "La Transfiguration du passé", *Le Monde des livres*, July 28 1995, p. 12. "The foreigners" are mainly the Jews.

[4] *Ibidem.*

[5] In the 1996 text, Boissau characterizes Liiceanu's approach as a "hagiography", a "real photo album".

[6] Pierre-Yves Boissau, "La Transfiguration du passé".

[7] *Ibidem.*

[8] See "Itinerariile lui Cioran" [The itineraries of Cioran], in *Cioran, Țara mea* [My country], quoted edition, pp. 37-77.

[9] *Ibidem.*

[10] *Ibidem.*

[11] *Ibidem.*

[12] Philippe Cusin, "Cioran: le mauvais proces posthume [Cioran - an unpleasant posthumous trial], *Figaro littéraire*, 24 April 1997.

[13] Jean-Paul Enthoven, "La Deuxieme Mort de Cioran" [Cioran's second death], *Le Point*, April 5, 1997. A previously unknown text written by Cioran in the form of a withdrawal had been published, however, in number 9 of the *Messager européen* – which Enthoven either did not know or considered unsatisfactory.
[14] See Philippe Cusin, quoted work.
[15] See *Figaro littéraire*, April 24, 1997.
[16] See Cioran, *Țara mea* [My country], quoted edition, pp. 89-96.
[17] See Philippe Cusin.
[18] „Cioran către părinți" [Cioran to his parents], April 17 [1946], in *Scrisori către cei de-acasă* [Letters to the folks back home], quoted edition, p.17.

Part II
Restitutions

Because we need a Cioran *according to the original,* even if our option ignores the will of the philosopher, we undertake here the restitution of chapter IV, "National collectivism", transcribed from the manuscript and compared with the corresponding one in the first edition of *The Transfiguration of Romania* (1936; this version has a translation: *Transfiguration de la Roumanie,* traduit du roumain par Alain Paruit, Éditions de L'Herne, 2009).

This is the chapter completely excluded by Cioran from the "definitive" edition of *The Transfiguration of Romania* (Humanitas Publishing House, Bucharest, 1990).

For the title of this chapter, we will opt, however, for one of the two titles in the manuscript: "Nationalism, Socialism, Judaism".

Nationalism, Socialism, Judaism[1]

For the vitality of nationalism, it is very important to know the source from which it springs, and what fuels it. If it is closed in itself and sterile in its roots, this stems from a useless consciousness of preservation, without the support of instinct and without any possibility of being anchored in the universal. If it is too open to the world, it lacks the resistance of the actual and the aggressive charge that sits so well with any nationalism. The life formula of a nation must be composed of a sum of elements, which revolve around two foci:[2] *force and social justice*. Any nationalism, which thinks it can solve the problems of a nation without resolving its conflicts and social inequalities, is not only reactionary, but also impossible. In the past, it could have raised the grandeur of a nation on the tacit or voluntary acceptance of inequalities; after the Russian revolution, this is no longer possible, except as a transient reality. Lenin has done more for nationalism than for communism. More. He saved nationalism. If it hadn't been for the Russian revolution, nationalism would have remained so reactionary that it would have given, in its own name, the wealth of the poor to the rich. Regardless of political orientation, Lenin created, in all ideological movements, an interest in social problems; sometimes a real inferiority complex. In the name of inequality and the intangibility of property, one can't even move a feather; Lenin,[3] crazy about social justice and with Klausewitz at his bedside, is the prototype of a politician of the future. In the vision of social peace, think about the tactics and methods of struggle! Even the rich – who are, for those lacking conscience, the flower; and for the poor – the leprosy of history, can't withhold a fearful admiration for the sublime fanaticism of the Tartar.[4] Humanity will only be able to call itself civilized, when the rich man is ashamed of the light of the sun, when he will hide in the dark. On the ground of history waits *the blinding presence* of the poor...

How come Romanian nationalism has remained alien to so many dramatic, I want to say, so many modern problems? Romania is a country that does not die of hunger, because poverty has been its natural state for centuries. A country of ugly and badly fed peasants, who for a thousand years endured misery due to the *foreigners*... Animosity towards strangers is so characteristic of Romanian national feeling - these two can never be separated. The first national reaction of Romanians is not pride in the fate of Romania, or a sentiment of glory, inseparable from the patriotism of the French; but a revolt against the foreigners, often exhausted by a curse or organized, rarely, into an enduring hate. From this phenomenon derive most of the deficiencies of Romanian nationalism. *If we removed all foreigners*,[5] *Romania's problems would be no less serious*. Then they would just start. Throwing foreigners dead into a pit is a target; but nationalism does not have to turn this into its central mission, because eyes focused too much on foreigners cease to see their own reality, our essential misery. For a thousand years we all lived under the yoke of foreigners; not to hate and not to remove them would be a lack of national instinct. The Jewish invasion of the last decades of Romania's emergence has made anti-Semitism an essential feature of our nationalism. Intelligible elsewhere, to us this fact finds its legitimacy which must not, however, be exaggerated. If Romania hadn't had any Jews, would it have experienced a less miserable existence? Would its historic level (the only important one) be higher? That there would be less corruption is obvious, but from here to history, it's a long way. The Jews, at most, *delayed* the solemn hour of Romania; they are not, in any case, the cause of our misery, of our eternal misery. A nationalism that does not see this is false and much too one-sided to be durable. A revolution cannot deal with false problems.

A healthy national body can always prove itself in the fight against the Jews; especially when they, by number and by impudence, invade a people. But anti-Semitism doesn't solve either the national or the social problems of a nation. It represents an action of *purification* and nothing more. The constitutional vices of that nation remain the same. The narrowness of vision of Romanian nationalism moves away from its origin in anti-Semitism. A peripheral issue becomes the source of movement and vision.

Our nationalism needs to arise from a desire to seek revenge for our historical sleep,[6] from a Messianic thought, from the will to make history.

A clarification of our own essence and a confrontation with our fate, in all its substantial immanence. Facing such problems, what does a minor reaction against a minority mean? Since there is no universal solution to the Jewish question, anti-Semitism is not a way of entering into history. What are, however, the deeper reasons that cause us to meet the Jews only with feelings of contempt and hatred? Why is there *no man on Earth* able to love the Jews naively, spontaneously, without *knowing*? Whence, the infinite drama of their existence?

Racial theory seems to have been born only to give expression to the feeling of precipitous separation, which distinguishes any non-Jew from the Jew. An abyss born not out of anti-Semitism or from any sort of conception, but of the antagonism, manifest or secret, which characterizes two essentially different beings. The Jew *is not our fellow man,* and regardless of how much privacy we share with him, a chasm separates us, whether we want it or not. It is as though they descended from another species of ape than us and were sentenced from the beginning to a sterile tragedy, to hope eternally deceived. Fittingly, we can't get near them, because the Jew is firstly *Jewish* and only secondly *Man*. The phenomenon happens both in their consciousness, and in ours.

The problem of Judaism is as complicated as [and] that of the existence of God. To talk of their vampirism and their aggression is to highlight one of their characteristic features, without diminishing the mystery of the nature of Judaism. This race, which fuels its inner fire with hatred, gave unique, inadmissible examples of love. Whoever knows Hasidic mysticism and the life of some of its rabbis cannot help but tremble in the face of examples of love which defy the laws of life, inhuman in their rarity and often leaving Christianity way behind. Only a doomed people can know such cases, which can only have the significance of large redemptions. Holiness, for the Jews, has a purely national character; it must save, by way of compensation, a people from perishing.

Viewed from the perspective of universal history, the Jewish problem is absolutely intractable. It remains the curse of history and a question mark, increased by the passing of time. There are only national solutions to the Jewish problem which, by being solved in one place, wouldn't get less complicated for the rest of the world. Centuries ago, Spain rid itself of its Jews; Germany liquidates them today, successfully, the whole problem. Does it seem that the plague of the Jews becomes less threatening in the world?

Whenever a people become conscious of itself, it falls fatally into conflict with the Jews. The latent conflict that exists forever between the Jews and the respective people shall be updated in a decisive historical moment, at an essential crossroads, in order to place the Jews beyond the sphere of the nation. More. There are historical moments that turn the Jews fatally *into traitors*. Due to the particular structure of the Jewish spirit and the orientation of their policy, which opposes all movements of national self-awareness, they are set at certain historical crossroads, so alien to the respective nation that any mutual adversity clamors to be resolved. Who sentenced the Jews to engage themselves passionately in the destiny of other nations, to place themselves artificially in the bosom and in the center of their lives, to be entangled in a fate that does not even interest them, for which they never suffered and in which they were never involved? That Jew who confessed to me that, if Romania lost Transylvania, it would be perfectly indifferent to him, expressed with sincerity an obvious, but deliberately obscured, state of the Jews. In all national failures, the only ones who don't lose their temper are the Jews. Germany's defeat in the World War has cost the Germans so much that desperation threw them into vice and decay. During this time, the Jews were making fortunes and occupying key positions. If indeed they felt that they have a right to involve themselves more deeply and to participate in the life of a nation, they wouldn't accept with so much cynicism the persecutions and the exile. Not feeling *at home* anywhere, they are unaware of the tragedy of alienation. The Jews are the only people who don't feel tied to the *landscape*. No corner of the world has shaped their soul; therefore, they are the same, regardless of country or continent. Cosmic sensitivity is alien to them. The gypsies, who have etched a living on the edge of villages and towns, with so many dusks and auroras in their souls, are infinitely closer to nature than the Jews, who wear throughout history the obscurities of the *ghetto*, with its nasty sorrows and its disgusting ironies, that have long removed the Jews from nature and keep them, reprovingly, in history. Although any Jew is a God compared to a Gypsy, anyone feels *humanly* closer to the latter. In everything, the Jews are small; they are alone in the world, bent under a curse for which only God is responsible. Were I a Jew, I would kill myself on the spot.

The Jews involve themselves in the life of a people in such measure that, if they are unable to create a rhythm of life, they can nevertheless pervert an existing one. Of all the species of beings, the Jew is the *least neutral*. That's why, in the life of peoples, he is a *catalyst*; he accelerates the processes. If the number of Jews in a country does not exceed the dose of poison lethal to any organism, they may be accepted as a regrettable nuisance, even with some indifferent sympathy. There are so many countries which don't even need to *know* that the Jews exist?! And wouldn't Romania's path be easier without a conflict with the smartest, most intelligent and wickedest people?

It is known that the Jews explain anti-Semitism as a reaction to times of crisis, as a distraction and a form of cowardice. This explanation is a hundred percent valid for the persecutions of Tsarist Russia, where the most imbecile regime that has ever existed in history organized pogroms to divert the attention of a dissatisfied population from the real causes of their misery, but this is not a valid explanation here, where, after the War, the political regime of Romania was filo-Semitic, meaning by this – not sympathy for the Jews (who absolutely no one loves), but tolerance and fear of them.[7] Hatred of the Jews, in us, has its deeper causes. I sincerely doubt that it springs from envy or out of rebellion against the situation of some of the Jews. Are Romanian capitalists any better than Jewish capitalists? There is the same bestiality in the one as in other. I can't conceive and I refuse to believe we could have a national revolution,[8] which would destroy the Jewish capitalists but would spare the Romanian ones. A national revolution that would try to save the Romanian capitalists seems to me something horrible.[9]

Jews have always resisted all attempts at Romanian national and political consolidation. Here must be sought the source of militant anti-Semitism, and not of sentimental anti-Semitism. They have always criticized Romania, but considered any attempt at consolidation outside a democracy as reactionary, barbaric, etc. In reality, there never existed a more reactionary press than the Jewish one, for which paradise was always to be found in the pestilent atmosphere of Romanian democracy, admirable in its intentions, but miserable in their achievement. I am criticizing in particular Jewry after the war.[10] Did it not oppose any attempts towards renewal for Romania? From a few morons and degenerates, who have managed to compromise an already flawed democracy, the Jews have made a tool of domination, wretchedly and irretrievably offending a whole country. We, the Romanians, can only be saved by a different political form. The Jews have resisted this with all the means available to their underground imperialism, cynicism and centuries-old experience. The democratic regime of Romania had no other mission than to defend the Jews and Judeo-Romanian capitalism.[11] We need to get it into our heads once and for all: Jews have no interest in living in a united and self-conscious Romania. We, as Romanians, have only got one interest: a strong Romania with a will to power.[12]

Each of us has had a time when we were moved by the sufferings of the Jews. However, since I realized that we, Romanians, have suffered in the past more than they did, I abandoned this kind of stupid sentimentality. If we don't concentrate all our forces, we will surely disappear, like a picture fading from the surface of history. Romania still has no substance. The Jews? Any man with historical culture will have to admit, with hurt in his soul, an axiom, the only axiom of history: the last people that will disappear will be the Jewish people. Were we to destroy the Romanian Jews, they will be reborn as *Jewry*, eternal and wandering as a rebuke to history or to God. Jewry survived the Roman empire and Hellas, and will clearly survive the West, ugly and despised by all other peoples that are born and die...

Of course, the inability of Jews to understand and to admit the gravity of the national problem is characteristic and revealing. Or maybe they don't want to understand. This people, the most Messianic of them all, whose nationalism, without geographical expression and thus with universal dimensions, does not allow for a similar case in all of history, this people is the deadly enemy of all other nationalism.

The Jews don't want to make peace with this fatality, which history checks at every step: *national conflicts are much more common than social ones*. How else can one explain the breath-taking frequency of wars and the appearance of the revolutionary phenomenon at intervals of centuries? This is very sad news, but you can't understand history without this eternal platitude, willfully neglected by the Jews. It is, however, a great merit of the Jews to have decried, all through the last century, the paramount importance of social problems, to have obsessively reiterated the need to solve them. If the world's conflicts were to be diminished just in the realm of the social, the Jews would feel at home in history. History is much more differentiated, and the irrational is its secret presence.

Had the Jews never introduced into socialism their materialistic vision, which is the essential attribute of their "spirit", every man today would be a socialist. That, through Marxism, the idea of collectivism has been infected by materialism, is the most serious vice by which Jews individualized themselves in the previous century. And when internationalism was added to materialism, the process leading to national disintegration began. The Jews are not for universalism, which is compatible with the specific nuances of a culture, but for a common and artificial set of values, without actual adhesion, which is internationalism. Universal is, for example, the European awareness of Goethe or Nietzsche who lived in a Europe made up of irreducibles, which met, however, in an ideal point of the perfect spirit.[13] Culture is universal in its essence. However, there is no internationalism in culture. Therefore, a phenomenon at the periphery of the culture, such as the press, could so often become the standard bearer of characteristic and appropriate expressions of internationalism. Only the economic has as much as value as the international. Hence, its generalization and absolutization by historical materialism. Jews are attracted to the idea of communism, in the first place for its internationalism, and only secondarily by the idea of social justice. They projected upon communism all items able to justify themselves and to ease their errors and wanderings in the world. It is interesting to note that, even if by communism they assert themselves politically, from an economic point of view, it is not Paradise on Earth.[14] Eliminating the competition and the spirit of enterprise, communism offers the Jews a refuge from persecution and even a political primacy, but no economic prosperity. Consistent communism would be a dead end for them. As it is not possible, Jews have a way out of their "dream". The situation of the Jews in Russia is characteristic. Once in a position of leadership in the field of economic life, they cannot exercise their own "virtues", which they dramatically emphasized in the capitalist world. In addition, Russia has isolated the Jews as a mass, giving them in exchange the satisfaction of having prohibited anti-Semitism. The theory aiming to make the Jews "responsible" for the Russian Revolution is unquestionably stupid.[15] Lack of comprehension of the revolutionary phenomenon is so great that this theoretical strain of nationalism revolts everyone. It can only be compared to some Marxist stupidities in the interpretation of spiritual phenomena. To cite two examples. In the Soviet history of art, the gloomy atmosphere, the deep shadows in the paintings of Tintoretto are explained by the fact that Venice lost the monopoly of the salt at the end of the XV-th century. Another author, a German Marxist, found that Calvin's theory of predestination has its source in the unsettled economic life of his time, which exalted or destroyed merchants, regardless of their qualities and their skills, in a game of fatalities. The anti-Semitic explanation of the Russian revolution is of similar intellectual quality. Actually, the Jews have exploited the turbulence of the spirit and they saw a means of revenge against a regime that had systematically persecuted them. But from here to making them the cause of the revolutionary movement is an enormous distance. The Russian revolution was built on all the centuries of suffering of Russia; in its veins flows the blood of all the Russian revolutionaries.

Although the pre-Marxist revolutionary idea was nebulous and devoid of political subtlety, its Utopianism is not as inconsistent as the pretentious scientism of Marxism wants it to appear. The Semitic spirit made the transition from socialist idealism to the basest materialism. If communist ideas, with so many correct concepts, but with a minor *Weltanschauung*, were ever to be achieved, they would necessarily constitute food for mortals *before* their achievement. But the myth of the revolutionary may no longer be an incentive once achieved, even partially. The era of preparation for communism can flare up from the fanaticism of its ideas; however, a humanity, which, in the communist "era", would only live for the same ideas for which it had fought, would be an empty humanity. The anthropological vision of communism is so minor, that you wonder if man was ever worthy of religion, the only thing able to give him a grandiose role in the Universe. Those dimensions which religion has given us seemingly exceeded our resistance, because how else could we explain why man has embraced, with such passion, the mediocre role Marxism has chosen for him.

If the ideals for which communism struggles were founded on another Weltanschauung, the religion of the future would already be established, and Christianity - only a memory.

Communism cannot be fought by nationalism, but by addressing social issues. If the reasons and causes that lead to revolt are not contested in themselves, if it does not end misery, nationalism is a phraseology that doesn't preclude serious social realities. Enthusiasm for a nation cannot replace the thirst for justice in man, which approaches more the essence of social life than the national one. Only those who suffer, with equal intensity, from an obsession with the grandeur of their own nation and a desire for social justice can build in an enduring way the exaltation of a nation.

In Romania there is enough interest, if not passion, in its national future. But the dream of national greatness relies too often on the extremes of irreparable misery and on the conditions of poor workers and the peasantry. The whole problem is reduced to knowing whether it is possible to have a collectivist formula in the context of national existence. If it is not possible, it means that from its origins, nationalism is forced to be reactionary.

Resistance to the formula of national collectivism is not offered by the actual life of the nation, but by previous theoretical crystallizations of the collectivist vision. Because of Marxism, a mandatory weakness for any collectivist guidelines of internationalism has been created. It is a pure generalized theoretical situation, which does not rely on any status quo. It would be fair if the nation were a transient reality or a simple historical stage, as Marxism thinks. True, a nation is born in history, but as a constant shaping of the latter. Humanity cannot evolve by convergence, and peoples may not keep the same step.

A group is both more dynamic and more aggressive, as it is more closed, and more tied to a set space. Unlimited space creates a vagueness of outlines and an artificial solidarity. Federated countries have never given birth to a specific style of culture. Heterogeneous associations give birth, in the best case, to a Switzerland or a North America. Although they too have humanity, it is not a creative force as such; any productive impulse has vivid and immediate roots; the abstraction of humanity is sterile by itself. The idea of humanity is based on all the centrifugal forces of man, the disintegration of his natural center. He cannot be integrated, except in *a rush towards the center*, the nation means focusing on immediate becoming.[16] One can only create in a concrete, actual framework. The more values are spread across the vastness of space, the more they lose their grip and dramatic pulse. Is it not revealing that the dawn of cultures has a provincial character? All cultures are *born locally*.

Man is too minor a being to be able to be creative without the limit of immediacy. Removed from the framework of the nation, he floats in a vacuum, which throws him into inevitable failure. It might be that a nation has no other justification than that of being an obstacle in the path of failure. The "ultimate" reason for the nation cannot consist in its own essence, but in the rescue of man; and it is this, which also constitutes its historical limits. The cult of force is no less a desertion, an escape from the arbitrariness, from the normal climate of subjectivity. Force is a guarantee in the face of irresponsibility. If man seeks in the nation and in force a resistance to failure, he will mitigate his allotted freedom.

There is no human being more inclined to failure than the Romanian. Besides other causes, the absence of a strong national consciousness was crucial. Psychologically, we never had a tendency towards effective solidarity, and historically, not being a nation, we lacked the context of this solidarity. The Romanian's vague nihilism finds in failure its natural significance. *A nihilistic people are a people that have no history and remains as such until it becomes a nation.*

At 30 years of age, the Romanian intellectual has returned to being just matter. Not interested in anything apart from his indifference. The inner seed is rotten; early maturity, as a collective phenomenon, is a sign of deficiency. Only the Russians and we have the problem of a constant deficiency, a lack of cultured classes, of "intelligentsia". Romanian literature has obsessively developed this theme, without reaching any valid conclusions. Because, according to it, our intellectuals have been uprooted and lost contact with the people; and only the people are healthy. The peasantry is full of virtues; the intellectual, just a void, devoid of the spiritual. But it is incomprehensible how the first generations of intellectuals, with rural blood still in their veins, could be nothing, worthy only of contempt when compared with the peasant, that repository of life and spirit. The truth is different: our peasant has never felt at home in culture. Otherwise, how can one explain so much confusion arising from the first contact with it? The problem of uprooted Romanian intellectuals was the most painful, and most shameful in Romanian literature. How artificially sad was this superficial country! There was a fear for the future of the nation in all this confusion, which took hold of the first generations of intellectuals. The inertia of the secular shuddered in the face of so many problems demanding to be solved. If all these nobles could have recanted, today Romania would have been declared a country suitable for ethnographic study, and people would have organized expeditions to it, as they do to central Asia. For our destiny, the problem of uprooting is a bad sign and a compromising memory.[17] [18] Romanians were smart enough to feel that it is not so good, as a country, to make your way in the world; a long time had to pass, with all the thrills of the beginning, in order for it to get a taste for the affairs of the world. Today, the problem of uprooting is no longer current, except in the history of literature. It is a sign of vitality to be able to defeat the temptations of resignation and numbness. It would still be an excess of optimism to believe that nothing remains, in our blood, from our initial timidity and maladjustment. The problem of uprooting disappeared, but it continues to smolder in our national inclination towards being losers. When you look at a Romanian aged 20, you are willing to believe him a genius; be sure that, at 30, he will be a failure. This rapid exhaustion involves many inner inconsistencies and a lack of congruence between the biological level and the spiritual. The life qualities of the base don't support a spiritual construction. It is as if our culture lacks a biological core. Actually, Romania always lacked an *inner form*. Either too rigid or too gelatinous, it looks for a way of life through the thickets of its own shortcomings.

The reason for our xenophobia lies in the fact that historical levels of inequality have always existed between the minorities and us. If we were a fully formed nation, our fight with them would take less dramatic forms because our historical level, representing an obvious superiority, would stimulate them to fit naturally into our rhythms. The Saxons feel tied to Romania only through *the landscape*. They don't have, like us, any kind of inner bond.[19] Proud of a tradition of culture that we lack, they isolate themselves, and they despise us. Do they represent a danger for Romania? No Saxon occupies a leading role[20] and they never tried to interfere in Romania's problems. Even if in the past they exploited us, from them we could always learn. Representing an isolated minority, which follows its own autonomous law of evolution, either integrated or misaligned in Romania, they do not represent any danger. Ten million Saxons would be less fatal to us than a million and a half Jews.[21] The 800,000 Saxons are a moral oasis in the Balkans. The Hungarians are bound to be honest and they hate us. It is not a big deal. Neither the Hungarians nor the Saxons have more political spirit than us. This explains why, after the War, they did not manage to subjugate us as the Jews did. How could the Saxons, who carry in their blood a whole world that makes them maladjusted to any other forms, do this? Wherever the German people colonized the world, they took with them traditions and their specific forms, which they imprinted upon the environment. When the Saxons came to Transylvania, they had in their blood the towns of Germany; they were pre-formed with these architectural treasures. In South America, in Africa, in Russia, in Romania and in all the countries to which they spread, despite the diversity of the landscape, which they nevertheless loved as such, they imprinted it with their own constructive vision, and they lived with the understandable fascination of Germany, always centrifugal. The colonists have rarely created their own culture (America, even today, has not developed one). All the colonists alight in the world in the quality of conquistadors and end up, hopelessly, as householders. Once again, the phenomenon of failure can be seen outside the nation.

All the objections we might have concerning the Jews from the point of view of the existence our nation must have as their prototype the attitude of the Saxons towards us. A minority cannot be asked to love us; nor to agree on any point with us; but if we are going to walk together, we should at least keep to the same path. A state like ours, troubled in addition by the curse of minorities, by this great inorganic fatality that turns any country without political instinct into a Switzerland,[22] cannot achieve a political balance, except by running parallel to all of the minorities that support this condition of maintaining an equal distance from the line of our evolution. Did the Jews ever walk in step with us? The Hungarians hate us from a distance, the Jews in our middle, in our center. How are we, a poor people, going to assimilate the most irreducible phenomenon of history? A people who have as its asset the victorious fight with the most brilliant peoples of history; how is it going to be assimilated by a nation, which saw the light only through the darkness of the Hungarians, the Turks or the Greeks? The vitality of the Jews is so aggressive[23] and their will to enrichment so persistent that our tolerance[24] of this hard working, and exploiting people, would mean certain bankruptcy for us.

The argument of so many Jews – according to which their rise in Romania is based on their unique qualities, which put them forever in a condition of superiority, and therefore anti-Semitism does not have a serious foundation - does not seem evident to me, not because these qualities aren't real, but because, after such a conception, any people that are more mature,[25] more experienced and more steeped in evil would have the right to exploit the naivety and the inexperience of a historically young people. What do the Romanian people know compared to the Jews? What can a telluric people do, when facing the most cerebral people? If we gave Jews absolute freedom, I am convinced that, in less than a year, they would even change the name of the country. In the end, we must admit, with melancholy, that anti-Semitism is the greatest tribute to the Jews. Our solutions to life are their moral death. And they are their moral death because they can't accept them except by giving up what defines their unhappy excellence. If the Jews care, just a little – in reality, they care enormously, even if they don't want to (but they are unable *not to want* to be Jews) – to remain what they are, meaning pariahs and the equivocal halo of history, then they should thank the anti-Semites. Are not they the ones who have *internalized* Judaism? The persecutions brought them nearer to the essence of their being, and liberal regimes, satisfying their lust for gain, have sweetened and alleviated them through freedom. Peoples who gain by their chains are dangerous. The great pride of a nation must derive from an exaggeration of its role in the world. Who, more than the anti-Semites, exaggerated the role of the Jewish people? If the prophecies of the Old Testament had been written after the justification for modern persecutions, they would be just boring platitudes. The gross tears of the Jews have shone like the stars of an inverted sky.[26] These people shall never reap the harvest of their tears. That's why he doth suffer from the obsession of a paradise[27] that other people's taste[28] just by looking at the earth.

How happy we would be, we Romanians, if someone would only exaggerate our role in the world, if we were to be embraced by a fate which we mysteriously desire, in holy grandeur! No prophet ever exaggerated our role in the world. But all of us have no other purpose than to project a reason for being until we become dizzy, to love the aspect imagined by our dreams. Romania's future might be our Utopia – or tragedy.

It might come to pass that Romania becomes a nation with a well-defined profile, established automatically by the force of things and by our will. We have to ask ourselves all the more if we want to build in our nation the vices of the old world, or desire to use all the advantages of a modern vision. Will we continue to grow, in the becoming of nations, leaning on a train of inequalities, on all the frightening misery of this people; or, on the contrary, will we find in national collectivism a solution to all our problems and disasters?

Some say: the ascension of modern peoples was not due to the idea of collectivism. The spirit of competition, of enterprise, of speculation, atomization and individualism, which are the soul of democracy and capitalism, were the reasons for their rapid ascent. Giving each individual the illusion of his enormous possibilities, these political and economic conditions have triggered unsuspected energies, hidden forces. *Arrivism* and *upstartism* assume the quality of specific virtues, from the strength of instinct to an excessive lucidity.

The passion to win has created a general frenzy, extremely fertile for a hoped for leap. Capitalism has been a unique jolt in the evolution of nations.

But these objections neglect two things: capitalism, with all its "virtues", is exhausted as a historical stage, and these virtues, prolific for one people, are the causes of disaster in another. Free competition, the spirit of enterprise, etc., has created in Romania a new world, and it is obvious that without liberalism it would be nothing but a backward country - forever. But inertia, passivity, lack of initiative are defects that, in a regime of unlimited liberties, condemn a nation to languish. That is why, in a democratic regime, foreigners have bestridden the Romanians in a stunning way. We didn't have the needed qualities to break through in a regime of competition and struggle, in which the state remains neutral to the rise and fall of the individual. Romanian democracy has manifested itself in the beginning, with a fecund and surprising impulse; only to be irredeemably compromised by maturity and decadence. Its merit lies in achieving the modernization of the country, giving it, however, a false universal consciousness and a totally misleading illusion of force.

Peoples without historical bones can't make leaps in a regime of uncontrolled freedom. Democracy, guaranteeing freedom to all, ends up not in anarchy, but in a collective slavery; I mean, in national deficiency. Clearly centrifugal, democracy has removed nations from their effective center, their will to power. For the minor nations, decentralization is a real catastrophe. They can no longer *find themselves*. Will Romania be able to find itself again?

Our bourgeoisie raised the historical level of Romania. But, totally lacking in national self-assertion, it has crystallized quickly into a mediocre balance and has sacrificed all the problems that we had to respond to, for its petty interests. Was Romania afraid of the revolution it was supposed to make? Otherwise, it would be hard to explain our lack of revolutionary tradition.

A people must prepare and wait for its revolution. That's the only way it can fulfill a duty towards itself.

Romania needs to break the barriers of its own mediocrity and to understand all the unsolvable data of becoming. Its political spirit should develop towards cynicism; it should be able to call *force* by its name and cease to find solace in the delusions of the right. The explicit belief of the politician has to be that there is no law, only antagonisms, or compromises between the forces. The concept of force in international relations is the only reality; it's not *decent* to express it overtly, but it is no less an act of theoretical sincerity.

Cynicism is never a challenge, but a false joy in the face of the irredeemable. It rests on a painful contradiction between the impulses of sensibility and the non-solvable intelligentsia. Any cynic would wish for things to be as knowledge puts them; but as it is the organic bias of the cynical, he doesn't sag under its weight. All the cynicism of this land has started, in a certain way, from the irreducibility of force – and was caught in the paradoxical conflicts between disabused intelligence and a corrupted heart. Any great politician must be a Fouché with the added bonus of passionate faith.

All conceptions of force are based on a pessimistic anthropology. Man is a fallen being, who can't be lulled by the illusion of freedom; on the contrary, it is a source of error. He can only create when tightly bound to an organization which goes beyond him and which imposes a rhythm on life. The pessimistic vision of man does not become a reality, except in the measure in which he dominates and is dominated. Power is the criterion of value. The generalization and absolutization of politics, its conversion into *Weltanschauung*, turns *force* into the axis of history. From a political point of view, a sergeant in the street has a greater reality than a wise man.[29] So, for a state in time of peace, a watchman is more useful than a general.

Of all these categories, the political was the one which most often tried to ride on the back of history. And managed to do it, to the extent that it does not import what historical form was imposed by *its values of dominance*, and not by its inherent qualities. Everything becomes, *at a given time*, political, as everything, at some point, becomes mystical. All the non-political institutions, because they constitute historical realities, must pass through a political moment. The era of domination of the Catholic Church determines a political moment of its evolution. The maximum effectiveness of an institution is identical to its political moment.

Everything becomes mystical, in the measure in which it achieves its values in its last movements. The contents of life and of the spirit, touching delirium, are raised to a mystical level. Even the economic may become mystical. Everything that unfolds in history but wants to jump into the absolute defeats its own law and touches eternity... for a moment. Through the mystical, history is saved from itself.

Notes

[1] In the manuscript, the chapter mentioned above was titled, originally, "Nationalism, Socialism, Judaism", over which Cioran has written, in pencil, "Nationalism and social problems". The following notes refer exclusively to the manuscript of *The Transfiguration of Romania*.
[2] Followed by "central ideas", cut.
[3] Followed by "is the type of the politician", cut.
[4] Originally it was said "bestiality", cut.
[5] Followed by "from Romania", cut.

⁶ Originally it was spelled "the fundament", cut.
⁷ Interleaved word, after which follows "the Jewish press", cut.
⁸ Follows the "generation of which I am a part", cut.
⁹ Follows: "To take the political force of the liberals in order to strengthen [their] economic force!", cut.
¹⁰ Follows: "and in particular the form in which it was presented in the past few years", cut.
¹¹ Originally it was spelled "political", cut.
¹² Follows: "Only now Romania has started to become conscious of itself. The actual historical moment is so important that, if we lose it, we will have definitively missed our mission", cut.
¹³ Follows: "The press is internationalist", cut.
¹⁴ Follows an unreadable word (perhaps "lost"?).
¹⁵ Originally it was written "guilty", cut.
¹⁶ Followed by "concrete/actual", cut in the manuscript.
¹⁷ In the manuscript it continues with: "Fear of history was the substrate of uprooting"
¹⁸ Follows "compromising", cut in the manuscript
¹⁹ Misprint in the book; "with", in the manuscript.
²⁰ Follows "in us", in the manuscript.
²¹ In the manuscript it is formulated otherwise: "would be less threatening than lethal"; emphasized words are cut.
²² In the manuscript, "the people", cut.
²³ In manuscript: "impressive", cut.
²⁴ Initially: "intolerance", cut in the manuscript.
²⁵ In manuscript: "old", cut.
²⁶ In the manuscript, follows: A upside-down sky wept for its fate in the sewage sludge of these times. There is no salvation for them", cut.
²⁷ Originally written: "salvation and heaven", cut.
²⁸ Follows: "unconsciously", cut.
²⁹ Follows: "and even a value", cut.

Abstract

The exegesis of Cioran to date may be seen as a grid for what might be called a Cioran *syndrome* in Romanian culture. The author, claimed both by Romanian and by French culture, is, at the same time, a *function* of Romanian culture, like Mircea Eliade or Eugen Ionescu.

Much has been written about Cioran, but very little about his youthful publications (his time in Romania), which includes the political compromises that he made with the legionary movement, and its rightist ideological orientation. These are texts that caused serious questions to be asked in the West about the author's Romanian past.

Distancing itself from everything that has been written up till now about Cioran's writings, the chapters in A *Dionysiac with the voluptuousness of doubt*, try to deconstruct the polytropic of Cioran the journalist. Cioran appears as a complex character, contradictory and tragic, atypical in the manner of his deep reflection, scepticism and seeming complicity with the assumed reader.

In the preliminary chapter "Shortcuts" I omit some controversial topics regarding Cioran's metaphysical meditations, Cioran the philosopher. In some *raccourcisseme* I plead for the following ideas, amongst others: the need for *critical editions* of Cioran's works; the need for the impartial reception of both his journalism and his books without ideological prejudices and political and ideological judgement (Cioran must not be turned into an ideological punch bag); the analysis of *grief*, the fundamental reason for engaging in thinking as explored in the manuscript *Amurgul gîndurilor (The Twilight of Thought)*; what philosophy meant for the young Cioran and how he approached it; what are *the stages of loneliness* in Cioran's work.

I deal with Cioran's youthful publications, which have a particular aspect and sense. They form an indivisible whole, with books written by him in Romanian, as well as texts from newspapers and magazines which appeared, sometimes not changed in any way, in the volumes of essays and aphorisms. Moreover, Cioran's journalism and, with it, the work written before his final departure in France, contain many of the ideas that Cioran subsequently developed and rewrote in French.

The books published by Gallimard disclose the character of a writer who became his own disciple, but in another language, freely living his own "theory".

I am interested in the texts of his youth in the chapter "The Overture of The Tragic", where I primarily analyse how Cioran responded to the phenomenon of religion in the third decade of the twentieth century. At that time, when he was young, he begins an *exercise of divine disobedience*, which will continue throughout his whole life. Cioran, the son of an Orthodox priest, was not against God, but he was addressing The Great Silent One (just as he does in Demiurgul cel rău) (*The Evil Demiurge*).

Cioran was not someone who was defeated but had the ontological status of an *outraged man*. He was always situated *against* or *against the grain (à rebours)*, to everything that was created from Adam onwards, a radical, dissatisfied even with the thought of suicide. Illness and pain subsumed into suffering, with metaphysical dimensions, boredom, melancholy and grief caused by an existential overflow lived on the edge of *the falling away of time-* were negative states that fertilized in Cioran *optimism and vigorous philosophical meditation*. As I show in the chapter "Bouts of Insomnia" Cioran's scepticism is atypical. We are not dealing with behaviour filled with gestures and reflexes of defence or failure.

In two chapters ("The Ambiguity of the epistolary Self" and "The erotic adolescence of a septuagenarian") I analyse the correspondence or "epistolary mania" of Cioran. Correspondence is part of his work and not an appendage to it, just as was the case for Goethe, for example. The philosopher appears to me in *Scrisori către cei de acasă (Letters to the ones back home)* (1995) to be a disguised thinker, one wearing a *mask*. And here I find homesickness and the image of someone who suffers from "metaphysical statelessness". In the exchange of letters with Friedgard Thomas, the last great love of the philosopher, I discover a frivolous Cioran, a "skirt hunter".

In the section "Impervious to the French Spirit" I examine the mistaken approach towards Cioran by a Romanian journalist living in Spain, Pamfil Șeicaru, who also writes about the months spent in prison by the philosopher, because of an error committed by retreating German troops about Cioran's identity.

In "Waiting for Cioran's *Reply*" I describe how Cioran's work was received in France immediately after his death, especially those works written in Romanian, with specific reference to his right-wing interwar publications and to the book *Transfiguration of Romania*.

The essay also contains a philosophical analysis of some major themes of Cioran's metaphysics, through which I come with the idea of the *philosophical dandyism* of the author, as it was expressed by those who were part of the generation of Mircea Eliade. I was particularly interested (see the chapter "Between falling in time and falling into the temporal") in Cioran's vision of time, which he did not approach systemically, but as an essayist interested in *style*, in the *how* of our means of expression relates to our historical development. As I show and how he "falls" into *temporality*, into *time*, through his right-wing political sympathies, to show what Julien Benda called "treason of the intellectuals".

Abstract

In the second part of the book, I bring to light a chapter that Cioran suppressed from the "final" edition of *Transfiguration of Romania* (1990). I transcribe the manuscript of that chapter, following Cioran's handwritten original manuscript ("Nationalism, Judaism, socialism") and I make a *parallel reading* of this with the same chapter from the first edition (1936). It seems to me as a gesture of honesty for those who want to have access to Cioran *according to the original.*

The type of academic readership it would appeal to: the book is very useful for teachers and students in *faculties of journalism and letters,* as well as researchers interested in the work of Cioran. In countries *where there is an intensive teaching of philosophy* in high school, it can be used as a reference book for students.

Bibliography

Emil Cioran, *The Transfiguration of Romania*, Bucharest: Vremea Publishing House, 1936.
Emil Cioran, *Amurgul gândurilor* [Twilight of thoughts], Sibiu: Dacia Traiana Publishing House, 1940.
Emil Cioran, *Pe culmile disperării* [On the heights of despair], Bucharest: Humanitas Publishing House, 1990.
Emil Cioran, *Revelațiile durerii* [Revelations of pain], Cluj: Echinox Publishing House, edition supervised by Mariana Vartic and Aurel Sasu, 1990.
Emil Cioran, *Singurătate și destin* [Loneliness and destiny], Bucharest: Humanitas Publishing House, 1991.
Emil Cioran, *Îndreptar pătimaș* [A passionate handbook], Bucharest: Humanitas Publishing House, 1991.
Emil Cioran, *Istorie și Utopie* [History and Utopia], Bucharest: Humanitas Publishing House, 1992.
Cioran, *Căderea în timp* [The fall in time], Bucharest: Humanitas Publishing House, 1994.
Cioran, *Mărturisiri și anateme* [Confessions and anathemas], Bucharest: Publishing House Humanitas, 1994.
Cioran, *Scrisori către cei de-acasă* [Letters to the folks back home], Bucharest: Humanitas Publishing House, 1995.
Cioran, *Entretiens*, Paris: Gallimard, 1995.
Emil Cioran, *Cartea amăgirilor* [The Book of Deceptions], Bucharest: Humanitas Publishing House, 1996.
Cioran, *Exerciții de admirație* [Exercises of admiration], Bucharest: Humanitas Publishing House, 1993.
Cioran, *Caiete* [Notebooks], II, 1966-1968, Bucharest: Humanitas Publishing House, 1999.
Cioran, *Caiete* [Notebooks], III, Bucharest: Humanitas Publishing House, 1999.
E. M. Cioran, *Exercices negatifs. En marge du Précis de décomposition*, Paris: Gallimard, 2005.
Cioran, *Opere* [Works], vol. I and II, edited by Marin Diaconu, Bucharest: Romanian Academy, National Foundation for Science and Art, 2012.
Cioran, *Opere* [Works], vol. III and IV (published works, interviews, correspondence), Bucharest: Romanian Academy, National Foundation for Science and Art, Romanian National Literature Museum, 2017.

***

Henri Bergson, *Gândirea și mișcarea* [Thinking and movement], Iași: Polirom Publishing House, 1995.

Henri Bergson, *Eseu asupra datelor imediate ale conștiinței* [Essay on the immediate data of consciousness], Iași: Polirom Publishing House, 1998.

Moris Blanchot, *La littérature et le droit à la mort*, 1948.

Lucian Blaga, *Despre gândirea magică* [About magical thinking], in *Trilogia valorilor, Opere* [Trilogy of values, Works], vol. 10, Bucharest: Minerva Publishing House, 1987.

Angela Botez, *Filosofia românească în dispunere universală* [Romanian Philosophy in Universal Disposition], Bucharest: Pro Universitaria Publishing House, 2012.

Mircea Braga, *Ecce Nietzsche. Exercițiu de lectură hermeneutică* [Ecce Nietzsche. Hermeneutical reading exercise], Bucharest: The Romanian Academy Publishing House, 2015.

Albert Camus, *Omul revoltat* [The Rebel], Bucharest: RAO Publishing House, 1994.

G. Călinescu, *Istoria literaturii române de la origini până în prezent* [The history of Romanian literature from its origins to the present], Italy: Nagard Publishing House, 1980.

*** *Convorbiri cu Cioran* [Conversations with Cioran], Bucharest: Humanitas Publishing House, 1993.

*** *Din istoria filosofiei în România* [From the history of philosophy in Romania], vol. I, Academy R.P.R. Publishing House, 1955.

Ion Dur, *Hîrtia de turnesol. Cioran inedit. Teme pentru acasă* [The litmus paper. Cioran previously unpublished. Homework], Sibiu: Saeculum Publishing House, 2000.

Mircea Eliade, *Încercarea labirintului* [The trial of the labyrinth], Cluj: Dacia Publishing House, 1991.

Silvie Jaudeau, *Cioran ou dernier homme*, José Corti, 1990.

André Lalande, *Vocabulaire technique et critique de la philosophie*, vol II: N-Z, Paris: Press Universitaires de France, 1993.

Gabriel Liiceanu, *Cearta cu filosofia* [The Quarrel with Philosophy], Bucharest: Humanitas Publishing House, 1992.

Geneviève Léveille-Mourin, *Le langage chrétien, antichrétien de la trenscendance: Pascal-Nietzsche*, Librairie philosophique J. Vrin, 1978.

Simona Modreanu, *Le Dieu paradoxal de Cioran*, Paris: Editions du Rocher, 2003.

Fr. Nietzsche, *Știința voioasă* [The Gay Science], in *Works, 2*, Bucharest: Humanitas Publishing House, 1994.

Z. Ornea, *Anii treizeci. Extrema dreaptă românească* [The thirties. The Romanian extreme right], Bucharest: Romanian Cultural Foundation Publishing House, 1995.

*** *Pro și contra Emil Cioran. Între idolatrie și pamflet* [Pros and cons of Emil Cioran. Between idolatry and pamphlet], Bucharest: Humanitas Publishing House, Edition by Marin Diaconu, 1998.

Paul Ricoeur, *Eseuri de hermeneutică* [Hermeneutical essays], Bucharest: Humanitas Publishing House, 1995.

Fernando Savater, *Eseu despre Cioran* [Essay on Cioran], Bucharest: Humanitas Publishing House, 1998.

Pamfil Șeicaru, *Scrieri din exil, I, Figuri din lumea literară* [Writings from exile, I, Figures of the literary world], Bucharest: Saeculum I.O. Publishing House, 2002.

Gh. Vlăduțescu, *Neconvențional, despre filosofie românească* [Unconventional, about Romanian philosophy], Bucharest: Paideia Publishing House, 2002.

About the Author

Professor Ion Dur, PhD, Doctoral School of Philosophy, Baia Mare Northern University Centre, Romania.

Research interest / Areas of competence: History of Philosophy; History of Romanian Culture; Aesthetics; Literary and Philosophy Criticism; Romanian Media and Collective Mentality in the 19th and 20th centuries; Media Critique.

Literary awards: Member of the National Writers Union of Romania, which granted seven awards for the published books; member of the managing committee of the Sibiu branch of the National Writers Union of Romania; „Mircea Florian" prize for philosophy, granted by the Romanian Academy; Journalistic debut: Romanian Public Broadcasting, 1973; Critical debut: simultaneously in both *Transilvania* 4/1981 and *Ramuri* 4/1981 magazines.

Works published: Attempts to Recognition, Craiova: Scrisul Românesc Publishing House, 1992; *Noica – Between Dandyism and the Myth of School,* Bucharest: Eminescu Publishing House, 1994; *From Eminescu to Cioran,* Craiova: Scrisul Românesc Publishing House, 1996; *Noica – The Portrait of a Journalist in His Youth,* Sibiu: Saeculum Publishing House, 1999; *The Litmus Paper. An Undiscovered Cioran. Food for Thought,* Sibiu: Saeculum Publishing House, 2000; *Caryatids,* Sibiu: Psihomedia Publishing House, 2007; *Noica. Boundaries of Journalism,* Iași: Institutul European Publishing House, 2009; *The spiral-bound notebook,* Sibiu: University of Lucian Blaga Publishing House, 2010; *Scraps and Days,* Sibiu: University of Lucian Blaga Publishing House, 2012; *The Third Meaning,* Iași: Institutul European Publishing House, 2014; *Cioran. According to the original,* Bucharest: Tritonic Publishing House, 2016; *Critique of Judgement of Taste,* Bucharest: Eikon Publishing House, 2017; *Domestic journal. Note of an in-former,* Bucharest: Cartea Românească Publishing House, 2018.

Translations: Hannah Arendt, *The Origins of Totalitarianism,* Bucharest: Humanitas Publishing House, 1994; a collaboration with Mircea Ivănescu; Hannah Arendt, *The Crisis of the Republic,* Bucharest: Humanitas Publishing House, 1999; a collaboration with D.-I. Cenușer.

Index of Proper Names

A

Acterian, Arsavir, 115, 122, 126, 127
Alexandrescu, Sorin, 97
Andrei, Petre, 15, 82
Anselm, 13
Antonescu, Ion, 41
Arendt, Hannah, 34
Aristotle, 19, 33, 89
Avram, Vasile, 4
Azi [Today], 115, 126

B

Bacon, Francis, 16, 113
Băncilă, Vasile, 82
Baudelaire, Charles, 19
Benda, Julien, 16, 89, 92, 133
Berdyaev, Nicolai, 16, 48, 82
Bergson, Henri, 16, 37, 58, 72, 75, 76, 77, 78, 82, 83, 84, 85
Berthelot, Réné, 85
Blaga, Lucian, 10, 22, 73, 74, 76, 78, 81, 95, 109, 117, 118, 119, 120, 127
Blanchot, Moris, 120, 121, 127
Boeriu, Adrian, 4
Boissau, Pierre-Yves, 111, 129, 130, 131, 132, 134
Bolboașă, N., 117, 127
Bollon, Patrice, 132, 134
Bolon, Patrice, 21
Bondy, Fr., 60, 91
Borges, Jorge Luis, 38, 95
Boué, Simone, 20, 34, 35, 37
Bourdieu, Pierre, 95
Boutroux, Emile, 16
Braga, Mircea, 55
Bréhier, Emile, 16
Brunet, Claude, 21
Brunschwicg, Leon, 16

C

Caillois, R., 97, 128
Calendarul [The Calendar], 66, 69, 71, 81, 82, 97
Călinescu, G., 17, 113, 117, 126
Camus, Albert, 57, 58, 59, 67, 68
Caragiale, Ion L., 122
Cassirer, Ernst, 16, 75
Cioculescu, Șerban, 61, 117
Cioran, Aurel, 4, 12, 16, 22, 27, 55, 57, 63, 119, 126, 127
Cioran, Emil, Adolescența, 55
Cioran, Emil, Aveux et Anathèmes, 39
Cioran, Emil, Căderea în timp [Falling in time], 96, 97
Cioran, Emil, Caiete [Notebooks], 25, 31, 81, 96, 97
Cioran, Emil, Cele două morale [The two moraties], 68
Cioran, Emil, Conștiință și viață [Consciousness and life], 82
Cioran, Emil, Copacul vieții [Tree of life], 96
Cioran, Emil, Creștinismul și scandalul pe care l-a adus în lume [Christianity and the scandal it brought into the world], 54

Cioran, Emil, Cultul puterii [The cult of power], 97
Cioran, Emil, Despre creștinism [About Christianity], 55
Cioran, Emil, Despre Protestantism [About Protestantism], 55
Cioran, Emil, Despre stările depressive [About depressive states], 69, 82
Cioran, Emil, Elogiul oamenilor pasionați [In praise of passionate people], 82
Cioran, Emil, Entretiens, 67, 68, 82, 97
Cioran, Emil, Exercices negatifs. En marge du Précis de décomposition, 22, 24
Cioran, Emil, Floarea de foc [The fiery flower], 67, 68
Cioran, Emil, Handbook of Passions, 22, 23
Cioran, Emil, Histoire et Utopie, 3, 41, 93, 94, 95, 97, 98, 99, 103, 113, 116, 128
Cioran, Emil, Împotriva istoriei și a istoricilor [Against history and historians], 82, 97
Cioran, Emil, Între spiritual și politic [Between the spiritual and the political], 97
Cioran, Emil, Intuiționismul contemporan [Contemporary Intuitionism], 81, 82
Cioran, Emil, Iraționalul în viață [The irrational in life], 68, 81
Cioran, Emil, Letter to a faraway friend, 41, 94
Cioran, Emil, Mărturisiri și anateme [Confessions and anathemas], 97

Cioran, Emil, Melancolii bavareze [Bavarian melancholy], 97
Cioran, Emil, Nae Ionescu și drama lucidității", 55
Cioran, Emil, Nu există nimeni [There is none], 97
Cioran, Emil, Omul fără destin [The man without a destiny], 97
Cioran, Emil, On the Heights of Despair, 9, 15, 16, 23, 24, 42, 58, 61, 113, 114, 118
Cioran, Emil, Pătimirea ca destin [Passion as destiny], 97
Cioran, Emil, Perspectiva pesimistă a istoriei [The pessimistic perspective of history], 81
Cioran, Emil, Précis de décomposition, 14, 21, 30, 34, 42, 99
Cioran, Emil, Provincial Letter, 55
Cioran, Emil, Reflexiuni asupra mizeriei [Reflections on poverty], 68
Cioran, Emil, Revelațiile durerii [The revelations of pain], 67, 68
Cioran, Emil, Scrisoare din munți [Letter from the mountains], 97
Cioran, Emil, Scrisoare din singurătate [Letter from solitude], 69, 82
Cioran, Emil, Scrisori către cei de-acasă [Letters to the folks back home], 31, 67, 126, 127, 135
Cioran, Emil, Seara [The evening], 97
Cioran, Emil, Sensul culturii contemporane [The meaning of contemporary culture], 81

Index

Cioran, Emil, Silogismele amărăciunii [Syllogisms of depression], 96
Cioran, Emil, Simbol și mit [Symbol and Myth], 71, 82
Cioran, Emil, Singurătate și destin [Solitude and Destiny], 24, 54, 67, 68, 81
Cioran, Emil, Sistem și viață [System and Life], 67, 68
Cioran, Emil, Structura cunoașterii religioase [The structure of religious knowledge], 68
Cioran, Emil, Syllogisms of Bitterness, 60, 61
Cioran, Emil, Țara mea [My Country], 25, 134, 135
Cioran, Emil, Țara oamenilor atenuați [The land of mitigated people], 81
Cioran, Emil, Tears and Saints, 3, 9, 11, 15, 60, 113, 130
Cioran, Emil, The Book of Deceptions, 10, 23, 24, 113, 115
Cioran, Emil, The Temptation to Exist, 23, 60, 117, 118, 127, 131
Cioran, Emil, The Transfiguration of Romania, 3, 5, 6, 15, 42, 61, 92, 93, 94, 95, 99, 100, 101, 104, 105, 107, 110, 111, 112, 113, 114, 115, 116, 117, 120, 121, 123, 124, 125, 126, 128, 129, 130, 131, 137, 151
Cioran, Emil, The Twilight of Thoughts, 11, 12, 13, 23, 24
Cioran, Emil, Timp și anemie [Time and anaemia], 96
Cioran, Emil, Tragicul cotidian, 55
Cioran, Relu, 99, 116, 122, 123
Codoban, Aurel, 4
Codreanu, Corneliu Z., 131
Constantinescu, Pompiliu, 115, 127
Contemporanul [The contemporary], 117, 118, 119, 127
Coste, Brutus, 43
Crainic, Nichifor, 114, 116, 117, 126
Curentul [The current], 23, 116
Cusin, Philippe, 132, 133, 134, 135

D

Débat, 129
Descartes, Rene, 19
Diaconu, Alina, 38, 39
Diaconu, Marin, 5, 23, 24, 33, 54, 100, 126, 127
Djuvara, Neagu, 43
Dur, Ion, 4, 23, 81, 82, 96
Duvingnaud, J, 93

E

Eco, Umberto, 13, 33
Eliade, Mircea, 4, 16, 17, 21, 22, 24, 43, 47, 50, 83, 89, 117, 127
Eminescu, Mihai, 5, 22, 65, 93, 97, 112, 119, 120
Enthoven, Jean-Paul, 132, 135

F

Fejtö, Francois, 131
Fichte, Johann Gottlieb, 16
Finkielkraut, Alain, 129, 131, 132
Florian, Mircea, 82
Furet, Francois, 133

G

Gândirea [Thought], 45, 67, 68, 81, 126, 127

Gazeta Literară [The Literary Gazette], 117
Glasul Patriei [The voice of the fatherland], 117
Goethe, J. W. von, 144
Graur, Doina, 4

H

Hartmann, Nicolai, 16, 58
Hegel, G. W. F., 29, 78, 82
Heidegger, Martin, 12, 29, 34, 117, 132
Hitler, A., 106, 133
Huxley, Aldous, 124, 125

I

Ierunca, Virgil, 22
Ionesco, Eugene, 131
Ionescu, Nae, 50, 55, 58, 64, 73, 74, 75, 76, 80, 85, 96, 113, 116
Isaac, Victor, 12, 116

J

Jaudeau, Sylvie, 95, 98
Junimea, 113

K

Kant, Immanuel, 13, 16, 19, 21, 25, 29, 34, 87
Keyserling, Hermann von, 16
Kierkegaard, Soren, 12, 16, 17, 42, 79, 113, 114, 118
Klages, Ludwig, 75, 76, 78
Kokoschka, Oskar, 57, 67
Koyré, Alexander, 16
Kroner, Richard, 85

L

Lenin, V. I., 106, 107, 139
Léveille-Mourin, Genevieve, 98
Lévy, Bernard-Henry, 132
Liiceanu, Gabriel, 4, 25, 60, 68, 82, 130, 131, 132, 134
Linia dreaptă [The straight line], 115
Lipatti, Dinu, 117, 127
Lovinescu, Monica, 22
Luther, Martin, 48, 49, 103

M

Macovei, Toma, 115
Mannheim, Karl, 125
Marcus Aurelius, 60
Marcuse, Herbert, 21
Marenco, Erica, 93
Maritain, Jacques, 16, 48
Massis, Henri, 16
Mateescu, Mircea, 12, 23
Mavrodin, Irina, 4
Michelangelo, 79
Mihăilescu, Dan C., 4, 111
Mişcarea, 54
Morin, Edgar, 11, 133
Motru, C-R., 118
Mussolini, B., 106

N

Narly, C., 82
Neamtzu, Ionel, 115
Negrici, Eugene, 33
Nietzsche, Friedrich, 14, 15, 16, 20, 25, 28, 29, 30, 31, 42, 49, 50, 55, 59, 60, 61, 62, 72, 75, 95, 98, 108, 114, 115, 118, 144

Index 167

Noica, Constantin, 4, 21, 22, 23, 28, 34, 41, 42, 43, 59, 94, 122, 127

O

Ornea, Z., 105, 116, 126, 131

P

Paraschivescu, M-R., 115
Pascal, Blaise, 90, 95, 98
Patapievici, H-R., 98
Petrașincu, Dan, 115, 116
Petreu, Marta, 5, 31
Petreu, Marta, The Transfiguration of Romania, 5
Plămădeală, Bishop Antoine, 4
Plato, 29, 103
Popa, Grigore, 12, 23, 116
Popescu, Gabriel, 4
Popescu, Radu, 117
Preda, Marin, 119
Primăvara literară [Literary Spring], 115
Protopopescu, Dragos, 115

R

Raddatz, Fritz J., 60
Radio France Culture debate, 131, 132
Rădulescu-Motru, C., 82
Ralea, Mihai, 82, 114, 115, 126
Reichmann, Edgar, 131
Reisner, Erwin, 45
Ricoeur, Paul, 94, 98, 125, 127
Riehl, Alois, 16
Rilke, Rainer Maria, 19
Roman, Toma, 4
Rosca, D. D., 117
Roșca, D.D., 117, 127

Rousseau, J-J., 103

S

Săndulescu, Ecaterina, 29
Sasu, Aurel, 67
Savater, Fernando, 67, 68, 81
Scheler, Max, 16, 78
Schopenhauer, Arthur, 16
Șeicaru, Pamfil, 13, 14, 23, 41, 42, 43
Semne [Signs], 115
Sfarmă piatră [Stone breaker], 116
Shakespeare, William, 16
Shestov, Lev, 16, 90, 115
Simmel, Georg, 16, 19, 75, 85, 120
Soca, Susana, 38
Sontag, Susan, 60
Șora, Mariana, 39
Spengler, Oswald, 16, 45, 50, 72
Stalin, Josef, 133
Stirner, Max, 16, 42

T

Tacou, Constantin, 28, 31
Tecuceanu, Stelian, 115
Thoma, Friedgard, 33, 34, 36, 37, 40
Thoma, Friedgard, Not for anything in the world. A love of Cioran's, 38, 40

Ț

Țincu, Bucur, 28, 115

T

Tismăneanu, Vladimir, 116, 127
Tolstoy, L., 79, 88
Țuțea, Petre, 28

U

Uricariu, Doina, 4

V

Vartic, Mariana, 67
Vianu, Tudor, 82
Viaţa literară [Literary life], 115, 116
Vlăduţescu, Gh., 17, 24
Vremea [The Time], 6, 54, 55, 81, 97, 101, 115, 126, 127, 128
Vrînceanu, Dragos, 12, 116

W

Weininger, Otto, 16
Windelband, W., 16
Wolfflin, H., 16
Worringer, W., 16

Z

Zapraţan, Mircea, 22
Zeletin, Şt., 16
Zeller, Ed., 16
Zola, Emile, 52

www.ingramcontent.com/pod-product-compliance
Lightning Source LLC
Chambersburg PA
CBHW052047300426
44117CB00012B/2011